Jeanette Li

Jeanette Li

A Girl Born Facing Outside

An autobiography translated by Rose Huston

Second Edition

© 2014 Crown & Covenant Publications
7408 Penn Avenue
Pittsburgh, PA 15208
www.crownandcovenant.com

Second Edition

Reprinted by permission. © The Reformation Translation Fellowship 1971

First English edition published by The Banner of Truth Trust 1971

ISBN: 978-1-884527-96-8
ePub: 978-1-884527-98-2
Kindle: 978-1-884527-95-1

Library of Congress Control Number: 2014952871

Printed in the United States of America

Cover design by Megan Wingfield. Interior layout by Shelley Davis. Text is in Adobe Garamond Pro 11 on 14. Illustrations, which first appeared in the 1971 edition, were drawn by Samuel E. Boyle, missionary and friend of Jeanette Li. Anglicizing of Chinese by John Qi and Shelby Winkel. Copy editing by Shelby Winkel, Rebecca Byers, and Linda Parker. Photographs courtesy of Faith M. Martin.

Unless otherwise indicated, all Scripture references taken from the New King James Version®. Copyright © 1982 by Thomas Nelson. Used by permission. All rights reserved.

All rights reserved. No part of this book may be reproduced or stored in a retrieval system in any form by any means (electronic, mechanical, photocopying, recording, or otherwise) without the prior written permission of the publisher.

Table of Contents

Foreword vii
Foreword to 1971 Edition xi
Translator's Preface xv

1. Almost a Castaway 1
2. A Girl at Our School! 5
3. The Griefs of a Broken Nest 11
4. No Hope from Idols 15
5. Found by a Heavenly Father 19
6. A House Divided 23
7. The School Ghost Destroyed 29
8. A Girl's Learning Tested 35
9. I Escape the Mocker's Snare 41
10. Mother Tells a Secret 45
11. Unwilling Betrothal 47
12. Bride with a Twisted Ear 51
13. Li Mu's Change and End 55
14. Alone—A New Beginning 59
15. Canton and Streams in the Desert 63
16. My Mother's Death 67
17. Temptations and Victory 71
18. On the Horns of a Dilemma 75
19. Calls in the Night 81
20. To Jinling Bible School, Nanjing 85
21. Timothy's Snare and His Deliverance 89
22. The Call from the Far North 95
23. A Thousand Perilous Miles 99
24. The Afflictions of the Gospel 103
25. Timothy Joins Me at Qiqihar 109
26. Winter Hazards 115
27. Come and Receive a Blessing 119
28. God Saves Only Sinners 123
29. Mrs. Zhao Locks Doors 129

30.	When You Pray, Believe	133
31.	False Gods Burned	137
32.	Idols Become Wallpaper	143
33.	Mr. Tian Finds Happiness	147
34.	Activities of the Church	151
35.	The Children of Daigang	157
36.	Worship the Emperor	161
37.	God's White Ravens	165
38.	Shadows of Pearl Harbor	169
39.	American Missionaries Removed	173
40.	Traps Laid for Me	179
41.	Still More Traps	183
42.	Russian Takeover	187
43.	Our Perilous Escape to Shenyang	191
44.	Souls Saved in Changchun Hospital	197
45.	A Dangerous Book	201
46.	Our Passport—My Bible!	207
47.	Back to Deqing Again	213
48.	New Work: The Orphanage	217
49.	The Story of a Gun	221
50.	Dissension at the Orphanage	225
51.	Hazardous Journeys to Hong Kong	231
52.	Annihilate the Christian Church	237
53.	Red Army Domination	243
54.	Communist Infiltrations	249
55.	Robbery by Daylight	253
56.	Prayer and Praise in Prison	261
57.	The Sighing of the Prisoner	265
58.	Brainwashing	271
59.	My Furnace of Affliction	277
60.	A Proselyte Communist Judge	283
61.	Testimony and Release	287
62.	Life in Canton	291
63.	Forever Free	297

Epilogue 305
Life of Miss Rose A. Huston 309
A Brief History of China 313
Outline of Jeanette Li's Life 317
Endnotes 319

Foreword

Although this is Jeanette Li's autobiography, it really is not about her. Rather, it is about the incredibly all-glorious, all-powerful, all-wise, and gracious God that she served.

Jeanette Li lived her life in the presence of God. When there was blessing from the Lord, she praised him. When she was convicted of sinning against him, she confessed her sin and God forgave her as he has promised. When she faced trials, she went to her knees before the throne of grace. When the way before her was not clear, she asked her Lord for wisdom and direction. God graciously responded to her prayers. She read and memorized the Scriptures and sang the Psalms. The memory of these verses served her well as God often brought to her mind the verses that would be a special blessing to her at those specific times of need.

This autobiography is of particular interest to me because I have heard about Jeanette Li from my youth. My parents are the Martins, who are mentioned briefly in the course of this book.

While a student at Westminster Seminary in Philadelphia, my father began a courtship with my mother. During that courtship, my mother became convinced that God wanted her to serve him overseas. Because of this conviction, she was ready to break off the courtship. But before she could mention this to my father, he asked her, "Would you be willing to go with me to China?" God's call on their courtship and missionary service was confirmed. They were married in Manchuria in 1938 by J. G. Vos.

When Mrs. Li and the other missionaries were forced to leave Manchuria because of the Japanese occupation—and later forced to leave the South China mission because of the Communist takeover—they lost contact with their brothers and sisters in Christ. What would happen to them? Would they remain faithful to the Lord Jesus Christ or would they succumb to the pressures of the world? Would the church of Jesus Christ in China be extinguished as her enemies hoped?

No doubt these dear people were often on the missionaries' minds and in their prayers. They longed to return to China to serve the church there. But in the meantime, while China was closed to Westerners, God used these missionaries to serve elsewhere in Christ's kingdom: translating theological works into the Chinese language for the training of church leaders in China, opening mission work in Japan, preaching the Word of God in churches in America, and teaching in Christian educational institutions. Their ministry was multiplied in China and in other nations of the world.

In this life, however, Mrs. Li and the American missionaries were not able to contact the Christians they had left in Manchuria and China to learn of their well-being in Christ. But the governments and armies of men could not drive the Holy Spirit out of China!

As Dr. Jerry O'Neill, president of the Reformed Presbyterian Theological Seminary reminded me, God declares, "I will not give my glory to another" (Isaiah 42:8 and 48:11). None of these missionaries who were driven out of China remain alive today. From time to time we have heard reports of a multitude of Chinese Christians in their homeland, but not about the specific Christians Mrs. Li and others had taught about Christ. After the missionaries, including Mrs. Li, had all passed to their heavenly home, we learned of many who are clinging to Jesus Christ with the same zeal for him that she demonstrated.

The church in China is flourishing with Christians who have been tested in the fires of persecution. Like Mrs. Li, they are being interrogated and even imprisoned. They are told that they are not to gather to worship the Lord but they do so anyway. They know that their Redeemer lives and has all authority, even over powerful governments. So they trust him and, like Mrs. Li, they live their lives in his presence, singing the Psalms, reciting the Scriptures and calling on him to praise him, to confess their sins to him, to seek wisdom and direction from him, and to ask him for mercy.

As the Apostle Paul approached the end of his life, he wrote to a younger pastor, Timothy, encouraging him to remain faithful to Jesus Christ. One striking verse in that letter is this: "All who desire to live godly in Christ Jesus will be persecuted" (2 Timothy 3:12). Read those words again slowly: "All who desire to live godly in Christ Jesus will be persecuted." Are you living your life conscious of this truth? Our brothers and sisters in China know its reality. But the church in America is also being persecuted—whether facing the same kinds of trials that Mrs. Li encountered or enduring the temptations of the evil one to turn away from Christ.

As the New Testament attests, the apostles spread the gospel while suffering great persecution. The Scriptures have much to say to the church today about remaining faithful to Jesus Christ in the face of persecution, whether from people who oppress us or the longings of the world that attract us. We need to know the Scriptures well, as Mrs. Li did. She sang psalms that had been forged in persecution, as David fled from Saul and later from Absalom, as he faced enemies from other nations, and as the Israelites were taken into exile. But David confessed that the psalms he wrote are the words of the Holy Spirit on his tongue (2 Samuel 23:2). They tell of the Messiah obeying the charge of our heavenly Father to "Ask of me, and I will make the nations your inheritance, the ends of the earth your possession" (Psalm 2:8). We join our Savior in seeking the nations to submit to Christ.

May Mrs. Li's autobiography encourage you to live your life intentionally for King Jesus in the presence of God for his glory.

—J. Bruce Martin
President of The Reformation Translation Fellowship
October 2014

Foreword to 1971 Edition

Many wise men have written thousands of pages about the failures of Western missions in China.

Many church conferences have spent hours of debate and study on the problem of ecumenical harmony and cooperation between the "younger" churches of those formerly colonial nations and the Western Christian churches.

Sometimes these criticisms are harsh and bitter. One book of this type was written by the late Indian diplomat, Dr. K. M. Pannikar, called *Asia and Western Dominance*. One whole chapter in this book is devoted to what the author calls "The Failure of Christian Missions."

Paul wrote in 1 Corinthians 1:27-29 that God chooses to work in this world through the foolish or the despised and lowly objects of his sovereign grace, "that no flesh should glory in his presence."

This autobiography is a living proof of that quiet but powerful work of God's grace in a humble Chinese woman's life. While scholars and ecumenical consultations spend many hours in discussions and write thousands of words about the improvement of Christian missions, this little narrative by Mrs. Li of Deqing, Guangdong, South China, so thrilling in its honest simplicity, shows how God works while men talk.

All the faults attributed to Western missions in China and in Asia are, no doubt, partly true. We who spent years as foreigners in these Asian nations, preaching Jesus Christ through our imperfect lives, have often been burdened with a sense of our failures. Mrs. Li's book will show that God is much greater than the failures of his servants. In spite of the worst that enemies of Christ may condemn in missionaries, somehow the love and the glory of Christ Jesus breaks through fleshly barriers to transfigure the souls of many Chinese saints like Mrs. Li.

Jeanette Li also demonstrates the happier side of fellowship between Chinese national leaders and missionary coworkers. How many times this Cantonese Christian woman was cursed by her fellow Chinese as "a running dog of foreign imperialism"! How she suffered under military and political suspicion because of her close friendship with American missionaries! Yet it was magnificently evident in Mrs. Li's close and loving friendship with Western brethren in Christ that God's grace can overcome all the friction, suspicion, and inequalities that arise between Western and Eastern Christian coworkers. "Not by might, nor by power, but by my Spirit, saith the Lord of Hosts." It is by grace alone that victory comes.

Christ told us that he will build his church. We may rest on that as a fact. While I was going around California to interpret for Mrs. Li as she gave her Christian testimony to American Christians, I once asked her whether she thought the church in China today would endure, or whether anti-Christian indoctrination would erase the knowledge of God from all China. Mrs. Li looked at me, surprised that I should ask such a question. Her answer was, "The church of Christ is his body. He purchased the church with his own blood. He has promised that the gates of hell shall never overcome the church. You ask me if the church in China will be destroyed? How could it be, in the light of all these great promises?"

So, in the face of all that seems to threaten his church in China and on earth, Mrs. Li's story encourages us to believe that God's grace is all-sufficient.

Many hints in the epistles of Paul show that primitive, confused conditions often prevailed in the early churches which Paul labored to plant and nurture in the Lord. He told Titus, "For this cause left I thee in Crete, that thou shouldest set in order the things which are wanting, and ordain elders in every city, as I had appointed thee" (Titus 1:5, KJV). Many problems in the church of Corinth caused the apostle deep sorrow and two epistles had to be written, if not more, to set in order the things within the church.

Western Christians in churches of the Reformed and Presbyterian tradition may misunderstand some things which Mrs. Li did in her remarkable ministry as a Bible woman in China and Manchuria. Accustomed as we are in the homeland to long-established rules and customs which strictly limit women from intruding on the ordained office of elder and pastor, the freedom and boldness of Mrs. Li in serving the rural Christians of her nation may give a sense of uneasiness to some readers. It is fitting therefore that I bear testimony from a long and happy fellowship with Mrs. Li and Miss Huston in the ministry of the gospel in China, that both these noble women held in the highest regard the limitations that Scripture places on the official, public ministry of the Word by ordained ministers. Nothing Mrs. Li says or did can be interpreted as careless indifference to the biblical requirements for bishops and elders in the church. Mrs. Li was well instructed in church government by Johannes G. Vos during his missionary career in Manchuria.

Much of Mrs. Li's labor and toil was done in primitive, rural churches and homes of Chinese poor people. Most of the women and many of the men were illiterate. Chinese ordained pastors were too few and the area to be evangelized was wide and the rural population was large. Sickness, danger, war, and Communist aggression complicated the work of Mrs. Li throughout all her able ministry for Christ. It is in these special emergency circumstances that her response to urgent human need when nobody else was within miles to do the task properly and officially caused her to exercise evangelistic gifts more freely than she might have done in a mature Chinese church.

The Reformation Translation Fellowship (RTF), for which Mrs. Li labored as a faithful worker up to the time of her death, was formed in Canton in late 1948. I was joined in the formation of this work by Chinese evangelist, Charles H. Zhao, and Dr. Johannes G. Vos. Mr. Zhao was a product of Scottish Presbyterian missionary work in Manchuria and had attended the Yingkou Bible School where one of his teachers was Dr. Vos of the Reformed Presbyterian Mission in Qiqihar. RTF has ministered to the Chinese Church over the past 22 years through the provision of sound Christian literature in Chinese.

We thank God for his gift of this Christian Chinese woman to the lay ministry of the church. We take this opportunity to pay respect to her memory and to urge that we all show more of the same devotion to Christ that she had through the grace of God.

—*Samuel E. Boyle*
January 1971

Translator's Preface

St. Augustine, in his exposition of the Psalms, wrote, "Confession is understood in two senses: of sin and of God's praise. Confession of sin all know, but confession of praise few attend to. The former showeth the wound to the physician; the latter giveth thanks for health."

In this story of her life Mrs. Jeanette Li, also known as Yin Wei Jie and by several other names, shows over and over again that she practiced these two confessions. Unlike St. Augustine, she had not committed flagrant sins, but whether for sins of ignorance or indifference, neglect or disobedience, she made humble confession of them and gave glad praise for assurance of God's grace of love and forgiveness.

Her early childhood was under the kindly influence of a devoted Buddhist father and a strict but superstitious mother. Even so, she very early learned to doubt, and dared to defy, some ancient beliefs and customs. She asked, "Do spirits of the dead return to earth, either for vengeance or for blessing?" Read her experience with the witch and also of the ghost she destroyed with a bamboo stick.

Mrs. Li's firm faith, at the age of eight or nine, that Jesus was her Savior, and God in heaven her Father, wavered and weakened but once in her sixty years as a Christian, and then God's Word restored her. She rejected temptations that would have brought her fame and wealth, and declined offers of high salaried positions because God had called her to serve him. She had "the breath of courage" to refuse emperor worship, and again to carry her Bible on a journey, though warned of the danger it would bring if Communist guards were to see it.

Left without support when mission funds were frozen, she raised chickens and peddled eggs from house to house in order to care for her daughter-in-law and baby grandson. Again and again she felt God's guidance, sometimes in dreams or visions, and she knew that she "could safely put her trust in him" for a future that otherwise would have looked dark and discouraging.

When communism was established in Manchuria, while her son was in America, Mrs. Li took her daughter-in-law and the two small children to her former home in South China. While there, she served as manager of the Mission Orphanage until the Communists imprisoned her on false charges, freeing her after seventeen months when they had become convinced by long investigations that the accusations against her were false and that she was one person who had never told them a lie. After more troubled years in Canton, she was given a permit to go to Hong Kong and return. However, she sent the return ticket to the Canton police and was forever free.

Through almost sixty years, her life of faith and service, of prayer and praise to God, bore abundant fruit. Her sturdy qualities of heart and mind won for her not only the deep affection and trust of Christian friends from the far South to the frozen North, but also the respect and admiration of those whom she withstood with high-hearted courage.

She passed beyond the body on May 9, 1968, after suffering a stroke while translating the account of a cruel experience during her imprisonment.

—Rose A. Huston
1971

1

Almost a Castaway

My great-grandmother was a tyrant. There was no doubt of that. The younger generations—all three of them—said so; and the in-laws—all women, naturally—definitely agreed. Though her husband was legally ruler of the Yin clan, Great-Grandmother actually reigned, and with an iron hand, over the whole household. One daughter-in-law became the target for jealousy and hatred because she was treated with respect and a leniency denied to the others simply because she had borne several sons while the others had only given birth to daughters.

Yin You Zhong, the eldest of these grandsons, had blessed Great-Grandmother with two great-grandsons and a great-granddaughter, but they had all died in early childhood. None of the other grandsons had even one son to carry on the family name. Failure to have sons has long been regarded as a major offense against filial piety, for without sons the proper rites toward parents cannot be continued. In such a case, not only will the living be disgraced but the spirits of the dead will be in misery.

Now, three years after his grandmother's death, You Zhong took the day off from his business because his wife was in labor with their fourth child. He had gone to the geomancer and was encouraged by his prognostication: "This child soon to be born has a good foundation for life, a long life full of blessings."

Sitting alone in the gloom of the windowless guest hall, he carefully reviewed his life: "I have been a faithful follower of Buddha; I have earnestly worshiped my ancestors; I have lived ever more virtuously. Surely the gods will grant me a son." Suddenly he was all agog. "This must be a lucky day. I have seen several wedding processions on the streets, gay bridal chairs accompanied by orchestras. If it's a lucky day for brides, why not for babies? The twelfth day of the twelfth month. Surely I shall have a son."

Still he waited—and hoped.

"Ha! Another good sign. As I came in I noticed that *li mei* (jasmine) shrub bursting into bloom. It hasn't bloomed for two or three years. So it is with us: death and years of grief, now life and hope."

His uncle's wife was acting as midwife while he sat, impatient at the long delay. "Will she come out to congratulate me, or to give me bad news?"

At last the woman came to him, looking glum, and she spoke with heartless disgust.

"Well," she said, "Taai So has given birth to another girl. I say, send it right off to the foundling house! The sooner the better. What do you say?"

There was a tense moment. You Zhong answered not a word, but went quickly into the next room, took the newborn child in his arms and carried her out to the altar which held the ancestral tablets worshiped by the clan.

As a matter of fact, any newborn child was considered unclean and unfit to be presented to the spirits of the ancestors until a period of purification had passed. That a newborn girl should be presented was unthinkable. But You Zhong was so stricken with this additional disappointment that he dared to defy whatever gods had sent this sorrow and ignored ancient traditions.

Standing in the awesome presence of the spirits of his numerous forefathers, in a low tense voice he prayed for this helpless unwelcome child—his daughter.

Then to the babe who understood not a word, he said, "You have come at an opportune time. You are my only child, my precious treasure. No one shall ever take you from me."

Turning to face his astonished aunt, he said, "I Shum, is not this child a human being? Then why do you want to cast her out to die? You regard sons as most precious simply because they perpetuate the family name, while girls 'are born facing outside,' only to marry into another clan. It is my desire and hope that this child may remain with us always, to be a companion and comfort to her mother and me."

On hearing these incredible words his aunt went away angry, embarrassed, and baffled.

Taking the baby girl back to his wife he said, "My heart has been empty, suffering bitter grief all these years. This child, though not a son, shall make up for all our loss and sorrow, bringing us comfort and joy. We shall never send her away."

From her inmost heart his wife replied, "We have only this one wee mite. Thank you for not even thinking of putting her away."

As he gently placed the child in her mother's arms he said, "Your words have saved me from the grief and sorrow I feared. Of every ten girls sent to the foundling house, nine are soon dead. But this child is our precious treasure."

Weeping tears of disappointment because she had not borne a son, she said to the child, "If you are a lucky one, very well. If not, we'll make the best of it. I am very sure of one thing: if your brothers and sister had not died, and if Grandmother were alive today, you would have no such welcome. She would cast you out to die. Even though you are only a girl born facing outside, you are better than none. We shall give you an opportunity to live."

So that is why my great-grandmother died: that I, this unwanted girl child, in the good providence of God should not die as a castaway. She died that I might be allowed to live and tell the story of my life and of God's goodness to me.

Believing more than ever in the geomancer's forecast, in the lucky day and the blossoming shrub, my father happily accepted his small daughter. Soon he came back and said to his wife, "That dried-up li mei shrub in the garden has come to life and is blooming again. So I have given our baby daughter a name: *Li Mao Ya* (Jasmine Bud), a name of hope and joy and new life."

My mother was not pleased with that name. She also had some superstitions, and she feared that a name with such a pleasant meaning might be the cause of shortening my life. Evil spirits might infer that such a child was very precious and thus might harm me. So she gave me a name that she hoped would deceive the spirits and be a protection to me. She called me *Zhao Ya*. Zhao means "noisy, unpleasant, ugly," and Nga is an imitation of the unhappy whimpering of a young baby.

My father had officially announced my name as Li Mao Ya (Jasmine Bud) but my mother always called me Zhao Ya (Ugly Cry-baby), and people were confused. They did not understand Mao Ya, but they knew why I was called Zhao Ya, and that name stuck to me. Because this displeased my father he gave me another name, *Dao Xing* (virtue and prosperity). He intended this to be my "book name" by which I should henceforth be known. But relatives and neighbors continued to call me Zhao Ya even to the time when I returned to visit my mother's old home after more than fifty years' absence.

2

A Girl at Our School!

For hundreds of years, until near the end of the 19th century, the Yin family had lived in Deqing, a city about 200 miles southwest of Canton and not far from Wuzhou on the border of Guangxi (Zhuangzu) Province. It lay in a poverty-stricken district facing the Xi River on the south and hemmed in by mountains on the north.

The mountains were largely stripped bare of forests and bracken for fuel. Heavy rains gouged great gullies in the mountainsides and washed down coarse gravel that destroyed rice fields in the valley. With the impoverished soil, frequent crop failures caused by drought, and occasional floods when the river inundated the whole valley, people depended on rice and other foods imported from Guangxi (Zhuangzu) and Yunnan. Though people were industrious, thrifty, and honest, all business and industry was unprofitable. They suffered hardship and poverty in hopeless patience.

The standard of living was low, and the mental culture had so deteriorated that the people imagined there lurked many dangers in the world beyond. They so firmly feared the powers of evil spirits that they did not readily accept anything new. Rather, they built up barricades of fear, ignorance, and superstition, hoping to hold back these harmful forces. They were as men with shackled feet unable to make progress.

There was not one wheeled vehicle in the district; all travel was on foot; all farm products and all merchandise were carried on the shoulders of men and women. Long after steamboats were known, because of superstitions, only small boats towed by men were allowed on the upper reaches of the Xi River, which was navigable far up into Guangxi Province. Such was the background of the life of the Yin family in Deqing.

Following the ancient Chinese custom, the entire clan lived together in the ancestral home. At the time I was born, the family consisted of about forty persons. According to tales told by my uncles and aunts of family affairs during the reign of my great-grandmother, what with the quarrels and jealousies, the hatred and the gossip, there was little peace or happiness in that household. When my great-grandparents had grown very old, on the insistence of the younger generations, the families, the food, and the finances were divided. But all the relatives continued to live under the ancestral roof though in separate apartments. All depended largely on the estate that had been handed down from their forefathers. The main business consisted of buying and selling tobacco leaves, and my grandfather, being the eldest son, had inherited the management of the business.

About that time, England had introduced opium into China by way of India. My grandfather, not knowing the great danger in opium smoking and supposing it was in the same category as tobacco, added opium to his stock-in-trade. My father objected to this but was not able to influence his father and brothers. Later, when as the eldest son, he, in his turn, inherited responsibility for the business, he refused it, and it was given to an uncle who unfortunately became an opium addict and brought the business to bankruptcy. In the meantime my father had opened his own business, dealing only in foodstuffs.

Formerly only men were given an academic education, and they studied mainly in the hope of becoming wealthy and famous as government officials. Every three years competitive examinations were held for ambitious scholars; those who failed to pass returned home to study more diligently in privacy and shame. The last to be accepted for literary degrees were those taught in private schools.

In Deqing there were no government schools for boys, much less for girls. As a result, there were no "literati" in the Yin clan sixty-five years ago. However, my father was determined that I should be educated as if I were a son. But since he was not wealthy and did not have much education himself, he was afraid he would be ridiculed if he hired an educated man to teach me privately. Therefore, he decided to send me to a private school for boys which was taught by a Mr. Liang. On the eighth day of the first month he led me to this school and, approaching Mr. Liang with the courtesy of a pupil bowing to his teacher, he arranged for me to enter school. Then he led me to the proper place to worship Confucius and left me in the care of the teacher.

Turning to the last page of the *Three Character Classic* instead of to the first, Mr. Liang began to teach me. Though I did not then understand what I was memorizing, I now know it was this: "Show by your life that you honor your parents;

the way before you will then be light. Afterwards good fortune will abound to you. Work diligently and you will prosper. Waste not time nor energy lest you suffer loss." With the learning of these lines, I had begun my education.

A certain Chinese proverb says, "Seven is the age when a child is divine," that is, exceptionally bright mentally. My father hoped I would be a brilliant pupil like the famous prodigy, Hong. By the Chinese way of counting age, I was seven, but actually I was only five years and thirty-six days old. Mr. Liang was pleased with me because I was the first girl to enter his school, and I was the smallest pupil. The second day my father led me to the door of the schoolroom and sent me in alone. Mr. Liang was not there yet, but most of the pupils had arrived.

One of the boys sneered, "It's a girl. We'll not play with her."

"It sure is a girl," said another. "Boys that play with girls get warts."

I had a sharp answer, and we had a fight with words until the teacher came.

He called me to recite first. I turned my book over, repeated what I had memorized, and sat down, thinking of those impudent boys.

"They hate girls," I said to myself. "They despise me. They say I have warts; they won't play with me just because I am a girl." The more I thought about it, the more fearful I became, so when the teacher was not looking I slipped out and ran home crying, "Those hateful boys insulted me."

"Don't cry," my mother said. "You are a little too young. But you did enter school. You paid your respects to your teacher and to Confucius. Just wait two years, and you can really go to school."

I stopped crying, but never again would I enter that school. Soon we heard the neighborhood gossip: "The Yin family sent a girl to school: she graduated with high honors."

In spite of that ridicule my father said, "My dear little girl, you really must learn to read. Don't ever give up merely because some people make fun of you."

My father and mother were of one heart and one mind as to the necessity for child training, but they used different methods. God provided me with a full measure of a father's gentleness and love and a mother's strict discipline. Sometimes, when she would have punished me severely, he would urge her to have more self-control, and often his serious instruction had more influence with me than my mother's stick.

Once when I was only five years old, while playing with a group of children, I saw a big boy maltreat a small girl. I hit him with my fist and he cursed me with vile language that I did not understand, but I used the same words to scold him in return. Just then my father came along and saw and heard it all.

"Mao Ya, come here," he said.

I left my fight and went skipping happily to him. Instead of the usual hug, he ignored me; he did not speak; he did not even smile. So I followed him home. He led me by the hand to my mother and said very sternly, "Our family is disgraced."

"What terrible thing has she done to disgrace the family?"

"Right out in the street," he said, "she fought with Ya Lun. They scolded and cursed each other with filthy words. What a shame for us! Punish her quickly. Have no pity," he said.

"Our daughter fighting with a boy? Right on the street? We can't have this. Of course she must be punished."

My mother went for a switch, and I knew I was in for a whipping.

"Papa, come quickly," I cried. "She is going to beat me. Take me up. Hold me tight!"

But he paid no attention to my cries. He turned his face away and looked outside. He could not watch while I was punished, though he approved of my mother's doing it.

"Don't you know shame?" said my mother as she whipped me. "Will you fight on the street again? Will you dare to keep on scolding and saying bad words?"

When my father thought I had been punished enough, he took me in his arms, while I cried, partly in pain, but more in bitter surprise that he had shown no pity for his beloved daughter. He carried me outside and sat down under a magnolia tree.

"Mao Ya," he said kindly, "because you did something wrong that we don't allow you to do, I told her to punish you just to teach you not to do those things. You know this, don't you?"

I did not answer.

"Mao Ya, do you hear me?" I nodded my head.

"You are really a good child; but because we love you we must give you good instruction." Then he gently stroked me where I was smarting most and asked, "Does it still hurt?"

Touched by his sympathy I cried harder than ever while he kissed my tear-stained face.

"I know you suffered," he said, "but don't ever forget this: we were suffering too. And remember, you are not to fight, and you must never, never use vile language. This is the custom and law of our home."

Clinging close to him I said in a soft low voice, "I shall not fight and I shall never say bad words."

He wiped away my tears, took some *lokwat* (a small fruit resembling an apple) from his pocket, gave me two of them and told me to take the others to my mother and little sister, then three years old.

Such was the love and severity of my parents as they disciplined and then comforted me. As I have been writing this, I have been moved to tears though more than sixty years have passed. Since then I have lost the never-to-be-forgotten love of my parents, but I accept the great love of my spiritual Father and confidently put my trust in him.

From my childhood I had an independent way of thinking and some characteristics that brought me into many difficult situations. I did not enjoy rowdiness, noise, or excitement. I did not admire facial makeup, though it was popular with brides and fashionable young ladies. I disliked wearing new clothes or gaily embroidered shoes. People said I was a strange child; uncles and aunts called me "The Rebel," and my mother said I was a child with a "hard neck." Because of my peculiarities many said, "She will come to no good end. She can never be happy."

Many superstitions and customs handed down from ancient times I could not believe; the old folk tales contained no truth for me, and I was sure they were pure myth. I refused to believe them, but I could not always give logical reasons for my opinions.

One old tale believed by the people was that the rainbow was a dragon who controlled the wind and the rain. When the rainbow appeared they said, "The dragon is out drinking water," though some said, "He is out to urinate."

Children were given very strict instructions: "Never point your finger at the dragon. This would show great disrespect, and he would be so surprised and angry that he would make your finger drop off. Point once, lose one joint."

Even as my mother told me this, I doubted it. I determined to prove that it was not true; so the next time I saw a rainbow, I pointed my finger just once. I was very careful of that finger; two days passed and no joint had dropped off.

So I held up my finger and said, "Mama, look at my finger."

She looked carefully for a splinter and found none. She squeezed it. "Does that hurt?"

"No, it doesn't hurt."

"There is nothing wrong with it. Go out and play."

Pausing in the doorway, I called back, "Several days ago I pointed at the dragon." Then I ran away quickly lest she punish me.

The next time I saw the rainbow I pointed at it and shouted to my playmates, "Look at the dragon; he's come down to drink."

"Oh, don't point at him; your finger will drop off."

But I kept pointing to show how daring I was.

My aunt Pai Gu saw and heard me, and shouted, "Look at that disobedient child. But her finger hasn't come off. How strange! But it will be off very soon."

A few days later, during a shower, Pai Gu told her little boy to look at the dragon, and pointed to it with her lips instead of her finger. I ran and told an uncle to come quickly.

"Pai Gu's lips are going to fall off."

He hurried out, supposing she had used vile language or cursed someone, but he found her playing with her son.

"You lied," he said rudely to me.

"But she pointed to the dragon with her lips," I said. "Won't they drop off?"

He went off and told my father, hoping he would punish me, but my father only said, "Don't blame her; we have taught her to believe that." Actually my father did believe it and had warned me, but after this he never mentioned it again.

Our house was built around a small courtyard called a light well, and there my father kept many pots of flowers. My mother loved to wear flowers in her hair, and when her morning work was done she gathered a few flowers and put them around the coil of her neatly combed hair. She would stick pink flowers into the pink yarn wound around my tiny braids but, strange child that I was, I did not like flowers in my hair. As soon as possible I would give them to some other girl or throw them away. One day I gave them to Ya Lun, the boy with whom I had fought. I told him to put them in his hair, as men and boys then wore their hair in a queue. I scurried into the house lest he fight me for the insult.

"Where are your flowers?" my mother asked.

"Lost," I lied.

"Dai hua bu kao ri ri, Si, mai bu shen," she said, quoting a local proverb: "If you don't wear your flowers all day, when you die you won't be buried deep."

It was a horrible idea, but I had an answer: "Can't you throw on a few more dustpans full of dirt for me? That would bury me deep enough."

"Good," my father said with a chuckle, "a young bamboo shoot got the better of a bamboo tree."

After that he seemed to regard me in a different light. At a feast for some relatives, he said, "I have decided to treat my daughter as a son and give her a good education. She shall be my heir and continue to live in my home just as a male descendant would do."

The uncles at the feast disapproved and went away without a word. After that my mother never put flowers in my hair, evidently regarding me as a son, and, of course, boys never wore flowers in their hair.

3

The Griefs of a Broken Nest

As an eagle stirs up its nest, hovers over its young, spreading out its wings, taking them up, carrying them on its wings, so the Lord alone led him. (Deuteronomy 32:11-12)

My father was a merchant who prepared his own merchandise from rice, beans, and such things. The refuse—the outer coat of these cereals—my mother used to feed to pigs. The buildings were old and damaged by frequent floods and, as the business grew, it was necessary to have new buildings. So my father borrowed 80 *liang*, about 110 silver dollars, expecting to repay it in about a year. Then, without warning symptoms, my father became ill, and his business did not flourish. Although we lived frugally, he was not able to pay off the debt.

A proverb says: "One never knows what the heavens may suddenly bring upon us, whether blessing or woe." Into our peaceful home trouble came suddenly: my father died.

Naive, and inexperienced, and barely six years of age, I could not realize what a calamity had come upon us. Though I was a bright child, I had no idea of the meaning of death. I simply thought he was going away from the place where we had been so happy together. Though my little sister cried beside the lifeless body, then clung to my mother, I did not weep. Instead I urged others not to cry. They told me I must cry, but I would not. They told me to kneel down and wail but I refused, even though Pai Gu beat me.

When my father's body was lying in the coffin many people came to pay their respects. My uncles had hired an eight-piece orchestra to play funeral dirges, but I thought it was a joyful and exciting occasion. Again Pai Gu beat me with a stick and forced me to kneel and wail, but I kept peeping through my unkempt hair to see what they were doing to my father.

In my home I had never heard idle talk about dead people, and that is the reason I had no idea what death involved. Afterwards I realized I no longer had a father. I saw my sister clinging to my mother and crying with her before the memorial tablet, but I wondered why. I had yet to learn the meaning of sorrow. While they wept before the tablet, I sat facing the wall behind the door, crying with loneliness and longing.

I often asked people, "Where is my father?" but they paid little attention to me, and I, formerly so full of happiness and energy, was greatly changed and spent my time weeping.

After observing the usual period of mourning, my mother had to make a living for herself and her two small daughters. So she went out weeping, to cut grass for fuel or to sell, to hoe the ground, to pick mulberry leaves, or to do any other work she could find. At such times, one hopes that friends might give timely assistance, but, after a time, hearts grow cold and indifferent, and nobody is ready to help.

This poor widow's creditors wanted her to pay back the silver they had loaned to her husband, so they sought a plan to force her to pay the debt at once in full. As she came home weary from her work one evening, a man representing her creditor followed her. At first, he spoke words of comfort and sympathy. Then he said they wanted her to repay the debt at once.

"I have two small daughters," she replied, "and it is not easy to make a living and pay the debt at once. I beg you to be patient, and I can pay it gradually during two or three years."

Speaking very gently, he said, "Let me suggest a plan that would quickly relieve you of this great burden."

"Under heaven on this earth," she replied, "there is no easy solution for this."

"Yes, there is; only listen to me," he said. "You owe Xu Dai twenty-four liang of silver. I know a young widow who has neither son nor daughter and she wants to adopt a girl. Give her one of your daughters, then ask her to give you twenty-four liang of silver. Then you can pay your debt, and all will be satisfied."

"Impossible!" my mother said. "I can never do such a thing."

"Then pay your debt to Xu Dai at once."

"Can he not give me a few days to try to find a plan?"

"Good!" he said. "I'll give you five days."

My mother led her two daughters to the memorial tablet and wept.

Five days passed. The next evening the man came again.

"Have you made up your mind to sell your girl?" he said.

"I shall never sell my daughter," my mother said. "I would rather sell this new house my husband built and be homeless."

"Then sell it, and pay your debt," he said.

Since my mother was not able to carry on the business alone, or to raise pigs as before, she consulted a real estate man about selling part of the property.

When the uncles heard about this they said, "Don't you know you have no right to sell this property? We shall refuse to sign the deed."

This was reasonable, for it was a well-known custom that no one could sell a part of the ancestral home or land, even if he had personally paid for it, without first getting the consent of all relatives. My father, having no living son, had intended to regard me as his son and heir, but he had left neither will nor instructions, and the Yin clan never had such a custom.

Since my father had no male heir, his brother had become head of the clan. It was his obligation to protect the rights of this widow and her children, but he had no regard for justice or mercy, and he refused to allow her to sell her property.

There were no kindhearted folk "to bring hot coals to give her comfort." On the contrary, many came to trouble and annoy her about paying her debt. So she was helpless in the hands of Zhu Dai her creditor.

One day Zhu Dai came with the representative as well as the childless widow and her mother. The man at once opened a paper covered with writing and demanded that my mother put her fingerprint on it. She refused, as she did not know what was written on the paper.

The creditor said, "If you will not sign this with your fingerprint, then pay me the money at once."

She wept and pleaded with them to be more merciful.

"Give me two days to consult with others and have this paper explained to me."

But they refused.

They began to force her, while she clung to the side of the doorway. Some pulled her hands, others pushed her. They cruely forced her hands to make a fingerprint, while we two little girls clung to her. Then they heartlessly dragged my little sister away. This paper was a contract for selling her daughter. In truth my mother did not know what it was.

She hoped as conditions improved to repay the money and redeem the child, but she was told that since her fingerprint was on the paper it would be difficult, if not impossible, to do this.

These grievous troubles had come upon us after the death of my father. The ancients said, "If the nest be broken, how shall the nestlings escape?" This sad experience still lives in my memory. I was now the solitary child of a friendless widow. When she went out to work, she locked me in the house, lest some harm come to me. I was a child "with only my form and my shadow to comfort each other." All day long I wept, calling for father and mother, but my cries were never heard. One kindhearted neighbor, sorry that I was locked in the house, took me into her home where I played with her daughter. But that pleasure was a passing mist, as Mrs. Liang became ill and again I was locked in the house with my sorrow.

Afterward, my aunt Liu Gu took me to her home, hoping the companionship of her children would cheer me. On the farm, they had eight water buffalo, so she sent me with her children to watch them as they grazed. Soon they left the herding to me. I was only six years old, and these wily beasts knew I did not know how to control them. When they ran away, I could only yell at them and weep in frustration.

Liu Gu sent me to sleep at their grandmother's place where the cows were kept. My pallet was in a small loft built over the cow stalls. I cried and could not sleep because I was afraid. The old lady scolded and cursed me, calling me an ill-omened, worthless child, as she sent me off with the cows. I cried all the while for my father and mother.

Liu Gu's husband was a farmer, a common laborer, but he was one who had sympathy for me. He often chatted and joked with me, trying to make me happy, but every time he spoke kindly to me, tears began to flow. He noticed that I ate much less than his children ate, and he understood and was sorry for me.

As soon as the busy season was over on the farm, he took me home. When I saw my mother, I ran to her and we wept together and could not stop. My uncle could not bear to see such grief, so with a few words of comfort to us he left without waiting to rest or drink tea.

4

No Hope from Idols

Superstitious belief in evil spirits has deep roots and very strong branches in the hearts of the people of my country, and it appears in many forms. People believe that spirits have all power over both good and evil happenings, even over life and death. To avoid death or escape calamity one need only burn gold or silver paper before the idols. The sacrifice of a fat animal, a tasty piece of roast pork, or other delicacy is supposed to induce the spirit not to send calamity.

My father had such beliefs as a faithful disciple of Buddha. He had a firm belief in cause and effect: that every sin had its appropriate penalty, and that a man's conduct in his former existence had its effect in this world. Good conduct would bring blessing; sins would bring suffering and hardship.

Buddhism teaches that the soul of man after death continually mutates, or is transformed through six paths or stages like a wheel in perpetual motion, becoming (1) a *deva*, a god of an order of good spirits; (2) man; (3) *Asuras*, a power for good or evil; (4) a beast; (5) a hungry ghost; (6) hell. Anyone who has lived a holy and virtuous life may escape these transmigrations; otherwise, he may be cast into a shoreless sea from which there is no escape. Therefore, my father sought salvation in Buddha, worshiping and sacrificing to idols in any temple he passed. He deceived himself with self-improvement and good works to avoid punishment. Sometimes he took me to a temple to worship, but I always asked questions and presented problems.

Once at the Temple of Joy and Goodness, as he worshiped the snake god, which was of stone, I said, "Who is this we are worshiping? Why do we worship a stone and put flowers on it?"

Before I finished my question, he put his hand over my mouth and said, "Say no more. You will offend the snake god."

Another time he said, "Little Bud, your body is very weak, so I am taking you to a temple to pray to the queen goddess to give you good health. She has the heart of a mother and will certainly have pity on you."

He lit the incense and candles, then worshiped the idol.

"Now kowtow three times with your face to the floor," he told me.

I did that while he burned offerings of gold and silver papers to the idol. Then we both knelt and bowed three times together, while he spoke in a low voice.

A priest dressed in a long black robe came in and spoke with my father, wrote something on a yellow paper, then folded it into a triangle. He put a thread through it and fastened it to a button on my dress.

"Now," he said very earnestly, "wear this always, and it will keep evil spirits away; it will overcome devils and prevent trouble."

He wrote a second paper, burned it before the idol, put the ashes in a cup, poured cold water over it, and told me to drink it.

"I won't drink it," I said. "It has ashes in it."

My father took the cup and said, "You are a good, obedient little girl, and because I love you dearly, I want you to drink it." So I closed my eyes and drank it at one gulp. But the medicine of the goddess did not heal me. All day and all night I was very ill with fever, nausea, and dysentery.

"She is so hot—as if she had a fire in her," my father said.

"You don't need to tell me," my mother said. "The ashes of your paper offerings are heavier than her body. What good is all your worshiping?"

And she berated him for believing in idols and evil spirits, and for his stupidity in making me drink the medicine of the gods, and probably causing my death. But by the next day I had almost recovered.

Even before we had heard of the true God and salvation through Jesus Christ, my mother and I had doubts about the idols and spirits my father worshiped. This truly was God's grace to us.

Nevertheless out of respect for his faith, on the night before his burial, my mother called a Buddhist priest to perform the correct rites and incantations for his soul.

To comfort her he said, "Because your husband had a good clean heart he will not fall into the eighteen hells to be punished, but will be raised to the highest heavens. He will not be forever changing, but will become a bird, free and comfortable, flying both east and west; he will be fat and hearty with no anxiety about food or clothing. Only in rain or cold will he suffer hardship."

My mother believed the priest, so with joy and relief she said to me: "Your father has gone into the heavens and has been changed into a bird. So you must never, never harm a bird, for there is one bird that is your father."

I believed this, and afterward every time I saw a flock of birds flying about I lifted my face to look at them, hoping that among the flock I might find my father. If they settled down somewhere near, I would quietly slip up close to them and ask softly, "Are you my papa?"

No bird ever answered; each flew away when I came near. I felt hopeless and cheated. Both my mother and I were deluded and fooled by superstition and the priest. We could not really believe a man could be reborn as a bird after he was dead, but we were being fools in order to find comfort.

5

Found by a Heavenly Father

While I was living with Liu Gu, my mother was very lonely, and now that we were together again I refused to leave her day or night.

One day I went with her to the mountain to cut grass. It was a long hot walk in the sun, and that night I became ill with high fever. She tried all the remedies the neighbors recommended, but I became worse. She could not leave me to go to work, and she had no money to call a doctor. She finally decided to carry me to a Chinese doctor.

Just as she carried me out of the door, Yin Liu Shu, a relative, came to see me, and she urged my mother to take me to the Mission Hospital.

"People tell me," my mother said, "that those foreign doctors take little children and dig out their eyes to make medicine. I'll never take my daughter to that hospital."

Liu Shu was a water carrier at the hospital, and she knew the doctors never did such things, but my mother could not believe it.

Just then I asked for a drink, and Mother went to the kitchen to boil water for tea. Liu Shu seized this opportunity to take me on her back, calling out as we went, "Shu Po, I am going."

"When you have time, come back and stay a while," Mother called in reply.

When she came with the tea, she could not find me, and she was sure that Liu Shu had carried me off to the hospital, so she came after us. On reaching the hospital almost a mile away, she found that Dr. Jean McBurney was already examining me. She watched, saying to herself, "I'll not leave her even half a step, and if they make one move to cut her eyes out, I'll beat them."

The doctor found I was suffering from malaria, hookworms, and other parasites, so she said I should stay in the hospital for care and medication. However, still fearful, my mother determined to take me home.

On the way out she peeped into a large ward and saw a mother with a little child. She carried me into the room and was surprised to see that the child still had her eyes, though her whole face was covered with bandages because of a burn. She talked with the woman and learned that the child was recovering and that the doctor could be trusted. Just then she saw Liu Ai Chen, the doctor's helper whom she knew, so she consented to leave me for the night.

During the night I kept calling for my father, and during the day I cried for him. Until she talked with my mother, the doctor supposed it was because of the fever. Then she used psychology as well as medicine, and I soon began to get well.

She often spoke to me about "Our Father in heaven," and I supposed she was talking about my father. She said, "If you want to see your Father in heaven you must believe in Jesus."

"Oh, I believe. I do believe. Please take me quickly to see my papa."

She then saw that I had a wrong idea, so she explained, "Our heavenly Father is not the father you had here on earth who died. He is God who created the heavens, the earth, and people and all things. So we belong to him. All who believe in him and love him call him 'Our Father in heaven.' He loves you even more than your own father loved you and he will care for you, embracing you with his everlasting arms."

When she said that, I threw my arms around her neck and wept: "Please take me to him," I said. "My heart is urgent."

"Our Father in heaven is a spirit," she explained. "He doesn't have a form or body like we have, and we can't see him with our eyes. His Son, Jesus, came to earth and had a body like ours. He died for our sins, so we must believe in him and he will forgive our sins and lead us to the heavenly Father. He will give you peace and will never leave you without comfort."

Again I said, "Take me to him quickly. The more you tell me the more eager my heart is to go to him."

She said, "Only Jesus can lead you to him."

This made me sad and I cried out, "O Jesus, lead me to my Father."

Many days passed and, seeing that I was really seeking the heavenly Father, she taught me to pray to him in the name of Jesus. We knelt together, and I repeated her prayer after her as she confessed that she was a sinner and asked his forgiveness because of the death of Jesus for sin.

We prayed, "Make me a clean new person, a child that will please God, and receive me as your child, for Jesus' sake. Amen." She said, "This is the way you speak to your heavenly Father, so every time you feel lonely and in need of your father who has died, just pray for what is in your heart. He is always glad to hear his children speak to him."

After this, I often prayed, and as I learned to pray, I was mysteriously changed. I ceased continually to cry and call for my father. As I now know, all these sad experiences were God's grace to me. He used sickness and death to break up the home in which I had been lovingly nestled. But he did not cast me off and forsake me. As the eagle he "spread forth his wings, caught me up in his wings," and carried me even to his own home to become his child, and to obtain such blessing and peace and joy as this world cannot give. If he had not done this I should have followed my father in his superstition and idol worship on the way to hell.

After I recovered from my illness, Dr. McBurney said to me, "Before you go, I want to take you to a place where there are many girls."

So I went with her, and my mother followed. She took me to the Love Doctrine School for Girls. I saw one girl I knew, Huang Jin Ying, a distant relative, so I ran and sat down beside her. When my mother called me to go home, I said, "I am not going home."

The doctor urged her to let me stay with my friend, as it would help me to get well and forget my sorrow. My mother remembered that my father had promised that I should get an education. She noticed how healthy and happy all the girls were and decided to let me stay and study. Then she could go to work as usual.

She went to Jin Ying's desk and told me I could stay in school. I was so delighted that I laughed aloud and danced for joy. This was what my father had promised.

So we went to the principal, who was the sister of the doctor.

She asked me many questions, and I answered so clearly that I was accepted as a student. When she asked my name, my mother said, "Yin Zhao Ya." The teacher said, "That is not a suitable name for a pupil in school. You should give her another name."

"I remember now," she said. "Her father called her Mao Ya (Jasmine Bud) when she was born. Then later he gave her a 'read-book name,' Dao Xing."

The teacher was pleased with that name and said, "Dao is for Dao Li, which means doctrine or teaching, and Xing is for Xing Wang, which means prosperity.[1] The doctrine of Jesus prospers." I did not understand until some years later what it meant for Jesus' doctrine to prosper.

So my mother went home alone, and I really began to "read book." Even this was not ideal, however, for when night came I began to long for my mother. Often I would hide behind my book, or pretend to search for something in my desk, so that no one would see my tears.

Mother was lonely, too, and she often wept, but on the Sabbath she came with Liu Shu for church services and always came to the school to see me. When vacation came we were happy to be together again. When school opened in the autumn she felt it was best for me to stay with her for companionship and comfort. But finally, her mother's heart could not endure my continual coaxing, so I went as a day-pupil, she going with me in the morning and calling for me in the evening. This interfered with her work, so I then agreed to stay at home.

They missed me at school, and Liu Shu told them why I could not go. Just then the McBurney sisters needed some one to care for the house, so they asked my mother to help them, and she was glad to accept. After that I lived in the School for Children and my mother lived in the School for Women. Now she had permanent work and an opportunity to learn to read.

During this time the grace of God came upon us both. In 1908 my mother was baptized in the Reformed Presbyterian Church. Even before this I had become a believer, but because I was very young and there were no other Christians in my home, the pastor thought I should wait until I was more mature.

After I had been absent from Dr. McBurney's Bible class because of illness, she gave me 2 Corinthians 12:9 to memorize: "And he said to me, 'My grace is sufficient for you, for my strength is made perfect in weakness.'" All through my life, this verse has given me strength, whether in physical or spiritual weakness. Apart from prayer, nothing has been so helpful and so delightful to me as the knowledge of this wonderful promise.

6

A House Divided

My mother had a heart to believe in Jesus, but she had never been to school, so she could not read the Bible. But, when she went to work in the home of the McBurney sisters, she spent some time in the School for Women and learned to read. Her faith and her hope grew, and that is why she was baptized.

Because I was always searching for my father, the heavenly Father found me. The doctor had led me to know and love Jesus as my Savior, and after I entered the Qi Li School we had a Bible lesson every day. I soon knew many of the stories and teachings of the Bible. When I saw my mother receiving baptism, I wanted very much to be baptized also.

Sometime during the winter of 1907–08, I went to the meeting of the church session to be examined. As I had not learned much church history, I failed to pass for baptism. At the spring communion, I went again for examination and showed satisfactory understanding, but once again I was advised to wait because I was so young. Though I had been deprived of the privileges of church membership, I did not show a bad spirit, but at the third opportunity some months later, I again applied for baptism. I was examined and the pastor admitted that he was satisfied that I understood the gospel and the meaning of baptism, but again the command was that I wait until I was older. This time I was not willing to wait.

Elder Liang said, "Why are you so very eager to be baptized?"

"I believe in Jesus," I said. "I want to be baptized as a proof that I am a Christian."

They all laughed, and with a red face I ran to Mr. J. K. Robb and said, "I won't wait. Jesus said 'Suffer little children to come unto me and forbid them not.' Why do you forbid me to be baptized?"

That very tall pastor smiled kindly, and as though speaking from heaven he said, "Tomorrow you may be baptized. You may go now."

I was so happy that I ran skipping back to school. The next day was Saturday. At the service that day, many were to be baptized—men, women, boys, and one insignificant little girl. All stood in a long row at the front of the church. I was at the end of the line near where Mrs. A. I. Robb was sitting. Next to me stood Mrs. Zhong, a rather large, tall woman in ample loose-fitting clothing with wide sleeves that completely hid the small girl beside her.

Pastor A. I. Robb performed the baptisms, beginning with the men and boys, then the women. After baptizing Mrs. Zhong, he was returning to the pulpit for the prayer, when his wife called, "You have forgotten the little girl." He came back and discovered the shy little girl close beside the large lady.

So at last I was baptized as a Christian in the spring of 1909 when I was not yet ten years old.[2]

Afterwards some people said, "You should not have been baptized that day. You could talk so glibly that the pastor let you leak through though you are so naughty."

"This," I said, "is God's will. Satan didn't want me baptized. God knows I am bad, but he loves me, I am sure. This is what we Christians say is God's wonderful grace."

When I said this I was very happy and sang:

> Jesus loves me, this I know,
> For the Bible tells me so.
> Little ones to him belong;
> They are weak but he is strong.

They said, "You are a naughty little girl," and went away. Jesus said to his disciples, "If the world hates you, you know that it hated me before it hated you.... Because you are not of the world, but I chose you out of the world, therefore the world hates you" (John 15:18-19).

While my father was alive he led me and taught me to worship idols and our ancestors. This was the customary thing, and after his death I also went for a time to worship the ancestors' spirits. My father had taught me much of the history of our ancestors, so I was pleased to light the incense for worshiping them morning and evening. On all special festival days and anniversaries, I worshiped with folded hands and the kowtow, because I reverenced them as being my own blood relations and forefathers.

After I received Jesus as my Savior, I knew that neither the idols nor my ancestors were gods; so I did not worship them nor burn incense to them. For some time after we were baptized, we lived at the schools and were seldom at home.

In 1911, China was at war. Because of the fear that the tragedy of the Boxer Rebellion (1898–1900) might be repeated, all foreigners were ordered to leave China. The missionaries living in Deqing went to Hong Kong, a British colony. The schools were closed, and my mother had no work, so we returned home. My uncle would not allow us to enter the house. He threw our baggage into the street, saying, "You two can't ever come in here. We decided long ago no longer to recognize you as belonging to the Yin clan."

"What reason have you for doing this?" my mother asked.

He replied, "I first ask you this: These three years, why have you not been living in your own home? Even your ancestors you have neglected. You have not burned incense to them nor worshiped them. How, then, can you pretend to belong to the Yin clan?"

Mother said, "I have sometimes come back to see you. But since my work is for another house, of course I couldn't live at home. Zhao Ya was living in school; she could not live here alone."

My Fourth Uncle said, "Since you work for foreign people and worship foreign gods, and do not worship our ancestors or idols, we can't allow you to enter this house."

On hearing this, my mother went out and called the village elders to meet in the room where my father had died.

"My husband lived and died in this room," she said. "Then my daughter was very ill, and no one helped to care for her. We went to the foreign hospital where she became well and strong. Three women doctors cared for her and healed her. Then I determined with my whole heart and mind to devote my life of widowhood to serving them, since I and my daughter are alone. I have not broken the customs of the Yin family.

"Therefore I wish to regard as my home the place where my bridal chair rested. I beg you, village fathers and elders, to speak just and equitable words in my behalf and do not cause trouble for my daughter and me. This was my husband's ancestral home. This the elders of the Yin family know, and also they know why I went to work for foreigners. But because we worship another God, they are displeased with us."

The village elders gave a stern command to my Fourth Uncle, who was then the head of the clan, not to cast us out of the home. They advised my mother to observe the customs of ancestral worship, at least until I grew up. Therefore, we were allowed to live in the home in peace.

Though the family was divided, living and eating separately, all worshiped at the same shrine which was in our section of the house—the one farthest back from the front entrance. Since we were Christians, we could not sin against God by worshiping ancestors and idols.

So I went to my uncles and said, "My mother and I believe in Jesus and cannot worship any God but him. So from now on I cannot worship at the ancestral tablets, nor burn incense to them. Nor can we share in the cost of incense and candles. Every year we shall go and help repair ancestral graves, but we can't join in the worship."

When my uncles' mother heard me say this, she very excitedly scolded and cursed and even beat me. My Sixth Aunt said to her, "Don't do that. The village elders may hear of it and say we insult the ancestors by mistreating this lone widow and her daughter."

So they stopped scolding and beating me, and I went home and told my mother what I had done.

After a few days my father's older sister came to visit us. Among all the relatives, she was the one who was kind to us. But she also reproved us for not worshiping as she worshiped, and she wept.

"Dai Gu, do not cry," I said quietly. "Please listen to me. When I was born, everyone said I was just a girl 'born facing outside,' and they advised my parents to send me off, unwanted, to the foundling house. But they refused. If they had sent me off to that place for foundlings, I certainly would have died. Wouldn't that be the same as for me not to worship here now? Since I was born a girl, would I not be married into another clan and not required to worship here? Just pretend that I was married off early and that, like the married aunts, I don't worship here."

My aunt quit scolding and went out to an uncle and said, "Uncle, this girl is irreverent toward her forefathers. She was born stubborn and with a sharp tongue. Leave her alone. I can't convince her." Then she went to her own home. This was in 1911, when I was just twelve years old.

At the New Year, my mother and I went to visit her elder brother. They had heard rumors that we were irreverent toward the ancestors, and also that she was an immoral woman. They refused to accept her explanation.

While I was playing with my cousin, he bumped his head against the wall, so they bumped mine until it bled. When my mother came to my help they beat her, until I ran out into the street and called, "Save a life! My uncle is beating my mother." Neighbors came and helped us escape from our relatives.

As we came home, I said, "Jesus knew these things would come to us, and he said, 'Rejoice and be exceedingly glad…for so they persecuted the prophets who were before you' (Matthew 5:12). We must be patient and endure it."

In the autumn of 1912, after the revolution against the Manchus, the country was again peaceful. The foreign workers were permitted to return, so the chapels, schools, and hospitals were opened again. I then really began to "read book."

One day while I was in class, my Fifth Aunt came into the classroom and said, "Mao Ya, come outside. I have something to tell you."

She took a stick she had hidden and began to beat me. I ran away and said, "Wu Gu, why have you come so far to beat me, without any reason?"

"I came representing your forefathers," she said. "I came to beat you for not worshiping them. You show no reverence; you burn no incense. There is no fire, no smoke. You don't even give them any food."

"Don't be so hasty, Wu Gu. Tell me a good reason for beating me, and I'll gladly take it."

"How dare you be so hardhearted and leave your own father with no light, no incense, no fire, no food?"

She purposely spoke of my father to move me to worship him and the ancestors. But my heart was as though half iron, and I could not turn and worship the devil.

I answered her in a surprised tone, "Did my father tell you he was hungry? Why does he not come and tell me? If he came to me, would I disappoint him? Now, Wu Gu, let me ask you this: Do our ancestors eat the smoke and fragrance of incense as food?"

"Don't ask so many questions," she said. "Only light incense morning and evening." And she gave me a hearty slap.

"Wu Gu," I said, "I haven't finished; I must speak of their food. We who are alive must have at least one bowl of rice at each meal. How many bowls of rice are in an incense stick? Do they all get enough to eat? Or do the last ones get none?"

Suddenly her manner changed.

"Burning incense is not giving them food; it is just asking how they are, morning and evening."

"Is that so?" I said. "Did any of them tell you they were unhappy?"

Again she was very angry and slapped me in the face, *kwack kwack*; this time I did not move.

She pointed her finger at me and said, "Your forefathers are unlucky. The Yin clan is unlucky just because you don't worship them. Your father worshiped Buddha, and said many prayers hoping for a son, but all he got was you, an irreverent, unloving, rebellious, wicked, and unlucky girl. Your father's incense bowl sits there empty. Instead, you sharpen that tongue of yours. It is not surprising that your own aunt calls you obstreperous, heaven-born-stubborn, and sharp-tongued."

After this no relation ever mentioned ancestor worship to me or troubled me about it. Among all the eight aunts and many cousins, Wu Gu was the ablest talker and had hoped to make me submit. But God was my protector.

7

The School Ghost Destroyed

When the first missionaries of the Reformed Presbyterian Church decided to begin work in Deqing, they had difficulty in finding a suitable place to live and work. Then someone suggested an old temple in an ancient graveyard east of the city, which was available because it was said to be haunted.

That land, including the building, was purchased, and the temple was repaired and used as a dwelling until other buildings were erected. Then the temple was used as a school for girls.

It was rumored about town that in clearing the land many skeletons had been found. It was very interesting and frightening to listen to the spicy tales told at tea houses and feasts about the angry spirits who often returned to earth to get revenge because worshipers had neglected them. However, when the school was opened, no one seemed to be alarmed about such things and even seemed not to know about them. Then a new teacher came from Canton, named Ni Liu Yong, and her mind was obsessed with fears and superstitions about evil spirits.

At that time I was only seven or eight years old and had no knowledge or fear of such things. But after Miss Ni came the older girls were soon infected, so that even the sound of grass or paper fluttering in the wind was a devil, and a strange shadow frightened them. At night they would push two or three beds together for safety. As an ancient proverb says: "Scarlet dye makes white scarlet; ink makes white black. So also may our minds be changed."

At home my mother and I never talked about devils, but in the school, now ghost-haunted and devil-fearing, I began to have some fears. But in times of fear I always prayed, "Lord save me from them; don't let them seize me." Then I could go to my own bed and sleep. My bed was just under the open stairs leading to the attic.

One night I was half awakened by something creeping across my face. I yelled, "A ya! Gui lai!" (The devil has come!)

Next day Mrs. Robb, our teacher, asked me why I screamed in the night.

"I was afraid of devils," I said, not trying to keep it secret as the older girls did.

Next night while I was sleeping I felt something moving about my bed. It scratched my toe.

"If that's a devil, I want to see it," I thought, so I lay quietly and soon it was nibbling at my big toe. I kicked with all my might and knocked it against the stairs. When I heard it go *pik-paak*, *pik-paak* up the stairs, I got up to see what it was but could see nothing.

Next morning I examined my toes, and I was sure the marks on them were made by very small teeth, and I said, "Of course it was not a devil. It was a rat."

In this way I had learned something about devils: they could bite, and they were rats. And the sounds that had frightened us were these "devils" scampering up and down stairs between the ricebags in the dining room cupboard and their hideaway in the attic.

Later a woman was hired to act as school mother. She was a wonderful storyteller; every night we gathered around her to hear very exciting tales about the fearsome doings of returned spirits. Some of the girls were so frightened that she had to teach them how to catch these spirits: simply tie a slip knot in a string, making a big circle, coax the devil into it, then gently slip the knot up around him.

A more plausible tale was of a certain person always dressed in white who often sauntered back and forth along the walk between the school and the house where the principal lived. This was supposedly the spirit of Miss Jennie Torrence, the first principal of the school, who died just before the school was opened.

That autumn, Miss Huston invited the pupils to her home for supper and a party on her birthday. We prepared to leave at nine o'clock. We had heard so much about the lady spirit in white that, as we started, we gathered in a close group for safety, but no one dared to go first. Being a venturesome child with a bit of the breath and blood of courage, I said, "I'm not afraid. I'll go first," and the other girls said, "We'll all hold hands and follow you."

As we turned at the corner of the house, suddenly I saw the spirit person clad in glowing white. It was quite tall and big and kept moving slightly.

"Who are you?" I shouted, "And why have you come here?"

I shouted again as there was no answer, "Why don't you say something?"

It said nothing but kept moving.

I looked around, but the girls had all disappeared. My legs became so weak that I fell.

Frightened I cried, "Lord save me." The whole school had run, terrified, back into the house, up the stairs, and across the bridge to the school. I ran after them as fast as I could go.

All the next day I kept thinking, "Actually, what was that thing I saw? I must find out and know absolutely."

So I got a strong piece of bamboo, and after dark I took it and went out to the same spot. With the stick in my hand ready to strike, I said, "If you dare to come here again, I dare to meet you face to face. I am not trusting myself. I am trusting in Jesus."

Then I prayed, "Lord, be with me."

There it was, exactly as before, glistening white and moving, but silent.

"Tell me who you are, and why you come to this place every night."

Still no answer.

"So you think I am afraid of you!" I said sternly.

With my eyes closed, gritting my teeth, I ran at this evil spirit and with my bamboo beat it again and again with all my might.

"It sounds like the leaves of a tree," I thought, so opened my eyes.

It was a tree with the moon shining on the luxuriant glossy leaves. Having gained the victory, I dragged my bamboo back to the corner of the walk and looked again. It was exactly as it had been. So I went cautiously to the tree and felt the leaves resplendent in the light of the full moon.

I went out every evening to watch this scene until the moon waned and the scene was entirely different. I had annihilated the rumor about the lady spirit that haunted the school.

In August of 1912, a neighbor girl said to me, "Last night several girls went to the temple to play with the fairy spirits. One of the girls said she saw your father, and that he said he longed to see you."

Being a Christian I did not believe the dead could speak with the living, but this aroused the memory of my father and a desire to see him.

"If you go again to play with the fairies, I want to go with you and see what it is like."

I told my mother, and she gave me permission to go.

In the temple was a bed, and on it a lighted lamp, a bundle of incense sticks, and a bowl of water. A woman called Ai Gu and two girls were lying there, so we also lay down. Soon an old woman came in, carrying lighted incense sticks, and she waved them back and forth as she muttered incantations that we could not understand.

After about half an hour of this, Ai Gu sat up and said, "The *xian gu* (immortal fairy) doesn't let me go down to *fen di* (the place of the dead)."

"No wonder you can't go," the old woman said. "For some strange reason when I call here and there, again and again, the spirits don't respond. Probably someone here is unclean and the spirit won't come up. So you may as well go home."

My heart was disturbed, and I went home—alone.

Next morning Shu Mei came and said, "After you left, the old woman called, and the spirit came up. Ai Gu saw your father again, and he said he was very contented there. He was wearing the same clothes as he wore when he went."

"I'm going with you again to see for myself," I said.

When we came to the temple I said to the old woman, "I also want to go to fen di to see the fairy spirits."

"Your eyes are too big," she said, "not suitable for that place. I fear you can't go."

Shu Mei had a plan. "I'll sew your clothes to Ai Gu's clothes, and when she goes she must take you along."

She brought needle and thread and sewed us together. The geomancer did the usual incantations for summoning the spirits, burning incense all the while. She kept it up until she was weary, and still no spirits came.

"I wasn't wrong," the old woman said. "It's because of you with the big eyes. The spirits are not willing for you to see them. You might as well go home."

I got off the bed so quickly that Ai Gu's clothes were torn where we were sewn together. She got up and hit me hard in the face, while Shu Mei cut the threads. I controlled my anger and went home disappointed and crying.

My mother asked why I was crying, and I told her all about it.

"They said my father wanted to see me, but the old woman said because of me and my big eyes the spirit wouldn't come up though I wanted to see him."

We wept together, then prayed about it, and God's good Spirit made us understand that those "good fairy spirits" were evil spirits sent out by the devil and used by him to deceive people by pretending to be souls of people who had died. I confessed my sin and asked God never to let me desire to see or be with my father as long as I lived.

Shu Mei came next day to tell me what happened after I left, but I said, "Don't tell me anything, and don't let that witch amuse you in that way. It is the devil deceiving you. The devil is a liar and the father of lies. I now know why I couldn't go to the place of the dead. It is because I believe in Jesus, and the devil knows that Jesus' blood cleanses me, and he dare not come to meet me."

All these experiences strengthened my faith in God's Word, and confirmed my belief that the spirits or souls of the dead do not become devils or unclean spirits or even "good fairies," nor do they bring to earth either blessing or misfortune.

Many years later when I was teaching Bible in Manchuria I learned that some Christians were still haunted by old superstitions of witchcraft and necromancy. Mrs. Xu was one of these, so I told her what Jesus said about the rich man who went to hell and the poor man who went to heaven. The rich man wanted to warn his brothers: why did not his spirit return to earth? When he asked that Lazarus, the poor man, be sent, neither did he go. Because the spirits of the dead cannot return to earth, either for good or for evil.

"But Jesus cast out demons and unclean spirits," said Miss Li, my coworker. "And the prophet Samuel was seen and heard on earth after he was dead."

"Yes," I replied. "These things are recorded in the Bible. Who are the unclean spirits? They came 'out of the mouth of the dragon' (Revelation 16:13). And who is the dragon? 'That old dragon…who is the Devil and Satan,' we read in Revelation 20:2. This Satan is also called 'that old serpent,' the same who deceived Adam and Eve.

"It was that same spirit who long afterward entered into the witch of Endor, disguised himself as the prophet Samuel, long dead, and deceived not only King Saul but also everyone who believes that the witch actually called up the spirit of Samuel. Though King Saul was disguised, the spirit in the witch recognized him and knew that the king had decreed death for all witches and diviners. Satan had won when Saul said no harm should come to the witch.

"Then, speaking as though he were Samuel, the spirit said (using the witch), 'Since God has departed from you, why do you call me? Tomorrow both you and your sons will be with me where I am.' Since Saul had departed from God and God from him, how could he go to paradise where Samuel was? Saul and his sons were slain the next day.

"These incidents show that Satan has superhuman powers and supernatural knowledge, that he is able to disguise himself, and to enter into the hearts of men or women. But the spirits of those who have died do not return to earth for good or for evil."

Mrs. Xu's heart was enlightened, and she was never again enslaved by the fear of the spirits of the dead, and she trusted God to protect her from Satan.

8

A Girl's Learning Tested

Before my mother learned to read and write, she had learned an ancient way of keeping records and accounts by tying knots in cords. For written records she had an educated man write them on incense sticks that had the wax burned off in worship.

After I had been in school a year or two, the Mission School was closed during the war against the Manchus, so my mother and I were at home weaving cloth, rearing silkworms, and working in the garden to earn a living. One day I noticed these incense sticks with writing on them, in a pot of earth. I climbed up out of curiosity, took one out and read it, then took the whole lot to my mother. She took them at once and put them back in the pot. Then she explained carefully that they were her family records and very precious to her.

I went to the bedroom and shook out a few coppers from my savings bank and secretly went out to a shop where they sold writing materials. I bought paper such as we used in school to learn to write, went home, and made it into a book. Then I asked my mother to tell me, one by one, what the sticks meant to her, and I wrote it in the book. The next day she asked me to read it all to her, as she hardly believed that I, a girl, could write it correctly. She was pleased when I read it just as she had told me to write it.

Then she said, "I wish you could learn to be an accountant like the one in my cousin's shop. She uses the abacus with her left hand and writes it with her right hand. Everybody in Deqing boasts of her ability."

Later my mother took me to her cousin's home, where I met Wan Sao,[3] the accountant, and at once we became friends. After that I had a great desire to learn to use the abacus.

By 1912 the war was over and schools opened again, and we begged Mr. Xie Zhong Liang to teach the abacus.

He said, "Girls are not merchants. You don't need to learn to keep accounts with the abacus."

We were angry because he belittled the ability of girls, and I said, "If I can't learn the abacus, I shall cut off the three fingers we use on it."

About that time a man came from Beijing to preside over the law court, and his daughter entered school. She asked Mr. Xie to teach her the abacus, and he gave her private lessons. She was somewhat stupid and asked me to help her, but I refused unless he would teach the whole class. He said he had not the proper equipment.

So I went to my uncle's shop, and he lent me his large abacus such as was used by special teachers. He told me what book to buy, and to tell each pupil to get a small counting frame. Next morning I lugged the heavy frame to school, and the principal arranged a time for this class. With this beginning I learned how to calculate and, after getting the foundation, I learned by constant practice, so that I saved my three fingers.

Until this time there had been only one school for girls in Deqing, and that was the Qi Li School. My relatives and friends were surprised that I studied in a school run by foreigners, and they were astonished that I believed in a foreign religion. And they doubted that I could get real Chinese learning.

During the revolution there was great unrest and trouble everywhere; bandits and robbers looted and killed, and there was no peace. Yet people were longing to know how the war was going. One day as I went to market with my mother, I noticed near the East Gate of the city, on the wall of the temple of the Goddess of Mercy, a notice "For the Community." There recent news was written large, and newspapers were pasted on the wall where merchants and educated people could read.

After we had taken our purchases home, I went secretly back to this place to read the news. That evening as usual, people of the neighborhood went to a certain place under a tree to hear Zhang Guo tell the news.

While they were discussing neighborhood gossip, I said, "Zhang Guo. Shall I tell some news?"

I didn't hear Zhang Guo's reply, but I did hear Li Pai Fu, an old man, say, "You baby girl! Your baby hair hasn't fallen out yet. You *mei ji* (little slave)! Can you tell the news to the people?"

Li Pai Fu was a very stern old man, and whenever children saw him coming one would shout, "Here comes Li Pai Fu," and all would run. So when he said this, it shut my mouth, and I was as silent as a cicada in winter. The whole crowd was silent as sleeping magpies, and my mother hid me beside her.

The old man broke the silence: "If you have some news, I'd like to hear it."

I took a deep breath and told what I had read on the city wall, in a voice loud enough for all to hear, and in good Cantonese instead of the local dialect.

"Where did you learn the Canton dialect?" someone asked.

"My teacher taught me at the Qi Li School," I said.

"And where did you get this news?" he asked.

Before I could answer, Li Pai Fu said, "She got it at the community newspaper; I saw her there. I wanted to know if she really understood what was there, so I came out hoping to hear her."

Then he went back home.

After this I went every day to read the newspapers on the city wall, and I always came home and told my mother. Once my Fourth Uncle was at the wall, and he ordered me to go home.

"But I want to read the news," I said, and I refused to obey him.

He said to the men standing about, "This child is stubborn and rebellious." They had often seen me there, so they said nothing, and my uncle went home in a huff.

When I got home he was there, scolding my mother.

"Mei Ya is not observing good custom. She went where men congregate to read the news. Girls should live in the privacy of the home and not walk in public alone. You must give her better instruction."

"She is only eleven years old," said my mother. "She doesn't go out to make trouble, so let her read the newspapers."

He replied, "You are letting her run into wickedness. If she brings mischief or shame upon me, I shall report it to the Yin clan." My mother did not object to my going to read the news, but because of the opinion of the others she kept me at home.

I was deeply chagrined and distressed.

It was not long before the revolutionary soldiers entered the city and ordered all official buildings and homes to put up notices or fly flags, saying, "Welcome to the Revolutionary Army," or other slogans. Everyone was out to see the excitement, I along with others. When I came home I saw the flag above our door, having eight characters written on it, and I shouted, "The Manchus are overthrown. The Chinese rule their own house."

Two uncles heard me and said, "How do you know that?"

I asked them, "How do you know it? I read the newspaper. It said, 'Overthrow the Manchus; let the Chinese rule their own house.' And that flag says it is done."

A few days later new excitement rocked the town. My ten-year-old cousin happened to be by the East Gate and came home crying. Someone had cut off his hair! Next day Ya Liang walked by East Gate, and they cut off his queue. He ran home holding his long clipped hair in both hands, and for several days would not go out of the door. My Second Uncle passed by East Gate, and they lopped off his long shiny black braid. He told them to shave his head, and they did so. He kept his head shaved all the rest of his life.

My older cousin came from Nanjing with his queue cut and his hair trimmed neatly, and I asked him to explain the reason for this.

"In ancient times," he said, "Chinese boys had long hair and wore it coiled around the head. Then about 1650, the Manchus conquered China, and all males were forced to wear the hair in a plait down the back with the outer rim of the hair shaved. This was a token of submission to the Manchus, and the queue remained as a humiliating badge until this revolution in 1912. So it is important to remove this sign of their shame and submission to another nation. It is also more clean, more attractive, and less troublesome. Men should get rid of this mark of shame quickly and gladly."

Up to this time the neighbors and relatives thought it very strange that I should study "foreign devil books," but after I read the newspapers on the city wall, learned about the revolution against the Manchus, and reported it to them, they gradually changed their opinion.

One evening Li Pai Fu, the old man, came to the neighborhood gathering. Suddenly he called to me and said he wanted to examine me and some of the boys.

"I am just a small girl," I said, "and have studied only a very little. Your nephews are older and have been in school six or eight years. But I am willing to try."

He told us to read the inscription written over the door of the home of a Mr. Hou. Then he sent us into the house. He called me out first and I gave the explanation, then the boys came out. At the end, he asked the audience to judge which was best, and I was given first place.

After seeing and hearing this, any doubts they had of the foreign school melted like ice, and their opposition collapsed like an old tile roof. The important impression left was not that I was brilliant and the others stupid, but that the teaching methods of the old-style private schools were not as effective as the newer methods of the foreign school.

So I thank God whose wonderful wisdom and providence and power granted to me the opportunity and the courage to attend a school run by foreigners who, they believed, would bewitch pupils and bring them to untold harm. And this was the school that made the people of Deqing realize that the minds of girls are just as able to engage in constructive thinking and reasoning as the minds of boys, and that they are capable of being educated and of doing things that only boys were previously supposed to be able to do.

9

I Escape the Mocker's Snare

My father believed that wine was beneficial; he said it dispelled the weariness of the day's labor. So he always drank one or two tiny cups of rice wine at each meal, taking an occasional sip as he ate. Sometimes a small girl's hand took the cup and drained it. Without seeming to notice, he would refill the cup, and if he did notice me, he did not reprove me.

But mother reproved him, quoting a proverb: "Bad habits of a father teach his children to do wrong." She told me that it was wrong, but neither I nor my father took her seriously. As a result, little by little I was forming a habit and developing a desire for this harmful drink.

Because my mother did not drink wine, after my father died I had none, though I longed for it and sometimes cried for it, but she never allowed me to have it.

Like many others, mother used a little wine in her cooking to improve the flavor, never realizing she had a "slave to wine" in her home since she did not serve it as a drink. But my heart was deceitful, and sometimes when she was away from home I would take not a little sip but a satisfying drink, and it never seemed to intoxicate me.

Finding the bottle empty a few times, my mother became suspicious, and then I was usually careful not to empty the bottle entirely. Once when the doctor ordered her to put a fish-head in hot wine and take it for dizziness, she found the bottle empty.

"Mei Ya, what happened to the wine? It is all gone."

"Perhaps it flew away," I answered.

"You have been drinking my wine again. Don't you know it will ruin your whole life?"

I had a quick reply. "I was thirsty. You have taught me not to drink unboiled water, and there was no rice water or tea so I had to drink it."

She wept bitterly as she punished me, saying, "Your dead father planted in you the roots of misfortune. Who knows what the fruits will be?"

After that she never bought rice wine for our own use in cooking.

The Chinese who worked away from home always returned to the old home for the New Year. The first fifteen days of the year were spent in greeting old friends and in feasting. My aunt, Liu Gu, was coming for a long visit, and, therefore, my mother bought wine for cooking special dishes. Every evening after the meal I always stayed in the kitchen to wash the dishes and drank some wine. On New Year's Day, when preparing a feast for relatives, my mother discovered there was no wine. She gave me a beating and pushed me out of the house just as my aunt came in.

My aunt tried to comfort me until she knew I had been punished. Then she urged my mother to try other methods of discipline. She suggested that I was old enough to be worshiping the ancestors, and that would help me to be obedient. Mother wept and said, "Her father was wicked and led her into this bad habit that distresses me and now embarrasses me exceedingly."

"What is it that has embarrassed you?" my aunt asked.

My mother explained about my terrible craving for wine.

At the New Year, when I was twelve years old, the seventy-first birthday of my Fourth Aunt was being celebrated and friends came in great numbers. Being the eldest of the grandchildren, I had the responsibility of sharing in the welcoming of the guests. Also, during the feast, I had to help my mother serve rice wine, urging them to drink as they ate. I was supposed only to pretend to drink with them, merely putting the tiny cup to my lips. But I made the most of the opportunity and sipped with them.

After the guests had eaten, the family ate. As the eldest, I was allowed to eat with the elderly aunts. When they were served rice wine, I drank along with the others.

Next morning my mother said to me, "You truly are like a low drunken slave. You are mad. You listen to nothing. You obey no one. You fear nothing. Are you not afraid to go insane like neighbor Hou? I tell you now, that if you come to that shameful state I shall not even look at you."

Her words came from her grieved heart, but they failed to touch me. I knew that if I had another opportunity I should drink as before.

However, at that time I was attending the Qi Li school where we studied the Bible, and had time morning and evening to worship God. I was eager to know the Bible. I believed it, and I believed in Jesus as my Savior. But there was, sad to say, a small viper lying dormant in my heart, though no one there knew it, nor did I realize it.

Some time later, Miss Huston taught us a lesson on temperance. I listened very carefully while she told us of the harm that alcohol does to the body and the mind. But my heart of iron refused to admit the truth.

"Do you think alcohol could cook an egg?" she asked.

"I don't believe it can," I answered.

So she took a glass cup, broke open an egg, and dropped the white of the egg into the cup. Then she opened a bottle of rice wine such as people drink, and poured it over the white of egg.

As we watched, the egg began to turn white as if it were in boiling water. I was amazed. Soon I raised my hand to ask a question.

"Didn't you first heat the wine to boiling?" I asked.

"Come and put your finger in it, and see for yourself," the teacher said.

When I got a whiff of the wine I longed to take the cup and drink it.

"May we drink this wine?" I asked.

"Oh, no," she said. "I am using it to teach you how harmful it is and how powerful. Some parts of our bodies are made up largely of the very same material as the white of egg. It is called albumen. The greater part of the brain is made of albumen, and so are parts of the stomach. When one uses alcoholic drinks such as rice wine, the alcohol in them little by little changes the albumen as you see it here, so that gradually the brain is damaged and a part of its usefulness destroyed. In time, great harm may be done to both body and mind, as well as to the character of a person. If a blood vessel in the brain bursts, it may cause paralysis or instant death." This had a powerful effect upon me, and I had nothing more to say. After class, we all went to the church for the worship service. I heard nothing of what the minister said. I kept seeing that wine-cooked egg white, and thought only of the possible fearful effect on my brain of all the wine I had already drunk.

I thought, "If I do not overcome this love for wine, how shall I escape the awful fate of neighbor Hou? How shall I ever get an education?"

The more I thought about it the more fearful I became, and at last I prayed, "Lord, I am afraid. Save me. Free me forever from the desire to drink wine. Cleanse me from the wine I used to drink so that I shall not become a worthless tramp. Forgive me for disobeying my mother and for stealing wine and for lying. Take away my fear. *Chen xin suo yuan.* (That is what I desire with a sincere heart.)"

I thank my God that he heard my prayer and took away both the craving for wine and the fear of its consequences. Later, at a wedding feast, I was seated with older ones who drank wine; I left that table and ate with the six- and seven-year-olds who were not served wine.

Six years later, when my son was born, that small viper raised its head again. At that time people believed that to relieve the pains of childbirth the expectant mother should eat chicken and glutinous rice cooked in wine, or drink wine heated with some very pungent ginger root in it. So my mother prepared this special dish for me. I ate it without comment and soon suffered from headache. When I asked for very simple food with no wine, she still brought the same wine-flavored food.

"Mother," I said, "when I was small you forbade me to drink wine. Why do you now compel me to drink it?"

"But I made this wine myself especially for you at this time. Don't you trust the wisdom of older people?"

"I won't eat it," I said. "And from now on I shall not let one drop of wine enter my mouth."

God knew what my future work was to be and he allowed me to have these experiences so that in later years I might be able to help others who were slaves to wine. More than twenty years later, while doing evangelistic work in Manchuria, I met a young high school teacher who was a drink addict. When I told him of my experiences and of the experiment with the egg white in wine, warning him of the dangerous consequences of the habit and that "wine is a mocker" (Proverbs 20:1), he too became alarmed.

"No wonder my father died as he did," he said. "He had just such diseases as you described, and I am sure alcohol was the cause of his death. Now that I know wine drinking was the cause of my father's 'wrecked cart,' I shall not wreck myself in the same rut."

He believed in Jesus as his Savior and trusted him to help him overcome the evil habit.

As he left me he said, "We shall meet again in heaven."

10

Mother Tells a Secret

My parents differed in their modes of thought and especially in their religious beliefs and superstitions in regard to me. Their two sons and a daughter had died when very young, and they feared that their only living child also might not survive childhood. Then they would have no one to care for them in their old age and worship them after their death and burial. My father earnestly worshiped the ancestral tablets and prayed fervently to the idols for my welfare.

One day as my mother held her baby girl in her arms, a very strange idea came into her mind. She decided to do a thing that no one, not even her husband, should see or ever know. She "cautioned her hand and her mouth" never to disclose it to anyone, because she believed if the secret leaked out she would lose the precious thing she hoped to secure from heaven for her baby, then her only living child. And she kept the secret for more than twenty long years.

After I had become a teacher, during a meeting of Christian women, I attended a lesson called "Jesus Raising Lazarus from the Dead." After the lesson, several women gave their testimony. Then my mother rose, smiled, and, pointing at me, said "This, my child, is also one who came out of the grave."

Everyone stared in surprise, and I was openly astonished. Then she told her story, which was the secret she had kept for so many years.

"Before I ever heard of Jesus or believed in him, I was a firm and fanatical believer in many superstitions and false gods. I had borne four children and had only this one girl child left, and my heart never was at peace, for I always feared this precious little one would die also. So I continually sought for ways to circumvent such a misfortune. This was the way I thought of to foil any evil plan of the gods or evil spirits for her death.

"One day when I went to the mountain to cut grass or bracken for fuel, I carried this child, then much less than a year old, on my back. On a pole across my shoulder I also carried two baskets to be filled with grass.

"Just before going out of the North Gate of the city, I took the baby down from my back and wrapped her carefully in a piece of an old quilt I had brought for the purpose. I followed the custom of those whose occupation is to bury children, as people seldom have a funeral for a baby. So I put her in the basket at my back and carried her to the place where coffins were often stored while waiting for a lucky day for burial. Then I went to Shi Zhong mountain and found an old grave from which the bones had been removed. There I put down my baskets, picked up my baby and laid her in the empty tomb as if she were dead. Leaving her there, I went some distance away and filled my baskets with grass as quickly as I could. Then I hurried back and snatched my baby alive from the tomb.

"I took off the old quilt and left it in the grave. I tied her on my back again, carefully, then joyfully carried my precious one home saying over and over, 'Life, long life! My child has been buried. And she lives. May she have a long life even to a hundred years.'

"My heart was greatly comforted; I truly believed she would be blessed with a long life.

"Now that I am a Christian, I know and sincerely believe that one's life is in God's hands. I shall not again be deluded and bound by such superstitions. I tell you this to boast in the Lord who saved me from such bondage. Then, I had no peace; now I have peace and joy unspeakable. My daughter lives, but not because of my crafty superstitious scheme."

I thanked my mother for recounting this interesting incident in my life. It impressed on me two important truths: One, that sinners truly are dead in sin, and God gives new life when we repent and believe. Two, that Jesus promises resurrection from the dead. We may say with Paul: "I have been crucified with Christ…And the life which I now live in the flesh I live by faith in the Son of God, who loved me and gave himself for me" (Galatians 2:20).

11

Unwilling Betrothal

From very ancient times, Chinese parents arranged the betrothal and marriage of their children, working through a matchmaker or other go-between. Their will and decisions were final and absolute. During negotiations the girl concerned was kept in close privacy. Important details affecting her whole future were kept strictly from her. She had to be passive and submissive to whatever the gods decreed, to the word of the matchmaker, and to the decision of the parents. If she became unhappy, she could blame that on the fact that she had been born on an unlucky day or on the fact that she was destined for misfortune. It simply had to be endured.

Within the last one or two centuries, schools, hospitals, and churches were established by missions from foreign countries bringing new cultures, wider knowledge, and higher goals. Girls were now given an opportunity for education; they emerged from their former seclusion and entered social and public life. Gradually, many broke away from the old customs of betrothal and marriage. But the Deqing of sixty years ago was still living in the 18th century.

Just about the time my mother became a Christian, she studied for a time in the school that the church opened for women. Li Tai Shu was also studying there. She, having been married into a well-to-do family, had engaged in study some time before she came to the school. These two women were widows, each having but one child.

Until 1907, the church had not opened a boarding school for boys, so Li Tai Shu's son studied in The Girls' School for a year or two, the only boy in the school. My mother saw that he was an intelligent boy and handsome, so she asked Liu Ai Chen to act as go-between and suggest to his mother that he be betrothed to her daughter.

Li Tai Shu knew me well as a girl who observed proper rules of courtesy, especially to older persons, and teachers praised my ability as a student. So she was pleased, and the engagement was arranged. That was in 1909.

In the summer of 1915, I was fifteen years and six months old. Li Yong Guan, the youth concerned, was just fifteen. Li Mu (literally, Mother Li) believed that when the girl was older they should marry earlier, so she chose a day to have the marriage ceremony. My mother's heart could be at rest with her daughter well married. So Li Mu told the go-between to notify my mother of her plan.

My mother had no objection, and she herself made the announcement to me: "September 14 is the day chosen for your wedding. You should prepare for it at once."

Those words were like a loud clap of thunder out of a clear blue sky, and they gave me a terrible fright. I knew that with marriage my opportunity for study would be gone. My life purpose to get an education in order to benefit the girls of my country was ruined. I urged my mother to take authority in her own hands and beg Li Mu to delay this step at least a few years until I should graduate from high school.

To our surprise Li Mu was highly displeased and was very impolite and arrogant to the go-between, saying, "Who would ever dare to mention a postponement? I am of the groom's family. I have the right to choose my daughter-in-law and the day for her wedding. The bride's family never chooses the day. Much less should the girl choose the time for my son's marriage."

The go-between, feeling that Li Mu had made a fool of her and of us, told my mother every detail. I was sitting in the inner room and heard everything clearly. After the go-between left, I came out and scolded my mother angrily and cried aloud. I knew that Li Mu had deliberately insulted me for my suggestion. My future mother-in-law was purposely "blowing aside the fur to seek for fleas." She was determined to thwart my plans for an education. I cried continually for days and pleaded with my mother to beg her to postpone the wedding.

My mother felt helpless in the matter. She asked my father's sister to explain everything to me and admonish me to submit. As soon as my aunt came she began to talk.

"Mei Ya," she said, "have you ever seen a grown-up girl not yet married? What woman ever lived to old age in her mother's house?"

"Aunt, I didn't say I would never marry. I merely wish to continue to study until I finish the middle school course before marrying. Also I am too young and inexperienced; I don't know how to serve a mother-in-law or to keep a home. Besides, 'the one facing me' (Li Yong Guan) is also young. In four years we shall be only twenty, and that is not too late."

She retorted, "You have too much lip. Even read-book people must submit to their parents."

As she went out she said to my mother, "Just don't bother her. When the time comes, put her into the bride's chair and see if she doesn't get married."

Those words were effective and no one brought up the subject again, but Mother began making preparations. "Educated people must also obey their parents."

Those words were too heavy. "As a great stone crushes a crab," so my heart was crushed and I could not utter a word.

After a few days I thought the school authorities might explain the disadvantages of early marriage, so I asked Miss Huston, then principal of the school.

To my surprise she also took the other side, saying, "If you refuse to marry, it may influence other girls to rebel against their parents, and then they may not be willing to educate their girls. They may even refuse to betroth their sons to educated girls lest they rebel and put their sons to shame. You should also remember that God plans the details of our lives, and this may be his plan. God makes no mistakes. Obedience to parents is the duty of children and is pleasing to God."

I pondered much about what she had said: "God plans our lives. He makes no mistakes." I finally decided there was sound reasoning in these words.[4]

Therefore, for the sake of the girls of Deqing, the girls of Qi Li School, and for the sake of the church, I was willing to sacrifice my own personal desires so that no ill fame should come to them because of me, so that my own name should not be dragged in the dust, so that parents should not be brought to shame, nor the name of the Lord be dishonored.

After this, in regard to marriage, I became numb and unfeeling. I paid no attention to preparations. I asked no questions and left everything to others to do as they wished, even to carrying me on their backs to the bridal chair. I allowed them to carry me away from my home to the home of others, to be despised, scolded, and mistreated even worse than many would treat a slave.

12

Bride with a Twisted Ear[5]

On the fourteenth day of the ninth month of 1915, I was married to Li Yong Guan. The Rev. A. I. Robb performed the Christian ceremony. An elderly man of the Li family was in charge of the ceremony that was held at the ancestral home of the Li family on Gui Bei Street, Deqing. The place was filled with relatives and friends who gathered to celebrate the occasion.

About a week after the wedding, we returned to our respective schools. I continued to live in the school until the New Year vacation, when I went to my new home. In my husband's family there were no such feelings of affection as is usual nowadays between those who marry. Gradually some such feelings did develop but, sad to say, "winds blew and rains came."

The ancient classics say, "When a woman marries she should have a home of her own." But in Chinese homes from ancient times many generations lived under the same ancestral roof, believing that thus they acquired great virtue and blessing, security and happiness.

Three days after a bride enters her new home, she goes to the kitchen to assume her duties as a daughter-in-law: taking over management of the kitchen and all work connected with it. This means cooking the meals, including pounding the rice to remove the husks, carrying water for household use, and always serving the mother-in-law. If her husband has younger brothers and sisters, she is supposed to serve them as well. She must be very dutiful and careful in attending to the wants of her husband, carrying water for his ablutions, combing his hair (in the days of the queue), always being careful to show proper honor and respect, and never refusing to do anything he demands.

We were three people in the home; life was very simple. We should have been congenial, but actually we were quite otherwise. My mother-in-law acted according to ancient usage, as though she were the wife of a high official: wealthy, proud, arrogant, overbearing. Her husband's ancestor several generations back had been such an official, but as the generations passed, through opium smoking and other delinquencies, they had lost position, prestige, and wealth, and the descendants now living were nothing better than the common run of people. But they tried to live and act as though they possessed the former glories of their ancestors, insisting on observing many vain and troublesome customs as though they were wealthy.

To serve in-laws is not so easy and informal as to serve one's own parents Since I had not mastered the art of serving my mother-in-law to her satisfaction, I often heard this proverb: "It were better to have married a slave from a large wealthy family than to take a daughter-in-law from a family of common people." According to this proverb, often quoted by my mother-in-law, my social status was even lower than that of a common slave. In such a situation one suffers unutterable shame in her inmost being.

Before I was married, my mother, knowing the hardships and suffering I might have to endure, told me how a good daughter-in-law should conduct herself. She said I had to endure secretly and silently whatever scolding, insults, and shameful treatment my mother-in-law might heap upon me. This is a proper and honored custom even to the present time, but the good reputation of such a daughter-in-law remains with her even to old age.

"In every way try to please your mother-in-law, even if she makes unreasonable demands. Never rub the fur the wrong way. Be agreeable even if she is entirely wrong. In the ordinary courtesies of the home you must be very humble and respectful toward your superiors. In serving, no matter what trouble or hardship it means for you, give complete satisfaction."

However, try as I might, I was not able to do all that was required of me, nor could I ever completely satisfy my mother-in-law.

In ancient times, when seeking a partner for marriage, it was invariably the man who sought the woman, first through a middleman. Then the parents of the woman investigated the character and standing not only of the man but of his family also, even for several generations. If all parents were satisfied, the marriage would be arranged.

But in my case, all concerned being Christians, my mother had spoken to a friend who spoke to the Li family suggesting this match. Since this was not according to the usual procedure, the Li family should have refused the suggestion; but they accepted it without making any objections.

Afterwards the unconventional procedure caused me much shame. My mother-in-law often reminded me of it, saying, "It was not that I was pleased with you and sought you for my son, but your mother brought you to my door."

These words pierced my heart like a knife; I suffered agony.

I hated the very earth because it did not open to receive me and cover me from this shame. I wished never to see this woman's face again, nor hear her hateful words.

Even though I was not "a virgin from a wealthy family," only an ordinary girl from a lowly family, yet I had come from a home of respectability, and I was a virtuous and self-respecting person. Now to be mistreated and unjustly despised made me murmur against heaven and complain against others. I marveled that my mother had so carelessly managed the details leading to my marriage. And I had no secret place in which to weep for the fierce and cruel taunts.

It was then that I wished to rebel against Li Mu and say, "It was the Li house who first sent the ceremonial documents to my mother; they sent gifts with flags flying; they sent the flower-chair to receive the bride, and it was accompanied by an orchestra of eight pieces according to the very best custom—a proper threefold welcome. Why should I now be shamed?"

But my mother had given me very explicit instructions: "No matter how your husband or your mother-in-law mistreats you, control your anger, swallow your angry words, and do not talk to others about them. If you lose control of your lips and irritate your mother-in-law, she will report it to the Yin clan and they will not permit you to return to your own mother's home."

So I dared not speak one rebellious word, but in my heart I said, "Oh, Lord, you know all this. Flow, ye tears, flow." I thank the Lord that his grace was sufficient for me and through such experiences I learned submission and self-control.

> For this is commendable, if because of conscience toward God one endures grief, suffering wrongfully....Because Christ also suffered for us, leaving us an example, that you should follow his steps: "Who committed no sin, nor was deceit found in his mouth"; who, when he was reviled, did not revile in return...but committed himself to him who judges righteously. (1 Peter 2:19, 21-23)

"Now, Lord," I prayed, "grant to me patience and strength to follow in your steps."

After this I wept no more for the things I still suffered.

But the devil continually comes with violent storms and floods of temptations to trouble and destroy the faith of those who believe in Jesus Christ. When this happened to me, the Lord put out his hand and gave me comfort and courage.

13

Li Mu's Change and End

Before three years of my married life had passed, my mother-in-law urged my husband to get a concubine. He asked for my opinion. I had never thought of the possibility of such a thing and did not know of the damage and danger it would bring to me, so I merely said, "As you wish."

He took my answer to his mother. In a fury, as one half insane, she engaged a middleman to seek a girl to be my husband's concubine.

"I was all to blame," she said.

My husband then brought a paper and commanded me to write these words: "Because I cannot bear children, I wish my husband to get a concubine."

Though I was young and inexperienced, I had courage to say to him, "You may be very intelligent; I also am no fool. How do you know that I may not bear many sons and daughters? I shall not write such a paper."

Without this paper, the girl in question was not willing to accept the "honor."

After this, whenever I was eating and could not escape her tongue, Li Mu quoted to me the ancient saying, "There be three unfilial acts, and the greatest of them is to bear no sons." And she vulgarly added, "We must get more hens and have more eggs."

Though these words were drummed into my ears over and over many times, never a word did I reply, but my heart was bitter. In all my life before I had never endured such torture and bitterness.

Again I prayed: "Lord, my suffering is too grievous. I can bear no more. Open a road for me to escape."

I cried so bitterly that I woke my husband from his sleep. But he was soon asleep again, while I cried in bitterness against the injustice, even murmuring against God.

I was like the Israelites murmuring in the wilderness until they were destroyed, and I began to fear. Then I seemed to hear the Lord speak of his own bitter suffering: "My heart was broken with grief; my sorrow was even unto death; I sweated drops of blood as I went to the cross. And who had any pity for me?"

My heart was reproved. I prayed for mercy, for patience and strength to endure, until he should show me a way of escape. He quieted my heart so that I sang softly:

> O my soul, bless thou Jehovah,
> All within me bless his name.
> Bless Jehovah and forget not
> All his mercies to proclaim.
> Who forgives all thy transgressions
> Thy diseases all who heals;
> Who redeems thee from destruction,
> Who with thee so kindly deals.
> In his righteousness Jehovah
> Will deliver those distressed;
> He will execute just judgment
> In the cause of all oppressed.
> (Psalm 103:1-6, from *The Book of Psalms with Music*)

Then peaceful sleep came to me.

God never fails those who put their trust in him. My husband did not mention the matter of a concubine again.

In the spring of 1918, my mother-in-law became seriously ill.

Her son was in school, so I gave up my plan for higher education in Canton, and began teaching in the Qi Li Girls' School. In addition to my schoolwork, I had the whole burden of the home, including the care of the one who was ill. My salary was only six dollars a month, and as I was the only wage earner, this had to cover the living expenses for the three of us plus medical bills.

Our home had the name of being that of the upper class, but we were an utterly impoverished family. We had by all means to guard our "face," while I paid the bills. It was a heavy burden for a girl of eighteen. So I took in sewing and crocheted lace to sell. After a year Li Mu recovered, and my burden was lighter.

On September 19, 1919, our son, Mian Chao (Timothy), was born at the

Mission Hospital. This was just five days after the fourth anniversary of our marriage, and I was not yet twenty years of age.

In 1920 my husband went to Canton to school, but I was not able to support him. Therefore, he worked in Hong Kong for a motor company and later got a position teaching in a village school at a salary barely enough to support himself, with an occasional visit home.

In the autumn of that year his mother became seriously ill again. Every morning I had to give her the proper greeting and a patient's care, besides preparing her food. Then I took the long walk to school, carrying on my back my son who was almost a year old. I taught my classes all day and came home in the evening to my home cares. God gave me a strong body and a joyful heart, so that I was able to do all that was required of me.

People who visited my mother-in-law praised me for my filial care of her, and at last she changed her attitude toward me. She then saw that my work was too great a burden and often urged me to rest, fearing that I might become ill.

I was so touched by this change in her and by her words of praise that I was moved to tears. Besides, I feared that the words of a proverb might be true: "When one is near death, her words are very virtuous: when a bird is about to die, its voice is sad and plaintive." This proved true in her case, and I was greatly moved to see how God could so marvelously change a heart.

In the autumn of 1921, she entered into her rest. Her son returned home to attend her funeral and pay proper respect and honor to his mother. My heavy burden I now laid down.

14

Alone—A New Beginning

After Li Mu's funeral, my husband returned to his teaching in Dai Bu, while I remained in the home with my son. After this, "like swallows, one flew east, one flew west" and husband and wife were living apart more than together. Gradually thorns came up where love should have grown, and love withered and died.

Not long after his mother's death, my husband laid down his teacher's ferule and pen and entered the army. He asked me to take our son and live near him, but I was teaching and could not get leave of absence at once. Besides, our second child was to be born in April. However, I wrote that I would go during summer vacation and asked him to prepare a place for us to live.

On April 10, 1922, our daughter Man Shi was born, and I was very happy. But after only eighteen days God took her to be with himself. I had become seriously ill, and for three weeks my life was in danger. I had tasted one more cup of sorrow, but I understood more fully the grief of my parents when their two sons and a daughter had died.

Before vacation time came, my husband wrote saying, "It is not convenient for a soldier to have his family with him," and he advised me to remain at home. This seemed sensible, and I remained in Deqing.

Within half a year, I was informed that a certain woman named Liao had given her daughter to him in marriage. Then I understood the reason for his advice to remain where I was. This was the first time a woman had come between us, and it seemed to have been very carefully and thoroughly planned. This was a very common occurrence among Chinese men.

My husband and I kept up some correspondence, but never was this other woman mentioned. I continued teaching. Some months passed and God healed my sickness, bound up my broken heart, and comforted me. He made me see that love and mercy lay in my great grief, for my little Man Shi would never be defiled by the evils of this world nor meet with its troubles and sorrows.

After this my husband never sought me, nor did I ever go to him. We were as far separated as heaven and earth, though occasional letters passed between us. Beginning in 1919, and down through the years, my son was with me, but as we had no settled home, he was like a float used by a fisherman, with no anchor, no roots, pushed about by circumstances. We lacked the warmth of a real home, and it was very difficult for him as well as for me. Looking into the past or trying to peer into the future, one could only weep.

The church was preparing the Psalms in meter for use in worship, and I was asked to prepare Psalm 73. I greatly loved it, for it spoke as the voice of my own heart:

> Yet evermore I am with Thee;
> Thou holdest me by my right hand.
> And Thou, even Thou, my guide shalt be;
> Thy counsel shall my way command.
> And afterward in glory bright
> Shalt Thou receive me to Thy sight.
>
> For whom have I in heaven but Thee?
> None else on earth I long to know.
> My flesh may faint and weary be;
> My heart may fail and heavy grow;
> With strength doth God my heart restore,
> He is my portion evermore.
> (Psalm 73:23-26, from *The Book of Psalms with Music*)

I thought, "Like a good shepherd, God saved my little Man Shi and carried her home where she will welcome me when I come to the end of my road in this world." When this thought came to me, I worried and grieved no more. I knew this was a lesson God had set for me to learn, so that I might be able "to comfort those who are in any trouble, with the comfort with which we ourselves are comforted by God" (2 Corinthians 1:4).

In 1921 the Qi Li School was overcrowded, so a suitable building was rented at Deep Pond Corner near my maternal grandmother's home, where everyone in the neighborhood knew me. A notice was posted on the city wall at the East Gate, announcing the opening of a school for girls with Yin Wei Jie (myself) in charge.

On the day the notice was posted, my Second Uncle had returned from Wuzhou for the New Year. Seeing many people reading and discussing the notice, he hurried away home to the tree where the people of the neighborhood were gathered.

There, too, they were discussing the school and saying the teacher was his niece.

"No, it can't be that child," he said. But when they insisted, he said, "Perhaps it is, but what honor or glory can a girl facing outside bring to the Yin clan?" He came to see me.

"Is that your name on the poster at the East Gate advertising a new school for girls?"

"Uncle, don't you recognize your own niece's name?"

He replied scornfully, "How should I know it was that little *mei ji* (slave) that was just recently born?"

Speaking in that way, he showed that he despised me for being just a girl, and for my youth, but I ignored it and said, "Uncle, won't you help? Won't you urge people to send their girls to the school?"

This brought results, for he even sent his own daughter and two children of his neighbors.

Forty-eight girls were enrolled the first day. The curriculum and books were the same as those used in city schools, but we used new methods of instruction. Every Saturday morning, I taught the more advanced classics and ancient literature. Sometimes curious people would stand outside the window to listen.

One person was so surprised that a woman could teach *Xiao Jing* (*The Book of Filial Piety*), that he went to Mr. Xie Zhong Liang, who taught at Qi Li, and said, "I want to know how the daughter of our neighbour and the niece of Mr. Hou can teach the classics just like a man."

"No mistake," Xie Zhong Liang replied. "She not only teaches *Xiao Jing* but also some classics you know nothing about—*Sheng Jing*, the Holy Bible."

In this way both men and women of the neighborhood came to listen, with the result that when the next term opened so many enrolled that it was necessary to enlarge our space.

So at last I was permitted to see not what I had formerly hoped—Deqing people replaced by more progressive people—but themselves awakened to the importance of girls and education for them. We had brought freedom to girls, though it took ten years to do it.

15

Canton and Streams in the Desert

"Until he was twenty-seven years of age, Shu Lao-chun did not really begin to study in earnest."

Those few words from the *Three Character Classic* came to my mind and encouraged me, for in the end he received a high literary degree. Even though I was now a mother and past the age when people usually go to school, I still wanted to gain sufficient education to perform suitable service to society. My mother-in-law was dead and also my baby daughter; I was strong and healthy, so I determined to continue my education through middle school.

Again words from the ancients haunted me: "While parents are yet alive, do not go far away from them." Here was my mother growing old, and I was her only child. How could I leave her lonely and sad? Already she was worrying about that problem.

"How can you establish a home if you are flitting east and running west? I must prepare me a rope to tie me to life in case I get sick while you are away."

"But, Mother, you need not be so anxious; the Lord will never leave you, and I would certainly come to your side."

She smiled and said nothing, but this scene was always before my eyes and her words were in my ears. Who would care for her in sickness, and who would care for my son? It was a growing burden on my shoulder, a responsibility I could not lay down. And yet I wished to leave because in my home town there was no middle school and no hope that one would ever be established there. I simply had to leave. I could not change my mind.

I prayed to God, laying my needs and problems before him. Early one morning the words of Jesus came to me as I prayed. I opened my Bible and read them over and over: "Do not worry about tomorrow, for tomorrow will worry about its own things." I took this as God's message to me, and I definitely decided to go to Canton to study.

Because I enjoyed teaching, I was advised to go to the Union Normal School in Canton for teacher training. And yet I could not forget the death of my little daughter, Man Shi. If it had not been the case that in the Li family there was no one trained to be "a receiver of babies," she might not have died. In this small city, numerous babies die for lack of proper care. Perhaps I should study medicine and save the lives of many children and their mothers. For that of course I would have to get a college degree, and I had not even enough money for middle school. I thought of learning midwifery, but my great interest was in teaching. Still undecided, I prayed for guidance and consulted my mother. She approved of my preparing for a life of usefulness as a midwife and volunteered to care for my son so that I could go to school.

Having my mother's approval, like Joshua of old, I went forward strong and of good courage. During the summer of 1923, I resigned from the teaching position in Qi Li School. Two other Qi Li students had just graduated from the Union Normal School and were ready to take over my work. So, with a promise of financial help, I left my mother and my small son, went to Canton, and registered in the normal school.

Lest I should fail to pass the entrance examination, I also registered at a school for midwifery where the scholastic requirements were not so high. To my great joy, the day before I was to take this examination, I received a notice that I had passed the normal school examination and was accepted there as a student.

On the opening day I entered the normal school and studied there for three years. God very frequently tested me severely, but he was always before me, leading me ever onward.

I recall a certain Sabbath when I seemed to be deep in "a dry and thirsty desert," I was led to read in Isaiah: "The wilderness and the wasteland shall be glad for them, and the desert shall rejoice and blossom as the rose.... The parched ground shall become a pool, and the thirsty land springs of water" (Isaiah 35:1, 7).

When I read this my heart was filled with joy, and I said, "It is true, Lord. Thou art a God who does wondrous things. Help me to look to thee with a sincere heart of trust."

For some reason unknown to me, my promised financial support had failed. Just at that time I was without money to pay my school fees, and it seemed as if I would have to leave school. It was then that this message was given me from

God's word, and I was sure that he would "open a stream in the desert" for me. So I asked the school treasurer if I might delay paying my fees for a week.

The very next morning, Miss Patton, the treasurer, said to me, "A certain person has sent some money to pay your tuition fees and other expenses."

After thanking her, I promised to repay this money when I began teaching. Then I sought a quiet place and thanked God for his wonderful provision for me.

In the autumn of 1923, I attended a conference for young people. The speaker was Miss Lin Mu Zhao, and the theme of the conference was "Who Will Go for Us?" I had often heard such a message, so it made no more impression upon me than water on a duck's back. But, the next day at the early morning meeting, her subject was "A Voice is Calling, Awake." She spoke of a drowning person calling for help; she compared unsaved people to those in a burning building who are awakened by smoke and fire and call desperately, "Save my life!" But there was no way of escape—no one to save them. Then, speaking of Paul's call to Macedonia, "Come over and help us," she closed with the appeal, "Who is willing to hold out their hands to help?"

I raised my hand and said, "I am willing to go," but this did not come from my heart.

At the evening meeting she seemed to sense that, though I had raised my hand, I was not wholehearted and sincere. She seemed to be speaking straight to me, drawing me so powerfully that I was dismayed and trembling. It seemed to me that if I could just take back that act of raising my hand I would be at peace.

The longer I sat there the more unhappy I became, until I prayed in my heart, "Lord, if you need me, I will go. Only give me peace in my heart."

Then I became quiet. But when I retired that night, I could not sleep. I knew that God could not accept a half-hearted sacrifice. He accepts only those who willingly and wholly devote themselves to him.

I prayed again, honestly and earnestly, confessing my doubting and half-heartedness, and he forgave me. Suddenly the song of commitment we had sung in the meeting welled up from my heart.

During the early 1920s, the Church of Christ in China started a missionary project. Groups volunteered to go to Yunnan, to Malaysia, to the Miao tribes, and to various other places. I wished to join the Malaysia group, but then I had an aged mother and a young son whom I could not leave behind nor take with me. Also I wished to finish my course at the normal school.

After my graduation, that missionary project was not being pushed, so I decided to teach until another opportunity should be offered. But God did not forget my promise to work for him.

16

My Mother's Death

I had brought my mother to live in the home of the Li clan, and then I had left my small son with her when I went to Canton to study. Of course she had lived many years in the ancestral home of her husband, but now only nine of that clan were left and, though I was married into another clan, I was her only close relative. Her one fear was that I might go far away and leave her alone.

"Mei Ya," she said, still using my "milk name," "When I gave you to the Li family in marriage, it was because our homes were not far apart and I could see you often. But contrary to my expectations you were soon going here and there, and the more you went the farther away you were. I thought I had woven a rope that would bind you to me all through my sorrowful life."

During the summer of 1924, although I needed to earn some money and was planning to find work in Canton, I remembered her words and decided to go back home to her and my little son.

Soon after my return to Deqing, the Xi River overflowed its banks, flooding the houses on low ground. We moved to higher ground but the water rose still higher. Therefore we moved to the girls' school until the flood receded. Then we had to clean the mud and filth out of our home.

The flood was followed by an epidemic of which many died. My mother also became ill. The mission doctor was away because of the flood, so I called a doctor of Chinese medicine whose treatment was not effective. Two other doctors refused to visit her, and she was convinced that she would soon die.

"Mei Ya," she said, "I belong to the Yin clan. I should not die in the ancestral home of the Li clan. Please take me home." Her husband's relations agreed, saying, "She really belongs to the Yin family. She must not die outside of her own home."

Actually they were afraid to have her die away from the Yin home because they believed that after death her soul might become an evil spirit. If they neglected her and let her die away from her home, her spirit would certainly return to get revenge by bringing trouble upon them.

I went every day and cared for her, but in spite of three doctors, she grew worse. Then she gave me her final instructions.

"Mei Ya," she said, "I want you to buy me a good coffin and bury my body on high dry ground. That will prove your filial devotion."

I promised to do this, and she said no more but wept silently. Thinking she wept because she feared death, I tried to comfort her through her faith in Jesus, and I urged her to pray. She said she had already prayed, yet continued to weep.

"What is on your heart to make you weep?" I asked.

"I can't bear to leave you," she said, "because I didn't find a good, dependable husband for you."

"Don't worry about that," I replied. "I have a good husband, and we have a good son."

"Don't try to deceive me," she insisted. "You told him to come home, and he didn't come. I want to see his face once more and give him a few words of reproof and instruction. I fear he intentionally stays in the dark because he doesn't want to face me even for a few minutes. He breaks my heart."

She spoke no more after that. The next morning, December 12, 1924, at ten o'clock, her spirit passed beyond the body and went to be at home with Jesus. She had lived sixty-five years and five months.

I was about six years old in 1906 when my father died suddenly and our happy home was broken. Until then I had never known sorrow, and this great loss was like a sharp sword stabbing my heart. My mother too suffered bitter grief, besides the heavy responsibility for her two daughters. Later I came to know how great was her burden, but her grace and lovingkindness were "high as the heavens and deep as the sea."

Often in the deep night when I could not sleep, I could think only of how I needed the love, sympathy, and wise counsel of my mother. What of my future? I was responsible for my son who was now five years of age. If I were to quit school now I would not be accepted as a teacher in any school. I had to continue my education, but how?

In facing my difficulties I saw no relief. In prayer I murmured against God, and he spoke to me in reproof: "Why are you stubbornly complaining? Where is your faith? What suffering of yours did I not know and prepare for beforehand? What prayer of yours that came sincerely from a full heart did I not hear?"

Humbly I confessed, "I look at my own misery and I weep. I have doubted the love and mercy and wisdom of God. Now I lay my too heavy burden on thee. Direct my life according to thy will." Then I sang from Psalm 37 and was given freedom from my burden.

> Set thou thy trust upon the Lord
> And be thou doing good;
> And so thou in the land shalt dwell
> And verily have food.
>
> Delight thyself in God, He'll give
> Thine heart's desire to thee;
> Thy way to God commit; him trust;
> It bring to pass shall He.
>
> And like the morning light he shall
> Thy righteousness display;
> And he thy judgment shall bring forth
> Like noontide of the day.
> (Psalm 37:3-6, from *The Book of Psalms with Music*)

I immediately wrote to my husband, telling him of this experience and God's leading. The Lord had mercy on me by giving him such a love for our son that he promised to support him so that I could continue my education until I graduated. Therefore, in the autumn of 1924, I took our son with me to Canton after arranging for his father to meet us and take charge of him.

In 1926, I completed the Union Normal School course and received a diploma. During those two years I had met with financial difficulties, but the Lord's grace was always sufficient for my needs. I was soon able to repay the money formerly advanced to me by the school treasurer, but they told me it was a special gift for me so they did not accept it.

About that time I learned that my husband had become an opium addict. Earlier he had taken a secondary wife. Therefore I took my son from his father and put him in the primary department of the Union Normal School while I went to Tai Shan, a town not far from Canton, and began teaching.

Not long after this, however, Timothy was once more taken by his father. It was only after other events, yet to be related, that God delivered me from the deep sorrow that this caused and led Timothy and me to praise his name together.

17

Temptations and Victory

During 1928 a storm of temptations almost overwhelmed me. The first came to me through a notice in a newspaper:

> [The] Government College at Nanjing is receiving both men and women students. Tuition free. A three-year course leads to diploma. Only students recommended by a committee of officers of the Nationalist Party will be accepted. Revolutionary students will not be received. After graduation students will be employed by the government.

This was just what I wanted—three years of free education and a good job! This advertisement captivated me, and naturally I sought an opportunity to register. But, as our proverb says, "Man makes plans, but the accomplishment is with heaven." God carried out his own plan for me.

The notice said clearly that one must be sponsored by a member of the Nationalist party. I was not a member nor did I have any relative or friend who was a member and who would recommend me. Naturally this one rule would keep me out. This was God's road sign. I should have noted it, turned about, and asked God's guidance, but I diligently studied the *Three Principles of the People* by Sun Yat-sen[6] and tried to get in touch with someone who would recommend me to the school.

I was ignorant of much that I needed to know. As I talked with a Mr. Guan, with a few words he made me feel that I was living as one in a dream. Yet he agreed to take me to a man who would recommend me.

"I have noted recently," he said, "that you have made great progress in your preparation. If you were not a Christian you could have been accepted as a member of the National Party much sooner."

Startled, I stopped in my tracks.

"What did you say?" I asked. "Do you mean to say that as a believer in Jesus Christ I cannot become a member of the Nationalist Party? If I were asked to renounce my faith in Jesus Christ, do you think I would enter that school?"

With that I took all the papers for registration, for instruction, my photographs and the name of the man who was to recommend me, and tore them to shreds right before his face and threw them into the air for the wind to carry away.

Mr. Guan reproved me for being so hasty, but I turned and strode the other way, thus showing him that I could never renounce Christianity in order to become a member of the Nationalist Party, even for the sake of an education and a government job. God certainly had given Mr. Guan the right words to startle me.

A second temptation came to me in the spring of 1928. Recommended by a friend, I obtained a position as teacher in a government school, but naturally it was not a Christian school.

After a time, I met six people who seemed to be strangers, and as they did not know the local manners and customs of the southerners, they constantly came to our school to talk. We had congenial and agreeable conversations. I knew they did not believe in Jesus and I hoped to give them the message. My own faith was so steadfast that I had no qualms about having fellowship with them.

What I stupidly did not recognize was that their aim was to drag me into their ditch. They used every wily scheme to entice me to depart from the Lord. At first they found no avenue of approach, but afterwards, when they learned that I enjoyed beauty, whether in pictures or in scenery, they invited me to go out with them to view beautiful scenes and to take pictures. So I stepped into their trap.

From my childhood I had been accustomed to observe the Sabbath, and was happy to spend the day with Christians in worshiping God. Now, every Sabbath, these friends came looking for me though I had told them very definitely how I always spent the day in service to God, a most important duty for Christians, and therefore I could not go with them for pleasure. I urged them to go with me to church and for three weeks I succeeded in persuading them to do so. But after that they absolutely refused to enter the church door.

Then they began to call on me in the afternoons when usually I would be visiting some who had been absent from church services. Because these six new friends came specially to see me, I sometimes went with them. If God had not graciously given me an opportunity to teach a Bible class, I fear I might have fallen into their trap even sooner. I was not a member of that church, but when I visited the Guang De Church School, I saw that the pastor's "tail was too big to wag": he wished to do this work but had not the ability. So I volunteered, hoping to lessen the pastor's burden and also to fulfill my promise to God to work for him.

I invited several students of the Normal Training School to help teach in this Sunday school, and they were a great help. I received the approval of the church board of education. At first I entered wholeheartedly into this work and enjoyed it very much, but after I accepted the alluring gifts from Satan, I began to feel bored with the work and even despised it. So I resigned, saying, "It interferes with my freedom."

But God had long ago bound me with the cords of his wisdom and love.

In the summer of 1928, the government opened a School of Physical Education to train teachers for the public schools. I went to Canton to take this course, and for three months I did not set foot in a church. By studying diligently I thought I had good reason for not attending church. I also neglected the habit of reading the Bible and praying until my conscience no longer reproved me. My heart became callous, without feeling or strength.

In November of the same year, being recommended by a former fellow student in the Normal School, I went to teach in Pu Ying School in Shuolong. My son was with his father. This was a church school, and I was very happy because the general management was good, and there was opportunity to worship God and have fellowship with other Christians. But in spite of this my heart was in great distress. Apart from teaching my classes and preparing for them, I did nothing and went nowhere; I simply stayed in my room, closed the door, and wept. At that time the whole country was in a chaotic condition. The school was in a sparsely settled district some distance from the church, and the pastor and school principal worried about my living at the school, so I moved into the guest room of the church.

In adjoining rooms were a woman evangelist and a young woman teacher. Only a thin board partition separated the rooms, so that everything one said or did could be heard in the other rooms. Whenever I wept, day or night, they always heard me. Thinking they should comfort me, they quoted Bible verses to me through the thin walls, but none of this helped me because my heart had its own suffering. Besides, I was proud: did not I know my Bible even better than they? So I paid no attention to them, while my displeasure and boredom increased.

One day, as I was thinking of my son and longing for him, I began to cry bitterly. Just at that moment, the evangelist passed my door and paused long enough to say, "You must remember from whence you are fallen, and repent, and return to your first love" (Revelation 2:5, paraphrased).

On this occasion I listened to her words and stopped my weeping. I recalled my past foolishness and how I had departed from the truth and followed the course of the world. I had fallen into the Slough of Despond and was not able to extricate myself. Unless I looked to the Lord to save me, I would have to die in this filthy ditch. The more I thought of it, the greater was my fear.

Then I said, "Lord, save me from this distress. I have disobeyed; I have rebelled. Do not condemn me for these sins: pride, despising thy word, refusing to hear the words of my friends, associating with people unworthy of my friendship, being bored with teaching a Bible class. Lord, lead me back to thyself to receive thy lovingkindess and have peace."

"If we confess our sins, He is faithful and just to forgive us our sins and to cleanse us from all unrighteousness" (1 John 1:9). These words gave me great comfort and were as a fountain springing up in my heart. Over and over again I sang psalms which speak of forgiveness.

After that I wept no more but trusted that the Lord had accepted me. Why had I wept? I have already spoken of this: my husband had long ago taken another wife; then he took my son from me. I had no husband—now no son. The wound made by the separation from my son was very deep.

The reason I had met with such trouble was that I had ignored the teaching of Psalm 1. I had walked and stood and sat with evil persons. Therefore I could not prosper. The leaving of my first love—my love for God—had drawn this suffering upon me. Now I determined to take time to read the Bible and pray daily. But I had no Bible. I had to borrow a Bible from the church. I decided to use a part of my tithe to buy a Bible and I increased my offerings to make up for the time I had not paid the tithe. I hoped soon to buy a gilt-edged Bible as a reminder of the prodigal child who returned.

Before I had saved enough for the Bible, Miss Weekes, who was returning to her homeland, gave me a parcel. I had no time to open it, but said, "How did you know that I liked candy so well that you are giving me a box of it?" After a few days I felt hungry for candy and opened the package.

"It isn't candy at all," I exclaimed. "It is the leather-bound gilt-edged Bible I was saving money to buy!"

I was so happy that I held it to my heart with both hands, hoping that I might keep it always. On the flyleaf I wrote in large characters: More Precious than Gold.

I am thankful to add that at this same time God heard my earnest prayers, and in the summer of 1929 he so moved my husband's heart that he returned our son to me.

18

On the Horns of a Dilemma

And the Lord said, "Simon, Simon! Indeed, Satan has asked for you, that he may sift you as wheat. But I have prayed for you, that your faith should not fail; and when you have returned to me, strengthen your brethren." (Luke 22:31-32)

Thank the Lord! He knew that I was being led astray by worldly people and leaving my first love. And he had already prayed for me that in my time of temptation I should not lose my faith, but that I should repent and turn about and do again "the first works."

My loving God now gave me some practical instruction for his own name's sake and caused me to escape this great peril. Even my husband reproved me for thinking of deserting the work that I had been doing for the church, for he knew that I really enjoyed it. At the time I became angry, but when I took time to think the matter over, I knew that every barrier that had been placed in my way resulted from the unbounded grace of God. If I had continued in my studying, I certainly would have been brought under the power of Satan. I was like a brand plucked from the burning by a merciful divine hand, after which the Lord led me in the way of righteousness.

After I repented and turned about I constantly sang Psalm 116:6-14. If anyone had asked me, "Why are you always singing a psalm?" I answered, "Because since childhood I have been taught the psalms, and we sang only the psalms of the Holy Bible in worshiping God. When I have some problem in my heart, some portion of a psalm comes forth spontaneously." In times of joy or thankfulness, when I need guidance, or in praise of his wonderful works, Psalm 23 is my favorite portion.

When the winter vacation began, I resigned from the school in Shuolong, having accepted a position in the primary school at Zao Wa, and planned to go with Miss Chen to Indonesia after the Chinese New Year. Just at the end of the old year, Miss Li Xue Qing wished me to accompany her on a trip to Deqing. I had not been there for several years, and because I had planned to go to what was then a very far-off land and did not know when I might return, I decided to accompany Miss Li to my birthplace. Though I now had no father or mother, I wished to return and renew my relationship with many uncles, aunts, cousins, and also my own sister.

On the twenty-seventh day of the twelfth month, three days before the Chinese New Year, we bought boat tickets for the voyage up the Xi River. Arriving before dawn at the Deqing pier, we went first to the school, then to Miss Li's home where we had breakfast, and from there to my former home in the Li clan. I paid my respects to the elderly members of the clan, the cousins, and the more distant relations who had come home to spend the New Year. I had been away six years, so there was much to talk about, such as weddings, births, deaths, and there was much feasting with great joy and merriment.

One person came specially to see me with a request from Mr. Kempf, principal of the School for Boys, that I come to his home for an interview. After our New Year feast I went first to my ancestral home to extend my New Year greetings to my father's relations, then went to visit Mr. Kempf. It was a most delightful meeting, for he and his wife treated me as an honored guest. After courteous greetings, Mr. Kempf told me of the situation in the *Chen Li* (True Doctrine) School for Boys and the need for a principal as well as for teachers, as he was due for a furlough. He then asked me to accept the position of principal of the school, but I humbly and politely declined it. I realized that since I was a native of Deqing, had been educated in the church school, and had become a Christian here, I should not refuse to accept the responsibility, but I had already accepted a position in Indonesia.

The next morning Miss Weekes came to see me and announced her errand: Would I go to a meeting at her room for an interview about the boys' school problem? I was surprised and said, "Miss Weekes, I am not connected with this school. Why should I attend this meeting? And besides, this is New Year's Eve and according to Chinese custom, every family is occupied with family affairs and has no time for outside business."

The next day was the Chinese New Year; it was also the Sabbath. In my own home, according to the usual custom, I paid my respects with tea and greetings to the older members of the family and gave usual New Year greetings to others in the clan. All then very informally partook of the New Year dainties. After this family meal I went to the church for the worship service.

As the group gathered, I took the opportunity to give New Year's greetings to all. Those who recognized me asked, "Where have you been all these years? What have you been doing? We have had no news of you."

So I had to tell them that I intended to go about the tenth day of the month to Indonesia to teach school and did not know when I would return, and that I had come early to church to see the faces of my Christian brothers and sisters once more, and to speak of God's grace to us all. At the close of the service all greeted me with New Year's wishes. The joy of that one day was greater than all the happiness I had had in several years.

That day, Miss Weekes came again and invited me to her home for supper on the third day of the New Year. At first I wished to decline, but my friend, Ruth Xie, persuaded me to go, saying, "You have been away six years and there is so much 'heart business' and many experiences for us to talk over."

We came to Miss Weekes's house at the appointed time. Mr. and Mrs. Kempf and the Deqing evangelist, Mr. Liang, were already there. After we had had our supper, Mr. Kempf began speaking of the needs of the boys' school and urged me to stay and help them.

"This puts me in a very difficult position," I said. "I have given my word to go to Indonesia and I cannot break my promise. I must leave here on the sixth and go to Hong Kong to take ship for Java. Please excuse me. I cannot accept your kind invitation."

Mr. Kempf said, "I can arrange for you to resign from that appointment to the school in Indonesia, so that they will not object. I can get a refund of the price of your ticket from the steamship company, and I shall pay your loss on the cancelled ticket. Isn't this reasonable? Think about it until tomorrow and let Miss Weekes know your decision."

"Very well," I replied.

Actually I did not wish to think about it, but consented to do it as a way out of the dilemma.

My heart was greatly disturbed: to go to Indonesia or to remain at Deqing? I did not wish to think about problems that were no concern of mine. But the Holy Spirit did a work in my heart; I had to look at the problem from every angle.

In case I accepted the position here, I would lose the confidence of Miss Chen and her sister; it would disrupt their plans, making it difficult for them to secure a substitute. I thought again of my real reasons for going to the East Indies. Was it not that my home was already broken, and that I hoped to escape more difficulties and disappointments? Here in Deqing I could not escape the questioning of friends: Where is your family? Your son? Why leave them? How should I answer them? Indonesia was an open door for me; I need not meet these embarrassing questions, and I could be happy in the school in Indonesia. Why accept this troublesome and difficult work in my birthplace?

But the Holy Spirit kept my heart stirred up: "Is not this the very thing you had in mind when you first had an opportunity to go to school? Was it not your highest aim to prepare in this wilderness of briars and thorns a smooth clear road for the girls of your native city? Now the door is wide open. There is only this one hindrance—your inclination to go the way of the world. Here is your original desire. Why not willingly accept it? You see the needs and difficulties facing the boys' school. How can you refuse to reach out a hand to help? This is your home; this is your church; you were educated in the Qi Li School, and here you got your freedom to live."

I thought, "If the Lord had not graciously loved me and chosen me—even this insignificant unlovely child—would I not be now living here in ignorance and superstition? 'As I drink water, I must think of the fountain from which it flowed'; I must remain here and accept the responsibility for the boys' school."

But in my inmost heart I was reluctant. I recalled the ancient proverb: "Home-grown ginger is not hot," that is, "No one is honored in his native place," as Jesus also knew.

While I was still determined to go overseas, the thought came to me, "If I insist on going there in opposition to God's evident plan for me here, suppose I get sick, can't work, can't live, and can't die while in rebellion against God—what then?"

I became fearful and wept.

Then I prayed: "Lord, I am pressed between two hard things. Guide me clearly in the way I should go." Suddenly God's Word came to answer me: "This is the way; walk in it." Though I understood the message, my heart was not entirely submissive.

When I went to Miss Weekes, still with a hard heart, I said, "I apologize, but I cannot accept the work here. My promise to go to Indonesia is still in my heart. According to right and reason, I should fulfill that promise."

She said, "Let us pray about it."

So we knelt together and, as she prayed, the Holy Spirit worked in my heart and I was exceedingly troubled. Again these words came to me: "Your ears shall hear a word behind you, saying, 'This is the way, walk in it,' whenever you turn to the right hand or whenever you turn to the left" (Isaiah 30:21).

As these words came to me the second time, they troubled me, heart and soul, and as I prayed I could only sob, "O Lord who loved me, because my heart was hard I have been in distress. But I belong to thee; I wish to live within thy will." Again I had the clear definite message: "This is the way; walk in it."

When we rose from our knees, I said to Miss Weekes, "I am willing to stay here and help my own people."

Holding my hand in a warm clasp she answered, "I was sure the Lord would give you definite leading."

She very happily sent a messenger to tell Mr. Kempf of my decision. He at once wrote to Miss Chen explaining why I was resigning from her school, cancelled the boat ticket, and made preparations for opening school.

I went back to Canton on the sixth day of the New Year, 1929, collected my baggage, and returned to Deqing on the twelfth. On the seventeenth I, as principal, opened the school. Through the guidance of God's Word I had been directed to this work, and although I lost the friendship of some people in Canton, the Lord became my most precious friend, with blessings and joy, both earthly and heavenly, in great measure.

During the following summer vacation, my husband brought our son back to me in Deqing. I took the Lord's way, and he took another. After that our son continued to live with me and we were a comfort to each other.

Before a half-year had passed, after my acceptance of the position in the Chen Li Boys' School, a new temptation was put before me. Miss Chen, my former classmate, returned from Haiphong and asked me to go and help her in the middle school there. The salary she promised me was ten times the salary I was receiving in Deqing. Because I knew that God had definitely directed me to the work I was doing, I dared not give her request a thought, but immediately declined her invitation with thanks. Many years afterward I saw Miss Chen in greatly altered circumstances and I thanked God for his goodness in preventing me from going with her where I would have been attracted by "the five lights and ten colors" of the world.

19

Calls in the Night

The prophet Samuel was very young when God called him. He did not at first understand that it was God calling him, so he went three times to Eli and said, "You called me." Then Eli said, "Go, lie down; and it shall be, if he calls you, that you must say, 'Speak, Lord, for Your servant hears'" (1 Samuel 3:9). Then the Lord told Samuel the message for Eli.

Like Samuel, I was slow in recognizing God's call to me. I heard but did not fully understand and so ignored it.

Three years before taking charge of the School at Deqing I had graduated from Teachers' College in Canton, after which I was preparing to teach in a school near the city. Very early one morning, I was in a deep sleep when I seemed to hear a voice calling, "Sister Yin. Sister Yin." I called aloud, "I am coming."

I looked out of the window and seemed to see dimly an old person facing our entrance. Still calling, "I am coming," I dressed quickly and went outside. I opened the door which was still locked, but saw no one, though I called all about the garden. Surprised that I found no one, I was frightened of the dark. I went back to the door, which meanwhile had swung shut and locked. Rather than rouse the neighbors, I sat on the step until the caretaker opened the door; then I returned to my room.

Later I asked, "Who called me this morning before daylight?" No one in the house had called me. One said, "You had a bad dream." Another said, "You have that dream-sickness. You must be very careful."

But I knew I was not in a dream after the voice awakened me. Nor was I a sleepwalker. Since I could not understand nor explain the incident I put it out of my mind. It occurred during the summer of 1926.

About the seventh or eighth month of 1929, while teaching in the Chen Li Boys' School, I was awakened from a sound sleep by a loud voice. It was a very powerful compelling voice, as if a person was pounding on the floor above me. When I was wide awake my heart was beating wildly, so I lay still until I was quieted. Then I heard a voice calling, "Teacher Yin. Teacher Yin," and the sound of someone knocking at the door.

As I lay in my bed I called out, "Who is there? Who is calling?"

There was no reply, but I rose at once, dressed quickly, and opened the door. No one was in sight. I went to the big outer gate and opened it, but again no one was in sight. I closed the gate and returned to my room, thinking that perhaps some pupil had called me, but it had been a woman's voice. In the school dormitory there were only boys from ten to fourteen years of age. Perhaps one of the boys was sick and when in pain his voice sounded like a woman's. I took a flashlight and went to the bedrooms, where everyone was sound asleep.

I went back to my room and could not sleep.

"Perhaps this is God's voice calling me," I thought. "But if so, why did he call me 'Teacher Yin' instead of by my name?" I studied this incident from every viewpoint—physical, spiritual and psychological—but found no solution. So again I dropped it from my thoughts, deciding it was simply my subconscious mind reviewing what I was continually doing during the day. So why worry about it?

At breakfast I asked if anyone had been sick or had called me. No one had done so. Then I told them of my experience.

"It was God calling you the way he called Samuel," a thirteen-year-old boy said at once.

"I thought of that too," I said. "But I don't think God would call me 'Teacher.' He would call me by my name, for I am his little child."

"You don't need to doubt," insisted Sheng Kuo Qing. "I believe this truly was God calling you."

"If I ever hear this voice again, I shall, like Samuel, say, 'Speak, Lord, for Your servant hears.'"

The boy said, "This is evidence enough. Do not doubt."[7]

I taught in the Chen Li School at Deqing for almost four years. During that period I spent my vacations in the Qi Li School for Girls in pleasant surroundings with friends.

One night in the summer of 1930, while in a deep sleep, I heard a voice calling my name: "Yin Wei Jie. Yin Wei Jie." I was wakened. An elderly person was looking at me through the south window of the small school room where I slept. This person was holding a small oil lamp but disappeared when I went to the window and called, "Who is there? What is your trouble?"

I then lighted my own lamp, thinking there might be a thief, and I searched all three rooms on the first floor. Then I went upstairs and roused Shan Shou Bing and asked if she had called me; she had not. I wakened Xue Jing, and she too had slept soundly and had not called. The woman who was caretaker slept in the adjoining house, so I crossed the corridor connecting the two houses and asked why she had called me. She was provoked and said, "Who would call you at three o'clock in the night? Don't bother me."

I returned to my room greatly puzzled. I sat down and thought over the whole incident: Could this really be God calling me? The last time I heard a voice, I said God would not call me "Teacher," and now he called my name. I should not doubt, but should accept it as a call from him. Thus I spoke with myself.

I knelt and prayed: "Lord, I am still but a child. If this truly is thy voice calling me, make me like Samuel, to hear definitely and accurately. Teach me to submit to thee and to do what is pleasing to thee."

As I knelt by my bed, I fell into a troubled sleep and in a dream I seemed to see at the top of a small mountain several people beckoning to me. All about them was fine green grass like a cushion, and fragrant flowers. Birds were chattering all about them as though singing praises to the power of the Creator for the wonders and the beauty all about them. These people were guests from afar, and as I went with them we sang songs of praise with great delight, using the words of Psalm 9. My heart was in an ecstasy of joy and I thought, "It is good for us to be here."

As I turned around in my dream, I saw at the foot of the mountain a wide road with clouds of dust as though there were tens of thousands of people travelling, some from afar, coming ever closer, some even to the mountain top where I stood. Suddenly I heard the moaning of someone in pain: a child's voice sobbing fretfully. There were laborers, faces wet with perspiration; many were old, bony, decrepit, pitiful. As I watched, more and more came.

What was bringing so many people together? They were so needy; so much should be done for them. And I was so unprepared to help them. I had gone to the mountain for my own pleasure, but suddenly, seeing so many miserable and troubled people, I was afraid and felt like running away. But once more I heard a voice: "Yin Wei Jie. Yin Wei Jie."

I answered in a loud voice, "Ah! Here I am. Where are these people now? Where have they gone?"

My own voice wakened me. I found that it was all a dream. The sun was already high, and the sunlight was streaming in at the window as I still knelt by my bed.

I got up and recalled the whole dream; it was as if a still small voice was saying, "Go and take the Word of God to these needy ones."

All at once I understood and answered, "Yes, Lord, I am now willing to go. I rebelled and ignored thy former command. Forgive me. Again I promise to do thy will and go." After making this promise my heart was at peace and exceedingly happy. God acknowledged me as his child. This dream or vision made me realize the great need of the multitudes for the gospel, and since I had submitted to God I could not be lazy and idle, or reluctant to do this work.

That afternoon the postman brought me a magazine. On the front page was this headline: "The Voice of Multitudes in the South." The article told of the multitudes in the Islands of the South (now Indonesia) who were dying without the gospel, living in deep darkness, walking on the road to ruin. It urged Christians to take the gospel to them.

To this day I do not know who sent the magazine to me, but, adding this to the three or four calls I had had from God, I accepted it as proof of his special call to me and of the assurance of his guidance.

I recalled the time when I thought I was ready to sacrifice myself—to go to a wilderness land, to islands, to cannibal peoples, to any nation, race, or class to teach the gospel of salvation, to give healing, comfort and help to the aged and serve them. But I had failed to go.

"Lord," I said, "what kind of a servant have I been? Rebellious and unworthy. And what great love and mercy and patience thou hast shown in reproving, instructing, and calling me, while I was slow to accept the responsibility. I pray for thy forgiveness. Give me a clean heart that I may become a submissive and fit instrument for thy use. Establish my heart in this, my sincere desire."

After unspoken prayer from my heart, I once again sang the song that I sang when I first heard God's call:

> I can hear my Savior calling....
> "Take my cross and follow me."
> Where he leads me I will follow,
> All my life, in blessing or in woe,
> I'll go with him—with him
> All the way.
> (*Where He Leads Me*, by Ernest W. Blandly, 1890)

Now the most important thing in my life is to tell the good news.

20

To Jinling Bible School, Nanjing

Often in the schoolroom, at the end of a class, I would give a special talk on some phase of the gospel or have a private interview with a pupil. When I had time I went to nearby villages to give gospel tracts or a gospel message. Even though people's hearts were hard as stone, and it was not easy to plant the seed of the Word in their hearts, yet I believed that some day the Lord's hammer would break in pieces those hard hearts.

There was a village ten miles from Deqing called *Ma Hui* (Horse Market) where we had a chapel but not always a resident minister. I arranged with the evangelistic committee of the church, and every Saturday afternoon Miss Jean Barr and I walked to this village, in the evening and conducted a class to teach children to read from a book of simple Bible stories. On the Sabbath we had a Bible class for children and a worship service, then in the evening a special meeting with a message for those who were not Christians. On Monday morning we again held the class for children.

Neither rain nor heat prevented us from taking this long walk. Through these weekend meetings we helped to revive and get into action a church that was benumbed. We also aroused the parents as to their children's need for an education and for the gospel of salvation.

I had decided many years before to give my life wholly to the service of God, but the things of the world intrigued and tempted me—education, high position, riches, fame—so that I turned aside to worldly things and failed to keep my vow to God. But he did not abandon me to the world; he pointed out the way I should go, leading and strengthening me until I was convinced that I should give myself wholly to the work of spreading the gospel.

During the winter of 1930, Mr. Kempf, the former principal of the school, having returned, I told him of my intention to resign from teaching and prepare for doing evangelistic work. But he did not give his approval.

A church council was organized to include all our churches in the Deqing and Luoding Districts, and I was chosen to represent the church at Deqing. At the meetings of the council I learned of the great need for evangelistic workers; every city and village where there was a chapel begged for evangelists, but there were not enough trained workers to supply the need.

A call was made for volunteers, and I went to Mr. Kempf.

"I have come to register for evangelistic work," I said.

"But you are not a trained evangelist."

"I came to register because I intend in future to give my life entirely to evangelistic work."

"But you have had no training for such work in a Bible school," he objected. "How can you be an evangelist? You don't know enough about the Bible."

"I am sorry I have not had Bible school training, but I do have a definite call from God to spread the gospel. I do wish with all my heart to do this work; therefore I came."

"But I can't accept you because you have not the necessary training."

"Shan Shou Xiong is able to do this work. I think I can do as well as she."

"I do not regard women as preachers or evangelists; I call them Bible Women," was his explanation.

I returned to my room and wept bitterly while I prayed, "Lord, it is not that I am unwilling to serve thee; others are unwilling to accept me and my services. Tell me what I should do now."

The searcher of hearts comforted me and with aching head I slept and put the setback out of my mind.

That afternoon I received a second copy of the evangelistic magazine, *A Voice From the South*. It increased my desire to spread the gospel, so I wrote to the Christian and Missionary Alliance asking for their requirements of qualifications for prospective evangelists.

"If one has been led of God to serve as an evangelist," wrote Rev. Huang Rong Shu, "it makes no difference as to age, sex, or denomination, but he should study at least one year in our Bible school. Also their church should be responsible for their living expenses, so that they can study without anxiety."

When I received this letter I again took my desire to the Lord, and he opened the way for me to go to a Bible school. During the summer of 1931, a spiritual life conference was held in Canton. After hearing speeches by Miss Deng of Jinling Bible College for Women and the Rev. Chen Zhong Kui of Changsha Theological

College, I had a desire to go to one of these schools. I discussed the problem with my son, who was now twelve years of age, and before the end of 1931, I notified Mr. Kempf that I wished to resign and would be leaving the school during the summer vacation.

Mr. Kempf was fully determined that I should remain at the school, but I dared not refuse the call of God, so I made plans to leave Deqing in the summer of 1932, and arranged all the details of the work I was leaving.

Letters from Miss Deng, principal of Jinling Bible College, told me that I had been accepted as a student. I was granted a scholarship by the Northern Presbyterian Mission, and a friend provided funds for my board and room. Miss Jean Barr had promised financial help for my son for three years. Two other students were going from Hong Kong, and she suggested we travel together.

The Bible school opened on September 15, but there was a special class for Cantonese students which opened two weeks earlier for the study of Mandarin. With my son I left Deqing on August 20, 1932. Upon arrival in Hong Kong we met the students who were to travel with us, then went to the steam ship company's office to arrange for our tickets and baggage. Another student then joined us, and, at sailing time on August 24, we were a party of five.

Arriving at Shanghai four days later, after a most miserable voyage because of a storm, we were met by friends who arranged for our train tickets to Nanjing.

21

Timothy's Snare and His Deliverance

When I first entered school in my childhood, the teacher gave me a new book. The very first sentence in it said: "Father-Mother love for children is beyond understanding." I repeated this sentence by rote until I knew it, but I was not then able to understand its full meaning. Not until I myself had a son and a daughter did I come to understand its deepest and best meaning.

Actually, only a father and a mother are truly capable of understanding the love that is beyond understanding. Love in the heart of parents for a child comes from God alone.

In my youth, I complained that my mother did not love me as my friend Ruth Xie's mother loved her. After my father died, my mother often left me to live in the school while she went to Wuzhou or Canton to find work, so I was deprived of the peace and warmth and love of home and mother. Every time my mother returned home, even before I spoke a word, I embraced her and wept. I hoped this would persuade her never to leave me again. But she did not really understand how empty my heart was and how urgently I needed a mother's love.

On one occasion she said, "You see how Xue Jing always smiles when she sees her mother; they seem very close. When you see me you weep. Why is that?"

But she did not take time to wipe away my tears. She did not cut open my sad heart to see what was there, and it left me more sad and bitter. I had no words to tell of the empty loneliness I felt so I became a shy, wordless, homeless child.

In time, my undemonstrative nature made my mother, my husband, and my son feel in turn that I did not love them. My son felt I did not love him as other mothers loved their sons. Actually, when did not my heart burn with love for him? But because of my inhibitions, I did not show my love in the usual words and manner.

His father and I had presented Timothy for baptism in the Reformed Presbyterian Church when he was an infant. When almost twelve, during the summer of 1931, he voluntarily made a profession of his faith in Jesus Christ as his personal Savior and was received as a member of the church on the basis of his knowledge of the Bible and public profession of faith.

In 1932, when I proposed to take my son with me to Nanjing, his father was strictly opposed to the plan. We had discussed every phase of the matter, including the love and relationship between parent and child, between husband and wife, as well as the duty of citizens. Because of the advantages of travel, he finally gave his consent, at the same time strenuously impressing on our son that sooner or later he must return to his ancestral home.

At Nanjing, the Christian schools for boys were already full so my son entered Sheng Mei City School. Every weekend he came to visit me, and we always had prayer together.

During the summer vacation of 1933, the Nanjing Bible School sent me with Miss Wu Pu Wen to Ban Qiao village to conduct a Bible school for children. The people of this village were Cantonese who had lived in America. As we also were from Guangdong Province—Deqing, my place of birth, is in Guangdong—we spoke the same dialect, so that our work there was very successful.

I had consulted with my coworker, Miss Wu, and she approved of my taking Timothy, now about fourteen years of age, with me for the summer. He soon became friendly with the children of the village and led many of them to come to our vacation Bible school. He was like my left hand in receiving and entertaining the children. However, he showed a proud, supercilious attitude towards our work because in his school he had been taught modernistic ideas about God and the Bible.

Once, on a weekend visit from school, he said to me, "Mother, you are superstitious."

"Son, why do you say that?" I asked.

"Mother," he replied, "I ask you not to talk to me about such things anymore. I already know all that about 'God so loved the world,' and that 'Jesus died on the cross to save sinners.' All this is not actually true. Isn't my high school principal more highly educated than you are? Hasn't he much more experience than you have? And is he not in a much higher position? Besides, he was formerly a pastor.

"He has taught me that even from the beginning of the universe there was no God, but just because some people's hearts are ignorant and empty they have let themselves be fooled into thinking there is a God. Faith and prayer are merely ideas someone thought up. Jesus was merely a man and was never accepted by his own people, the Jews. Only you women, ignorant uneducated men, and some children believe what is taught in the Bible about God and Jesus."

When I heard these words I was greatly distressed and said, "My dear son, such talk is a sin against God."

He interrupted me by saying, "Mother, you need not talk to me about such stupid things. I am a grown man—an adult; in fact, I know more than you do. I have 'read book' as well as you. It is useless for you to try to instruct me, because I have definitely made up my mind not to believe those things any longer."

I knew at once that this was from Satan, the evil one, and that it was useless for me to admonish him.

I simply said, "Son, I shall pray without ceasing for you that God may protect you from this false teaching." He then returned to his school.

Surely it was God's grace to cause him to tell me frankly and honestly what was in his heart. Otherwise I could not have known what he was being taught in his school. I could only pray God to save him from a fearful future. Believing in the efficacy of united prayer, I asked my fellow students to pray with me that this straying lamb would be saved from Satan's clutches. Despite Timothy's attitude, he came with us in the summer of 1933 to help with the Bible school for children. At every opportunity he told the children the very things he had said he did not believe. He talked to men as they worked in their fields, and sometimes he asked me to explain something he did not fully understand, so I knew that he had not entirely shut God out of his heart. I thanked God and prayed still for the Spirit's working in his heart.

My son and I and Miss Wu were living in the home of a woman who was not a Christian. Every morning and evening we had family worship together. As we sang praise to God, my son also sang, but not always the same words. While we read the Bible he sat with eyes closed. Sometimes our prayers were long and he did many things to disturb us, and annoyed us by coughing, scraping his chair noisily, dropping his books, and in other ways.

I said to him, "Son, if you are not pleased to join us in worshiping God, I do not compel you to come. You may leave any time you wish. Don't force yourself to come out of politeness." He paid no attention to my words and continued to come and also continued to disturb us. I knew that because of his youth he had been unduly influenced by the atheistic teachings he had heard. I also knew that what I had been taught of psychology and philosophy was not always trustworthy. Therefore, apart from gentle remonstrances, I gave him into the Lord's hands and also prayed for the many young students who were being taught such heresy.

One day Timothy had promised to go swimming with Li De Zhang, who was just learning to swim.

While we were at supper, Ya[8] Zhang's mother called, "Timothy, Ya Zhang is waiting for you to go swimming and he wants you to hurry."

He quickly finished his supper and went.

After a while a woman called, "Mrs. Li! Mrs. Li!"

I went outside, and she said, "Your son is out on the river bank drowned!"

We were soon at the river. A little distance away I saw my son sitting on the ground, pointing towards the river.

Now I realized that it was not Timothy who was dead, but Ya Zhang, who had the same surname. The two were about the same age. My son was a good swimmer, but the other boy was just learning to swim.

A little girl had seen Timothy struggling to save him and had called some men. When they found Timothy's body it seemed to be lifeless, but, after life-saving efforts, he was revived, though those who saved him had at first declared he was dead.

They soon got a net and searched for Ya Zhang's body, but it was not found until the next day. But for the Lord's mercy my son would have been dead with Ya Zhang.

Even though Timothy had been saved from death in the river, he had been so terribly frightened that he was not normal physically and his mind was not at rest. He could not eat, his sleep was disturbed by fearful dreams, and he had no vitality or spirit left.

I had told Ya Zhang's mother, when she urged me to let my son go to help her son learn to swim, that she must take the responsibility if anything happened to them. Yet she kept calling from the street for Timothy to "go and bring back Ya Zhang." Her continual calling and crying disturbed us and hindered our work, and it really amounted to persecution.

Finally I asked Miss Wu to take Timothy back to Jinling and put him in the care of Mr. Liao for a few days. Mr. Liao not only cared for him physically but prayed for and with him daily. The Holy Spirit humbled my son so that he saw his disobedience and confessed his sin to God with repentance. In this experience he came to know that there is one true living God. His faith was restored and established.

Later this was Timothy's testimony: "Today I am one who was dead and am alive. My former self—my old nature—died at the village by the river and was buried there. I was dead spiritually, and by the power and love of God I was saved from physical drowning. Speaking of spiritual life, I was a dead person who had separated himself from God, in spite of the fact that long ago the grace of God had been granted to me. I had opposed him. I denied his existence. I refused to believe that Jesus Christ had died on the cross to save me from my sin.

"But when I realized that Ya Zhang was in water too deep for him, I was not able to save him and myself. I was without hope, knowing that I must die. Then, trusting a strong power within me, I cried out, 'Oh God, save me!'

"How I was saved from the water I do not know, but God not only saved the life of my body, but his Holy Spirit enlightened my heart so that I repented and confessed my sin. He graciously forgave me and restored my soul, and I was reconciled to him. Speaking for both body and soul, I am a new creation. And I accept this new creation as a result of this experience.

"One who does not believe or acknowledge God, or who denies his existence, will obtain for himself only suffering and sorrow and death. He stores within his heart misery that it is impossible to express in words or to write with pen and ink. If anyone tries to persuade me by deceit or by persecution to doubt the existence of God, he cannot convince me that there is no God. I do believe there is one true eternally living God whose Son Jesus Christ died on the cross for my sins, giving me assurance of salvation. Because of this experience I can never deny the grace of God that gave me moral standing before him, and I cannot refuse his guidance for my life. This is my testimony as to how I obtained both physical and spiritual life. 'Do not be deceived: God is not mocked'" (Galatians 6:7).

After Timothy was restored, he earnestly sought God, and God did not fail him. God fulfilled his promises for help and guidance. Timothy was enabled to achieve his aims, and God greatly blessed him and his home and family. This incident is separated from today by thirty-four summers and winters, and Timothy is like a tree—green, flourishing and producing much fruit. May God protect and preserve him "until that day"!

22

The Call from the Far North

In the summer of 1934, I completed the two-year course at Jinling Bible College (Nanjing) and received a diploma. I had hoped to do further study, but the Reformed Presbyterian Mission in Qiqihar (the Black Dragon, or Heilongjiang Province) in Manchuria was in urgent need of workers and asked me to go to their help.

As I have already said, it was through the Reformed Presbyterian Church in Guangdong Province, South China—the place of my birth—that I was saved. That church had taught me in spiritual things; they had built a strong foundation for my faith, my life, and my work so that in this sinful world I should not be confused and deluded by false teachings. And now that I was able to give true and faithful testimony to the teachings of the Word of God, they gave me a work to do.

From first to last, with many interruptions, I had studied in various schools a total of fourteen years, but I had not obtained a full college education, though I prayed God many times to lead me to this. Through it all I realized that great ability and much learning may prove a hindrance when bearing witness to the gospel. Sometimes when I have compared my lack of education with the accomplishments of others I have felt embarrassed, but God sent his Word to comfort me: "'Not by might nor by power, but by my Spirit,' says the Lord of hosts" (Zechariah 4:6).

In witnessing for Jesus, I have learned not to think of how poorly qualified I am or how much more education my hearers may have. I simply tell of what God has done through Jesus' crucifixion for sinners, and I am not frightened or confused. On the other hand, I all the more joyfully wish to glorify him. But for his grace to me, I should be utterly ignorant.

In the spring of 1934, before I graduated from Jinling, I wrote to my son to tell him that I had been asked by the Reformed Presbyterian Mission to go to North Manchuria to help with evangelistic work there. I asked Timothy's opinion as to whether I should accept. But because Japan had then taken over the government of the Three Northeast Provinces and now wished to swallow up China, he did not wish to be a *Wang guo nu*—a slave in a subject nation. So he said, "I do not wish to go with you; I prefer to stay here."

He was then studying in high school where he was making good progress. After his faith in God was restored, he had advanced both physically and spiritually, so I gave my permission for him to stay in that school. He made arrangements with the school, then returned to Nanjing to see me. He urged me not to go to the Northeast Province.

Knowing the great crisis he had been through, I understood what was in his heart, so I cancelled my ticket to the North, and spent the summer in Nanjing, where we lived together through the vacation. Just before Jinling was to reopen after summer vacation, he was in excellent health and restored to his usual good spirits, so I talked with him about plans for the future.

"Mother," he said, "I think it is God's will for you to go to the Northeast to make known the gospel. I have grown more mature. I know God is with me and will help me. I shall not be sad and you need not be anxious about me. I still do not wish to go to the North but prefer to stay here and study."

When I heard these words I wept and said, "Son, since you are willing, I shall go and leave you here in Anhui. During vacation you shall visit me or go to Nanjing with your friend, Fan. He will welcome you. An ancient Chinese proverb says: 'Sons look toward the West; soon or late, they expect to leave mother. This separation is unavoidable.'"

He was very happy to hear this, as he already had a desire to go abroad to study, so I gave our future into God's hands. This heart-to-heart talk formed a good relationship and a strong tie between mother and son. Our friend, Mr. Fan, sent his brother-in-law to the same school, so Timothy had good companionship. He was to spend weekends and vacations in the Liao home in Nanjing, so I was quite willing to leave my fourteen-year-old in Anhui, and made preparations to go to Qiqihar in Heilongjiang Province in the northwest *Manchukuo* (Manchuria).

"Why go to faraway Manchuria to make known the gospel?" many friends asked.

I answered, "Didn't Jesus command his followers to take the gospel to all the earth? Compared to other parts of the world, it is very close; it is a part of the original China. We are one flesh and one blood, one race. Though the North and the South of China seem far separated, they are one country."

I truly believed that the will of God from eternity was now being fulfilled. Jesus Christ, who chose me, gave me the right to become a child of God whom he afterwards called and sent out. Like Paul, I was not disobedient to the call from heaven, and now, under his guidance, I prepared to go to that "frozen heaven and snow-covered earth," to a strange language and a new type of living.

My desire was not to go to prosperous cities where others had proclaimed the good news, nor did I wish to go to those who had heard the Word until they were bored with it. I wanted to go to neglected people, whether in backward localities or on far-off islands. I wanted to share the bitter and the sweet with those who hungered and thirsted for words of comfort, those who truly needed the gospel.

We accepted the work that God had prepared for us, to labor and struggle, sowing diligently in a field of hardships. Otherwise how could there be a harvest? I went to the North, to spread the gospel in obedience to the command of Jesus.

23

A Thousand Perilous Miles

God's promises fulfilled to me all the days and years of my life have been most remarkable, and on the long journey to the North his faithfulness was manifested in many ways.

I boarded the train at Nanjing on the morning of August 24, 1934, and arrived at Tianjin next morning at four o'clock. I had to wait seven hours for my train to Shanghaigang. No other people were waiting for the train and no one was about the station, so I felt afraid in this dark fearsome place. I found a man with a rickshaw and asked him to take me to a hotel. He took me to a shop that was not lighted and had no hotel sign.

"This is not a hotel," I said. "Why did you bring me here?"

"It is an inn," he said, and called out, "A guest has come." A man came and led me to a small room and said, "Breakfast will be at eight o'clock," then left and locked the door on the outside.

Before eight o'clock they brought water to wash my face and demanded ten dollars. Then they brought me some breakfast and asked for another ten dollars. Surprised at the demand for so much money for a scanty breakfast and a little water, I said, "Why didn't you ask for one hundred dollars? Ten dollars is so little." They said nothing and I paid the bill, though what I had received was worth only fifty cents.

They did not allow me to use the telephone but directed me to a drugstore on the corner of the street. At the drugstore a man who saw that I was a stranger said, "I advise you to leave that place at once and go to the railway station. It is a long way, and you should start immediately."

As I left the inn, they called a coolie to carry my baggage. Halfway to the station he stopped and demanded two dollars. I paid it and carried my own baggage. Very soon the train arrived, and I boarded it for Shenyang via Shanghaigang.

On the train I thanked God for his protection and sang Psalm 121 softly. I soon discovered that a woman sitting near me was a Christian; she recognized a favorite psalm of the Chinese, so we were happy to talk together. She assured me that there were many in these parts who cheated strangers.

Geographically Shanghaigang has for many generations been an important place, the door into China. There the Manchus entered and became the rulers, making China a united nation with one person as ruler both inside and outside the Great Wall. It was regarded as one undivided country.

However, on September 18, 1930, the Japanese invaded the Three Northeast Provinces and usurped authority over the whole land. The Chinese then began to fear for Shanghaigang and the territory north of it. The main military force of China, the 19th Route Army, was largely made up of men from Guangdong, and Japanese hatred of them was very deep.

Now I was in Shanghaigang and going into the land ruled by Japan. Some felt that I was like a lamb going into the mouth of a tiger and feared I might have trouble with the officers as I entered the country. I had therefore written to Miss McCracken, hoping to meet her here so that we might travel together. As Miss McCracken was not there, I waited for the next train. Again a coolie tried to overcharge me.

As I argued with him, a young man said, "What is the trouble?" I recognized him as a Cantonese by his speech. He was certainly sent there to help a stranger from the South. He arranged for my baggage to be carried, then took me to a money changer to have my Chinese money changed to the currency used beyond the Great Wall, because it was of greater value than that used in Manchukuo. He took me back to the station, returned the ticket I had bought with Chinese money and bought another ticket with Manchukuo money at quite a saving. He put my baggage through customs and stamped it officially, so that it was not examined again.

The same young man helped me board the train and made me comfortable, checked my time of arrival and leaving Shenyang, warned me not to talk freely with strangers, but if a railway official questioned me, to answer him freely. He also bought food for me to eat during the long trip. I followed his instructions and had no difficulty. After an hour's wait at Shenyang, I boarded the train for Qiqihar.

No one of my friends knew the time of my expected arrival, but to my surprise, when the train drew into the station at Qiqihar, I saw Miss Huston on the platform. A letter that I had sent had been delivered only an hour before I arrived.

Now that I had come, everyone was filled with joy and thanksgiving. This journey of more than a thousand miles alone and through strange places taught me that, trusting in that eternally stable Rock, one may have perfect peace.

24

The Afflictions of the Gospel

The Reformed Presbyterian Mission in South China had purchased property, erected dwelling-houses, churches, hospitals, schools, and a hospital for lepers. However, the mission in Manchuria was begun with the principle of building a group of Christians and churches that would be indigenous and with church buildings that they could afford to build, working toward a self-supporting church. So the work had begun in whatever suitable buildings could be rented.

The building in which Miss McCracken and Miss Huston lived in Qiqihar was very small and, naturally, when I was added to the family, it was inadequate for a dwelling and for carrying on our work. So we searched for a larger house. A Jewish friend led us to a suitable one owned by a Muslim, a once wealthy leader in that religion who was now in financial difficulty on account of his gambling. He said he was glad to rent his premises to us because Christians, like Muslims, were clean. Nevertheless, before we moved in we had to clean it, even whitewashing the walls of every room. However, we did not at once discover the shy vermin that kept out of sight in cracks and crevices during the day. The place was infested by hordes of living creatures which, though not so fearsome as lions and tigers of the forest, still gave us plenty of trouble.

The first night we spent in the house, we slept on pallets on the floor because the brick-and-tile beds had been repaired and were not dry enough for use. I was no sooner asleep than I felt something crawling over my face. I turned on a light and saw on the floor, on the walls, on the ceiling—everywhere—these horrible creatures. The "fire-wall," a sort of zigzag chimney built in the wall for heating, was warm, and from top to bottom was a solid, shiny brown mass trying to get warm after their long day in hiding.

By the next night we had filled cracks with candle wax, put cotton in our ears, prepared flyswatters, folded newspapers, and filled a spraygun with insecticide fortified with Lysol. We fought with all our might until we had slain a great host of the enemy, swept them all together, folded them up in newspapers, and cremated them in the new brick cookstove. Then we sat down to rest.

Shortly after the lights were out, we heard the sound of a myriad of tiny tapping feet. We turned the flashlight around the room. A whole army of reserves had come out against us, from where we never knew. Without courtesy, timidity, or regret, we set about total destruction. Never one insect was in sight during the day, but every night we had three or four battles. This war against cockroaches dragged on until the last of them had been tempted with their favorite food and trapped.

After we were rid of cockroaches, we were plagued with rats and mice. We did not use poison lest they die in the mud walls of a lean-to at the back, or inside the *kangs* (beds built of mud brick and heated from beneath). We used traps in runways and dark places, scrubbing or burning them to remove traces and odors of former victims. The rats were so daring they would face us in broad daylight after we had filled all their holes for escape. Then we battled with broomsticks and umbrellas. Finally we were rid of rats as well as cockroaches.

Mr. Ma, the owner of the house, claimed to be a very exemplary and virtuous Muslim. As such, he was permitted to have several wives. Consequently, he had two wives and four concubines, or secondary wives. One of these he got as payment of a gambling debt. Whatever advantage this may have been, it resulted only in quarrels, hatred, and jealousy. Each woman tried to escape as much of the work in the home as possible. According to an old Chinese proverb, "Where there are three monks, there is no one to carry water, so no one eats. One can carry two buckets; two can carry one; but three do nothing." Mr. Ma was growing old and had neither the ability nor the strength to rule such a complicated household.

When urged to believe in Jesus, Mr. Ma would say, "It is of no use to urge me or to preach to me. I once studied the Christian religion. I understand it thoroughly, but I do not believe in it. Jesus and Mohammed were sons of God and his prophets. Jesus, the elder brother, was sent to die on the cross to save men. Mohammed can also save, but by a different method. Christianity is good, and I do not oppose it. I approve of your urging people to believe in Jesus. But I cannot believe in him."

In this way he rejected Jesus as Savior but, strangely, he did urge some of his friends to come to our church and believe in Jesus. His friend Mr. Fu was an officer in a bank where his son also worked. The son was baptized and joined the church, but the aged father feared to do so lest he lose his position with the Japanese. Yet he and his family attended our church regularly.

After Mr. Ma's death I went to visit his family. The elder Mr. Fu also went and spoke of how often Mr. Ma had urged him to go to church. He gave me the reason why Mr. Ma had not gone: "Once a Muslim, always a Muslim. All the days of your life you may not change your belief."

Having been born in Guangdong Province, I was accustomed to food that grows in the tropics—rice, green vegetables, and many fruits. Our clothes were suitable for the climate: shoes made of cloth, or a sort of sandal made of wood, or we went barefoot. Every day we refreshed ourselves with a sponge bath.

In the North country I found many things different from those of the South; many local manners and customs were strange to me. People here often asked personal questions, and for a time I was not sure whether it was through friendliness or mere curiosity, so I was embarrassed. I soon learned their ways in order to become their friend and win them for Christ. In all these difficulties, the Lord truly helped me. Every time I longed for white rice, tropical fruits, and the vegetables of the South, he satisfied me in other ways in this frigid land, and he has truly restored to me a hundredfold whatever I gave up for him.

While studying geography in my youth, I learned that Heilongjiang Province was part of China, and that its climate was very cold, necessitating fur clothing. Also I learned that the principal crops grown are *kaoliang*,⁹ millet, wheat, corn, and soy beans. But when I entered the great Northwest all this became real. In the shops I saw cereal grains, with a great variety of beans, the most important being soya beans, which are used for food and for oil. As far as the eye could see there were great fields of kaoliang, corn, millet, and wheat. At harvest time, there were immense heaps of grain on the stalk—ready to be threshed by treading, beating by hand, or, in some cases, by small machines—and huge stacks of sacked grain waiting to be shipped abroad.

Practically every family ate kaoliang and millet, occasionally with coarse ground corn. Kaoliang had to be boiled about three hours, and millet two hours. As I had little time to spend in cooking and could not eat regularly, I ate what could be cooked quickly. I was not accustomed to the coarse grains, so my digestion became impaired, and I suffered. I became so thin and weak that I had to spend two months in a hospital in Shenyang.

Peiling Hospital in Shenyang had been established by the Seventh-day Adventist Mission and was an excellent and efficient hospital and sanitorium. I thank the Lord for my two months there for rest and healing. During my stay I came ever closer to the Master and learned new spiritual lessons. I also learned the teachings of the Seventh-day Adventist Church, which were a preparation for the work I was to do and for the opposition I was later to meet.

This two months' rest, with a little time spent in the Bible school there, was a great opportunity. Moreover, because of his love for the Lord, the physician reduced the cost of my board and room by half. My indigestion was the first great hindrance to my work in the North. But in the end, God sent me grace upon grace, renewing my strength and health, both physical and spiritual, so that after leaving the hospital I was able to eat the coarse grains of the North without ill effects.

The second hindrance was the cold. In October 1934, I went on my first evangelistic trip to Mingshui with the Rev. J. G. Vos[10] and Miss McCracken. At first we held meetings in the home of Dr. Zi; later we rented a larger building which could seat over a hundred people. Besides the large room there were two small rooms and a kitchen. The location in the town was quite convenient for our purpose.

The building had been vacant for two years and had not been kept in repair; cracks, crevices, and holes let the cold wind drive in. Though we had a fire, it was impossible to overcome the cold, and we could not endure it. Water left in the room turned to ice; tea froze in the teapot and cracked it. I, who was born in a very warm climate, had never experienced such extreme cold, and my body was not able to adjust. The church, as yet, had no plan to make the room sufficiently warm for comfort; the room was large and the people few; the north wind cut like a knife, blowing through cracks in the ill-fitting windows.

Mr. Vos and Miss McCracken returned to Qiqihar after some weeks. Later Mr. Zi and I also succumbed to the cold, and admitted our defeat before the wind, with severe colds and coughs.

In February 1935, I was transferred to Qiqihar. There we lived in a more suitable house and also had the services of a physician when needed. Nevertheless, my cough became worse until I coughed some blood, and that greatly alarmed Miss McCracken and Miss Huston. During this time I had stopped all work and was resting in bed.

As they were overly anxious, I said to them, "Why are you so distressed? God only wants to test me by means of this sickness to see if I have physical endurance, patience, and the heart to do this work. I know that God definitely called me to the Northeast to spread the gospel. I have done nothing as yet, and if I should die now, would not God violate his own plan? There is still much work for me to do. Will God take away my life at this juncture? No! Don't be downhearted; only be more earnest in prayer for me. Let me rest a few more days, and you will see God work marvelously in my body."

The following week my strength was somewhat restored, and in two weeks I took up the work again. Invitations were received for speaking in churches and visiting in homes, but I did only the work in our own church and sometimes spoke to other churches in the evenings. I did not become wearied, and when I spoke a long time, I was not troubled with coughing anymore. Despite cold weather and wind, God was taking care of me. But the roots of the trouble remained for three years and even to this day the X-ray shows scars of this former lung infection. The doctor tells me these are the protectors against germs that might have caused trouble again. So my mind is at rest, for which I thank God.

In the summer of 1938, I went again to the hospital, suffering from severe headaches. The doctor found my body quite normal, with lungs stronger than before. However, other symptoms indicated that an operation was necessary. After that I soon recovered. He advised a longer rest, but I felt it important to return to my work.

Dr. Pei said, smiling, "Are there not many patients here whom you can teach?"

I made no reply, but that evening I read Jeremiah 29:11: "'For I know the thoughts that I think toward you,' says the Lord, 'thoughts of peace and not of evil, to give you a future and a hope.'"

These were God's words to comfort Jeremiah while his people were slaves in Babylon; and it was also his word to comfort me in my weakness. Why should I refuse to accept the goodness of the Lord in giving me this opportunity to rest and fully recover my strength?

I was in a second-class ward with many other patients, paying reduced rates, and I had an opportunity to talk with many who were not seriously ill. The patient in the next room was there just for a rest, and so we had satisfying conversations. She was a member of a modernistic Presbyterian Church, and God opened her heart to understand clearly her spiritual need. He changed her former beliefs so that she became a new creature in Christ. A Mrs. Yao in the ward also accepted Jesus as her Savior. I was thankful to Dr. Pei and to God for giving me this opportunity to witness for him.

After this complete recovery, I remained in good health until 1952 and 1953 when I was in prison.

25

Timothy Joins Me at Qiqihar

While I was experiencing the rigors of northern life, my son, Timothy, wrote from Anhui: "Mother, I am keeping your letters in a special book which I made of special paper. I file them in order as I get them. At times when I feel lonely and long for you, I read over these letters and am happy."

I understood his heart. Was not my own heart longing for him?

During the winter vacation of 1935, he wrote me: "I was the only one left in the school, so a fellow student invited me to his home for the New Year. We were very happy with feasting and fun. But seeing the whole family—father, mother, and children—so happy together, I was filled with longing for the same happiness. I wondered when my family might have such a happy time together."

Before I had read through the letter, tears filled my eyes.

Truly we had never had such a complete family gathering. Before Timothy was a year old, his father had gone to a faraway place, leaving us alone. When he was four years old, he was sometimes with his father, while I was going to school and lived in the dormitory. After I graduated and was teaching, he lived with me, while his father worked in another town. Now his father was 5,000 *li* (a Chinese length, about .31 miles) to the south of Timothy, and I was 5,000 li to the north, leaving our only son sad and lonely. I wondered where I had failed to be a proper wife and a good mother. I was so distressed that I was ill for two weeks, but the Lord had mercy on me and my son, as you will see by the following story.

While Japan, like a tiger, glared fiercely at the Three Northeast Provinces of China and wished to capture them for herself, China, hoping to protect her own territory, took steps to train and equip an army in readiness for war. Fearing that in case of war I should be forever separated from my son, I urged him to spend his winter vacation at Nanjing. At the same time I sent money to Mr. Fan, asking him to make arrangements and to buy a ticket for Timothy to travel to Qiqihar.

By this time the Three Northeast Provinces were a part of Japan and were given a new name: Manchukuo. In order for a Chinese to enter this new country, he had to go through the red tape of many troublesome details, and it was especially difficult for young students. Fortunately Mr. Liao, a teacher in the school at Anhui, was a native of Liao Yang in Manchukuo and knew the conditions my son would meet, so he made the arrangements.

Just at that time, Miss Dorcas Wu was returning to the Northeast, and she agreed to accompany my son on the long journey. Kindhearted friends arranged to go with him as far as Tang Ku, the port for Tianjin where he would meet Miss Wu. Soon afterward, I received a telegram saying, "Timothy should arrive Qiqihar the day after tomorrow."

"The day after tomorrow" passed and yet another "day after tomorrow" until twelve days had dragged by with no news of him. I sent letters and telegrams, all with the same reply: "We have not seen this person." Mr. Vos wired to Dalian and again there was the same reply. We prayed earnestly and were comforted by the words of Psalm 121.

From Tang Ku to Dalian was only six or seven hours travel by sea, and from Dalian to Qiqihar was twenty-four hours by fast train. We had fears of foul play because at that time the Japanese were naturally suspicious of Chinese students and used devious methods in dealing with them. High school students were known to have been arrested and put to hard labor. A family might send a son on some errand only to discover later that he had mysteriously disappeared. Naturally I feared that both my son and Miss Wu had been taken prisoner by the Japanese.

On the morning of the thirteenth day I received a wire from Miss Wu from Dalian: "Both arrived safely in Dalian. Timothy leaves immediately for Qiqihar." On March 1, 1936, we went to the railway station at 6 a.m. in weather eleven degrees below zero and gave Timothy a warm welcome when he arrived. We had never had a more joyful meeting. I praised God for his care and protection. Afterwards, Timothy told me of his experiences:

"We went aboard the ship at Tang Ku and set sail for Dalian. All that night a strong north wind blew. It was so cold that the water froze and the ice became so thick and solid that the ship could not move forward or back into port. The ship had no radio, so no message could be sent. We sat frozen fast for twelve days."

How could we know that the delay was a blessing? It was at that time that the Japanese were seizing students who were suspect. Of course Timothy had arrived too late to enter school, and this also proved to be a blessing.

The first day Timothy was in Qiqihar, I went with him to the high school, but because he was more than a week late they would not accept him, though they had registered him earlier. The principal, out of sympathy, referred us to the minister of education for the state and city. There I met the Japanese officer who was the head of the administration. He appeared to be very stern, showing displeasure and no sympathy for a Chinese student.

"Chinese students do not have good minds," he said. "They are evil-minded; they can't understand our Manchukuo books. I cannot give him permission to enter school."

As he said this, he turned away to leave, but I followed him and begged him to give this young student an opportunity. He was then so gracious as to allow us a three-minute interview. Afterwards he wrote a few words on a paper which permitted Timothy to apply at a special school for underprivileged students who wished to study Japanese. If a student did not understand or speak the Japanese language, he could not enter a higher school and could hardly find employment.

So for his first year Timothy's most important study was Japanese, as all schools were required to study the Japanese language and history rather than their mother tongue and Chinese history. However, with two hours of Japanese in the morning, and Latin and German, which Mr. Vos taught him in the afternoon, Timothy got a good foundation for the three languages needed for his pre-medical course in college.

The closing of the Tang Ku port by ice caused a delay that proved to be another blessing. Since Timothy was a student direct from China, it seemed impossible for him to escape being conscripted into the army or imprisoned as a rebel. Even though the principal of the school knew he was from China and was of military age, yet he accepted him. Truly, "And we know that all things work together for good to those who love God, to those who are the called according to his purpose" (Romans 8:28).

Early in May 1936, Miss Huston and I were sent to Yi An to work in the church there. Timothy had been in the North only two months when I had to leave him at home alone to take care of himself. We went by train to Tai An Chen, expecting to go to Yi An by bus, but after going only three or four miles the bus skidded into a ditch. After using all their strength and many plans, the men got it out, but it refused to run. A cold wind blew, and the passengers were cold and hungry, so we returned to Tai An, arriving at the village very weary. We spent the night there, and after breakfast next morning, all passengers returned to where the bus was, but it still refused to move. We were delayed three days and still could not travel.

By that time my heart was in distress, as I thought of the unfortunate delay. I prayed, "Lord, this delay of three days must be according to thy will and purpose. If we are facing some danger, I regard this delay as thy protection. If I have sinned against thee in taking this journey, I do not know it. If we have disobeyed as Jonah did, when thou didst use a storm to hinder him, I pray thee graciously to show us the way we should go, because we desire to do according to thy plan."

After I prayed I slept.

At daybreak, word came that the bus was not going and that all should remain in Tai An Chen. Some recovered their tickets and waited for a bus next day. I learned from the stationmaster that because of impassable roads there would be no bus for at least five days. So we took our refund, certain that it was God's plan for us to return to Qiqihar.

There I learned that the third day after we left home, the Japanese began going into schools and arresting students, teachers, and principals. Among the students were many who were originally from China, where there was an organization which had the slogan, "Rebel against Japan; oppose Manchukuo." Now they were arresting all who might belong to that organization.

Timothy was living in his own home, quietly and peacefully studying. He had never before met with such a terrifying circumstance and, moreover, his mother was away from home. In the midst of such fears, the Lord was compassionate toward the needs and weaknesses of his children. So, by means of an impassable road, he stopped us in the midst of a 200-mile journey and brought me back, so that mother and son could be a comfort to each other in a time of trouble. If I had gone to Yi An and begun to work, it would have been difficult to leave until after three months at least. The Lord, knowing all things, had brought me back home.

The work of the Reformed Presbyterian Mission in Manchuria was begun in Qiqihar, the capital of Heilongjiang Province. It was quite a large city for that country, though it was neither famous nor beautiful as were so many cities in China.

The religions of Manchuria were the same as those in the rest of China. Most people believed in Buddhism or Taoism. Since this province adjoined Mongolia, there were many who were Muslims, as they were called farther south, but here called Lama. The Lama were not so well established in numbers or in power, but they had their special type of monks or priests who wore voluminous garments with decorations. They did not have temples as the Buddhists did, but conducted their religious services in private homes. Their Muslim faith was handed down by tradition, the children of Muslims being declared Muslim at birth, and taught that they could never change their faith. If a man became a Roman Catholic or a Protestant Christian, he was excommunicated and persecuted, his parents disowning him and his spouse deserting him.

We knew a teenage boy, the son of Muslims, who, through the witness of a Christian boy, had accepted Jesus as his Savior. He saved the money his mother gave him for his school breakfast and bought a New Testament. When the Muslims learned of it, his parents cast him out and he ran away to Hailar, 170 miles northwest of Qiqihar, to live with his mother's sister. After three years his father died and he returned home for the funeral. His brokenhearted mother received him again. He secretly attended our services until it was found out and he was again persecuted, so he returned to his aunt.

26

Winter Hazards

By the time the Reformed Presbyterian Mission started work in Qiqihar, Christian work had been carried on in Manchuria for about a hundred years, though in Heilongjiang Province for only about twenty years. Therefore this section of the country was regarded as neglected, though there were several sects or divisions of the Christian church in the province, to begin with, the Church of Christ, the Baptist Church, and the Seventh-day Adventists. They all used the Mandarin Chinese language. Later, the Norwegian Lutheran Mission came in, as well as the Japanese Methodist Church, which used the Japanese language. The Russian Greek Orthodox Church started work in the larger cities, and, last of all, the Manchukuo Christian Church was established.

When I went to Qiqihar the work of the Reformed Presbyterian Mission was well started. The itinerant work had its difficulties, as I afterward experienced in the towns of Mingshui, Lintan, Yi An, and Daigang, as well as other parts of the province. The farthest from Qiqihar was Mingshui, and the nearest was Daigang, which could be reached by train. All other places could be reached by going partly by train and continuing by two-wheeled horse cart or by ordinary freight trucks. But a trip from one of these stations to another required one or two days by cart.

In summer many roads were over swampy land, and travel was difficult. Though the winter was very cold, travel over the frozen ground was less difficult than in summer, both for man and beast. Also, the days were shorter in winter.

After the Japanese occupied Manchukuo, business prospered day by day. Manchukuo soon had over 6,000 miles of railways extending in all four directions. However, not one of our outstations had a railway passing through it. The roads were not paved, nor even graveled, and in rainy weather they became practically impassable, so that neither cars, trucks, nor buses could travel. This made evangelism in the country places very difficult.

Public vehicles were not like those in modern use; they were ordinary freight trucks. In addition to his freight, the driver was often willing to take one or two passengers in the cab with him. But apart from these, all others had to ride in the bottom of the truck or on top of their baggage. Some trucks had seats along the sides with freight piled in the middle. Sometimes latecomers had to stand, and sometimes they were packed so tight that they could not move.

The first time I went on an evangelistic tour was one winter day when I was still in school in Deqing. It was during a school vacation, so I went with Mr. Chue and an evangelist from village to village to teach for two weeks. Some criticized me and said I did not know shame. Truly I did not feel any shame. The more I spoke the gospel, the more stimulated and uplifted I felt. I wondered at this, for I was still only fifteen or sixteen years of age. And to this day I feel the same.

On October 11, 1934, I started on my first evangelistic tour in Manchukuo. With me were Mr. Vos, Mr. Zhi, Mr. Chen Tsai Min, and Miss McCracken. We went by train to Keshan where we held meetings in a church for two days. Then we traveled two days by cart to Paichuan and held meetings in the Church of Christ for five days. From there we hired a two-wheeled cart and started for Mingshui, a distance of about thirty miles.

With good roads and fast horses we could have made the trip in one day, but it had rained for two days and the road was as muddy as a ploughed field. Besides, after a few carts had gone over the road, we traveled in deep ruts. If not in a rut, we sometimes slid into a ditch. All this was very hard on the horses, and the passengers on the cart suffered as well.

We were not far out of the town when suddenly it began to drizzle; then a strong wind blew. There was no canvas cover for the cart. Having had experience in such weather, the driver offered his solution: "Probably it will soon be raining hard. It is better to have no cover, for it would withstand the wind and make it much heavier for the horses to pull, slowing them down," he said.

With both wind and rain it was very cold, so we each unrolled a blanket from our baggage and wrapped ourselves in it. Knowing that I, a southerner, could not endure this cold, Miss McCracken wrapped me up as though I were a child. I closed my eyes and looked to the Lord.

Even as I prayed, the cart gave a lurch, and we all slid into a ditch. Because of the mud, the horses could get no footing, so they went in too. The horses halted on the edge of the water, the cart and passengers in the water, which fortunately was shallow. We climbed over the horses and got safely to land, where we stood in the wind and rain. Wearing only clothing suited for autumn weather, I was huddled in a bunch, shivering, yet I could laugh at myself.

The driver was not able to get the cart out of the ditch, so at his request the people of a nearby village came in a group to help, some perhaps to see something exciting. With a plank they had brought, they helped the horses out and extricated the cart from the ditch. We all thanked the villagers heartily and gave them a gospel message and some tracts. The driver cleaned up the cart, and we rode on.

We had not gone far when night fell and a dark cloud appeared as well. We were out in the wilderness where we could not see the smoke of people, and no habitation where we might escape from the gathering storm. The driver left the main road and drove across a field of kaoliang, circling about until we saw a building in the distance. In half an hour we came to a road.

"This is not the road to Mingshui," the driver said, "but this inn will lodge both men and horses, and we ought to spend the night here. No one can say certainly that we shall not have a heavy snowstorm. Before us is a wilderness with no place to lodge. What do you say?"

"You are a man of experience," Mr. Vos replied. "We shall do as you advise."

So we stopped. The driver helped us disembark and led us into a clean, tidy room where the innkeeper and his wife welcomed us: "Please get up on the kang and rest. There will probably be a heavy snowfall. Stay until tomorrow."

They were courteous and cordial and we were grateful.

We were shown to a room with two large kangs, and there were no other guests. After helping us with our baggage, the man's wife served us hot tea and asked if we would like some food. Mr. Zhi said, "We would be glad for anything you have on hand." They soon served us cornmeal cakes, cabbage, carrots, and bean curd. Except for Mr. Zhi and Mr. Chen, we were not accustomed to eating cornmeal cakes of coarse ground corn, but we all enjoyed the meal very much.

Soon a strong wind was blowing with heavy rain, and more travelers came in looking like drowned rats, until probably fifty people were lodged at the inn. How thankful we were for the comforts and safety here!

After all had eaten, we took the opportunity to tell the others of Jesus, dividing them into small groups. They listened eagerly.

"Never before have I heard that the Son of God came and died for our sins," one old man said. "Alas, I do not know how to read. Please tell me again, that I may understand it more clearly."

I sat beside him and talked quietly, teaching him to pray, and urging him to find a church or a Christian in his village and learn more.

He said, "If there is One who can save us from bitterness and hardship, good."

He took tracts, folded them, and carefully put them in an inner pocket.

The next morning the weather was fine and, though very cold, the air was invigorating. A strong east wind was blowing. The ground was frozen hard with a thick blanket of snow. It was truly a beautiful scene. The earth that was soft yesterday was now as hard as cement. The cart wheels could not sink in deep mire; the road that had been a swamp was now so solid we could drive over it safely, and the driver was in high spirits.

But the ruts were also frozen hard, and the cart lurched from side to side, bumping into deep ruts, so we got off and walked at times for a rest and to make it easier for the horses. It was also easier to keep warm by walking. When we were within a few miles of Mingshui, the driver stopped at Liu Shu village to give the horses a drink. A large group of children, then women and men, surrounded us, eager to see the two tall Americans of the party. Miss McCracken began giving out tracts while I explained them. Among those who gathered about us was an elderly man who asked for a tract. A year later this man came to Mingshui to the market and recognized me as he passed the chapel. The next day he came again and we found he was still carrying the two tracts we had given him.

27

Come and Receive a Blessing

Our party arrived in Mingshui on a late afternoon in October 1934. We entered the east gate and found an inn where we spent the night. The next morning we prepared a poster in large characters announcing meetings, with a psalm also in large characters. Mr. Vos led the procession, and Mr. Zhi followed with the poster. I rang a bell while Miss McCracken gave out tracts, and invited people to come to hear the gospel: "Come and hear about Jesus and how to be saved. Come and receive a blessing."

Many came, both old and young, great and small. First were children who left their play to see the excitement. Then came mothers to see that the children came to no harm from these strange foreigners. Many idle workmen or clerks came from shops along the street, and our parade grew larger and longer.

Coming to a cross street in a residential section, we stopped where there was no traffic and plenty of room for standing. Holding the banner high, we began to sing. Supposing we were attracting a crowd, as medicine vendors did to sell medicines, many gathered about us. We sang and spoke, over and over again, while more and more people came to listen.

Mr. Zhi went to a nearby shop and borrowed a stool, and I stood on it to speak. My topic was "Faith in Jesus Christ for Salvation." Then Mr. Zhi spoke, and after him Mr. Vos. His dialect showed that he had learned the pure Mandarin of Beijing. It was very surprising to hear a tall, white-faced foreigner speak this language. After each had taken a turn at speaking, followed by singing, we each spoke again, as our audience was not willing to leave, though it was already three o'clock in the afternoon.

Suddenly an elderly man worked his way through the crowd to where we were standing and said very courteously to Mr. Vos, "Sir, what is your honorable surname? My name is Jian, and I also am a Christian. I invite you to come to my home; we have plenty of room. And afterwards make my home your headquarters."

Then he turned and spoke to the crowd about us, "Friends, brethren and neighbors, I invite you to come tonight at seven o'clock to Dr. Zi's home on Big Fourth Street. We have much more of importance and interest to tell you. Do not lose this opportunity to hear our important messages."

Still no one was willing to leave, so Mr. Zhi said politely, "Come and receive a blessing."

"Neighbors and friends, it is now time for the evening meal. These speakers also need to eat and rest. Please come to Dr. Zi's home at seven."

Mr. Jian helped us to gather up our things and led us to Dr. Zi's house. At the time Dr. Zi was in South Manchuria, but his wife received us kindly.

Dr. Zi and Mr. Jian had come to Manchuria together, and they were in business together, so Mr. Jian felt free to invite us to their home. These two families and that of Mr. Liu Chih Hsien were the only Christian families in the whole Mingshui district. They had real faith, though it was very weak, like a lamp with poor oil that could give out no light. Therefore, no one had learned that they were Christians. God used our coming to revive them from their sleep of indifference and make them the light and salt for the community. Their sons became believers, and Dr. Zi's married daughter was born again. People marveled greatly at the change made in this family, and it was a strong testimony for our Christian work.

Mr. Jian's son was bedridden, having suffered from dysentery for half a year. We gave a special prayer for him at the father's request, and God graciously heard our prayers and he was healed. His wife became a believer, and a year later they were blessed with a baby son, their first child in six-and-a-half years of married life. Mr. Jian was now a continual witness for what God had done for them.

After being revived, Dr. Zi's elder daughter, Mrs. Hong, entered a Baptist Bible school, but while there changed to the Pentecostal assembly, the members of which claimed to speak with tongues.

Our Reformed Presbyterian church had been established in Mingshui for three years when the Baptists started a church there with Mrs. Hong as evangelist. She was strongly inclined to "spiritual" songs and "spiritual" dances. To young Christians, this seemed very stimulating and entertaining, and a few of our members became involved until their husbands attended a meeting and forbade their wives to go. The Zi and Jian families followed this young woman until God's Spirit enabled them to see the fundamental difference, and they voluntarily returned to us.

The day we were preaching the gospel on the street, when Mr. Jian led us to the home of Dr. Zi, I thought of Paul and Silas going to the riverside at Philippi, where Lydia and the women were having a prayer meeting. Paul preached to them, and Lydia and her household believed in the Lord. While we were witnessing in that home, the Zi family were revived, sons and daughters believed, and Mr. Sung Kuei Chou and his whole family were converted. This was the work of the Holy Spirit, and a living testimony to the glory of God.

The room at the Zi home was not very large, seating only twenty or thirty comfortably. There was a large open court outsie. Dr. Zi's son built a small platform there, from which we could speak to the crowd; he also provided some long benches. The women sat inside on the warm kang, while the men sat outside. For more than ten days we held meetings there, but later the weather was too cold for anyone to sit outside, and the house was too cold when the door and windows were open.

We then decided to look for a more suitable place for our meetings. Mr. Jian and others found a large building that was vacant; in addition to two small bedrooms and a kitchen it had a large room that could seat more than a hundred people, and the rent was not high. This was God's further provision for the church. Benches were purchased and meetings were held every evening.

Since we were having regular meetings, Mr. Vos asked the Christians to choose two men to act as deacons and to attend to any business connected with the church. They chose Mr. Liao, Mr. Jian, and Mrs. Hong.

Mr. Fu, a native-trained Chinese doctor, attended every meeting from the first, but he gave no evidence that he believed in Jesus, nor did he ask any questions. So I made this announcement: "If any of you wish to ask questions about anything you do not understand, or if you have any objections to what you have heard, please stay and discuss it."

Mr. Fu waited after a meeting and I learned that he was a doctor from Tiehling. I asked if he had any problems about what he had heard.

"Up to this time," he said, "I had never heard of Jesus Christ. Now that I have an opportunity, I wish to listen until I understand it clearly. So I come every day."

I urged him to not merely sit and listen, but sincerely and openly to profess his faith and accept Jesus as his Savior. He agreed to join the Bible class, and I encouraged him, saying, "Do not set your mind on things outside of the church, but enter into life with Jesus, and trust him."

He replied, "I do already believe in him."

"Then," I asked, "why do you not acknowledge your faith before others?"

"I believe he is able to save me," he admitted, "but I do not fully understand many things. I fear I might fall into sin and fail to be a good Christian; then I would be ashamed before others. Therefore I do not have the courage to confess him."

To encourage him, I said, "We, of ourselves, can do nothing; we can only trust the Holy Spirit within us to lead us in right paths, and to understand the truth. Trust him, and you will experience his guidance and support."

"At the beginning of the New Year," he said, "I shall make my faith in Jesus known. It will be easy for me to remember when I was born again and became a Christian."

When he had finished speaking, we prayed together; he most earnestly and sincerely confessed his sins and prayed for God to help him escape the sorrows of death. After this, he stayed every evening to discuss points he did not understand clearly. He also wanted advice about his personal problems, and Bible teachings. In March 1935, he made his public profession and received baptism, becoming a member of the church.

28

God Saves Only Sinners

The Bible records many stories about children. For instance, when the disciples were quarreling about who was greatest, Jesus set a child among them and said, "Unless you are converted and become as little children, you will by no means enter the kingdom of heaven" (Matthew 18:3). Even though the disciples reproved mothers for bringing their children to Jesus, he said, "Let the little children come to me, and do not forbid them; for of such is the kingdom of heaven" (Matthew 19:14). He put his hands on children and blessed them. These incidents teach us that the instruction of children is a very important part of the church's work.

As we went about the street ringing a bell and calling men to hear the doctrine, many children followed, hoping to see some excitement. When we stopped at the street corner and preaching began, suddenly a seven- or eight-year-old boy, his face red and hot from running, forced his way from the edge of the crowd with the shout, "Lend light, lend light!" (Make way!)

Then he stood close to us, listening intently.

When Mr. Jian led us to the home of Mr. Zi, the boy followed and, standing close to Mrs. Zi, took in all he saw and heard. He seemed to be so eager for something, that I turned and asked his name.

He answered me with a question: "Are you a *Ta Bi-zi* or *Lao Mao-zi* (Big-Nosed One or Old Hairy One)?"

I said, "I am a Chinese; I don't know what you call a 'Big Nose' or an 'Old Hairy One.'"

When Mrs. Zi heard his question, she said, "She is neither a Big Nose nor an Old Hairy One. She is one of our own countrymen."

Glancing at Miss McCracken, he said, "Look at her nose. Isn't she a Big Nose—or the same as an Old Hairy?"

"Don't add any more to your foolish mistakes," Mrs. Zi told him. "Go home and eat your supper, Deng Sheng, then come back and hear more about Jesus."

He blushed with shame. To save his face, I invited him to come back, asking about his home and family and inviting them to come, too.

He seemed surprised and said, "Do you know how to read?"

"Yes, I do," I said.

Surprised, he said again, "You do? I have heard that no woman understands how to read. My mother doesn't. How did you learn?"

Mrs. Zi said, "She went to school and learned. Isn't that the way you learned to read? Run along home, now. Your mother will be waiting for you to eat rice." Then he left.

While eating supper he told his parents, "Just today several Old Hairy Ones came to Dr Zi's house. They can speak our language, and they are living at Dr. Zi's home."

"If they speak our language," his father said, "they are not *Lao Mao-zi*" (Russians, or foreigners).

"Papa," the boy said, "you go and see for yourself who they are."

"I am not going to see them," he said, "and I don't allow you to go to see them. They may be people who steal children. Deng Sheng, remember, you are not to go to the Zi house."

"But many people go; I am not afraid, and I intend to go. How can they steal children? I want to go and hear them."

The father did not take the boy's talk seriously. Deng Sheng ate his supper and went again to the meeting, helped to arrange the benches, then sat beside Mr. Zhi. At the close of the meeting he went home at once but did not say where he had been.

This happened every evening until we moved to the building we had rented.

Now, with preaching, answering questions, discussions, and Bible study, the meetings were much longer, and Deng Sheng's father wondered why he was not home. He went to Mrs. Zi's home, but found neither his son nor the strangers, and asked in alarm, "Isn't Deng Sheng here?" He then learned about the meetings at the chapel, so he went there and read the sign, "The Covenanter Christian Church. Please Enter." He went in and saw his son sitting at the front, very quiet, and listening intently. Seeing that the whole audience was as interested as Deng Sheng, he sat down, and when the meeting closed, he took his son home.

As they walked home Deng Sheng said, "Papa, they preached about Jesus; he really is God. He saw men on earth were sinners, and he came to earth to save them. Those who believe in him need not be punished in hell, but go to heaven where they live with God and all is happiness and peace. This Jesus made blind men to see, healed the sick, and even brought a man alive from the grave. As they told these things, it made me want to receive this salvation. Father, you should go and hear this."

The father said, "Son, I am not going to hear this, and I shall not allow you to go."

"But what they say is good," the boy insisted. "I want to go and hear more. If I could see the wonderful things Jesus does, I would follow him every day. He is able to make dead men live again. Isn't that most interesting?"

Next evening, Deng Sheng came as usual, and, in his care for his son, the father came also, sitting as before near the door. At the invitation to remain for questions or the discussion of anything objected to, this man at the back clearly showed that he was displeased about something.

"Teacher," he said, "I object to your inviting my son to come to these meetings. I do not know what you are teaching. You may bewitch my son."

I courteously asked, "Sir, what is your honorable name?"

"My name is Zhao. And that boy sitting at the front is my son."

"I am greatly pleased to have you come to the meeting. I should be glad to hear your valuable thoughts about what you heard. If you wish to know what we are teaching, you should come every evening and study together with us."

He made no reply but led his boy home. To protect his son from possible harm, he came daily to listen. Satan made use of all his doubts and superstitions to hinder Deng Sheng from faith in God. But "we know that all things work together for good to those who love God, to those who are the called according to his purpose" (Romans 8:28). God used this small thread to lead Deng Sheng and his whole family to Jesus. And God was glorified.

Mr. Vos and Miss McCracken had returned to Qiqihar, leaving Mr. Zhi and myself to carry on the work in Mingshui. One day after we had closed the meeting, I noticed Mr. Zhao still sitting there, looking as though he had something on his heart, so as I passed by, I spoke to him.

He said, "Teacher, what you speak is every word true. I do believe this Jesus is able to save me. I must receive him into my home. I ask you to teach me how to do this, how to establish him there."

"Mr. Zhao," I said, "Jesus is the Savior of sinners. He saves only sinners. If you wish to enshrine him in your home, are you ready to confess that you are a sinner?"

"I do confess that I am a sinner," he said. "If I were not, I would not suffer so much. I know that after death men suffer punishment, and I fear that. Therefore,

I have taken many gods into my home and worshiped them faithfully, hoping that they might protect and save me, so that when I die they may show kindness and save me from punishment and suffering. But I seem not to have been kept from sin, so I am still fearful and I am more and more in bitter misery as I think of it. Now, hearing you speak of Jesus, I am beginning to feel that these gods I have can't really protect me. But in this Jesus, my heart seems to have protection and peace of heart and mind. So I believe that he truly can save me. And therefore I shall receive him into my home."

"Mr. Zhao, the Holy Spirit is now working in your heart, making it possible for you to know that you are a sinner, and that only by faith in Jesus will God save you from fear and from suffering. This is absolutely true. 'For there is no other name under heaven given among men by which we must be saved' (Acts 4:12). Jesus is different from idols. Jesus is not such a god as your idols, not like a man who is dead. He is truly a living God. He is not limited by anything in this world. He is not dependent on any created thing to do his work. He needs nothing to represent him. He is not concerned with place, position, or comparison with other gods, such as who is higher or who takes first place. He is the First and the Last. He is God, and he is also man. He is the origin and Creator of all life. Therefore, though he suffered and died on the cross for sin and was buried, after three days he rose again and is now seated at the right hand of God, acting as our Mediator and praying for us. He will come again to earth to receive believers into heaven to live with him.

"You should confess that he is your God and your Lord. You should keep your heart open to receive his teaching. Be prepared to repent and confess your sins, turn about, and live as a new man. Put away the idols you have worshiped in the past. Then Jesus will wash away all your unrighteousness and make you clean. He will become Lord of your home, your whole household. Then that day of peace and rest will come to your house.

"Mr. Zhao, do you believe Jesus is able to take away your sins?"

"I do believe," he said earnestly. "I had never heard that Jesus died for sinners, to enable them to escape their just punishment. Shall I not believe in such a God?"

"If you truly believe, you will naturally pray to him," I told him. "You will voluntarily confess the sins of your life, pouring them out before his face."

"But I do not know how to pray."

"Then let us kneel and pray. As I pray, you may repeat the words I use, until God teaches you to use your own words and desires in speaking to him."

We knelt and prayed. At first I led him in the prayer, then I told him to pray whatever was in his heart. He prayed for himself most earnestly and sincerely. I then gave him some special verses from the Bible to read; then he and his son went home.

The next evening he came with his son and brought the New Testament. I turned to John 3:16 and asked them to read it.

Suddenly Mr. Zhao said, "Teacher, Jesus saved me; can he save my wife?"

I turned to Acts 16:30-32 and asked him to read it. Then I explained it, saying, "When a person believes in Jesus and is saved, he alone is saved, not his whole family by his faith. Now that you are saved, you should take Jesus to all in your home, so that they may be saved. Moreover, since you have received Jesus and new life through him, you are a new man, with new thoughts and actions—all is new. For example, suppose you formerly were easily angered, often scolding and cursing others. Now you must follow the example of Jesus, learn to be humble, patient and kind. Nor should you do some things you formerly did in your business life, such as drink wine, gamble, cheat, and defraud. You must turn from former sins and live as a new, born again man.

"People will be astonished at the change in you; they will desire to know the Jesus who changed you, and will believe and be saved. From today you should teach your wife to have faith in Jesus, so that you may walk the heavenly way together."

It was now time to open the meeting, and we began to sing praise to God. That day Mr. Zhao bought a Bible, and began to read it and to pray with his family at home.

29

Mrs. Zhao Locks Doors

Burning incense has always been an important part of Chinese worship offered to idols and false gods. The urn in which incense sticks are burned was also important and had to be kept on a table before the idols or ancestors to be worshiped. When Mrs. Li, an elderly woman, worshiped the gods, she took the urn with the burning incense, put it on her head, and bowed herself before them. This was to show her earnest devotion.

The very first day we preached in Mingshui, she definitely and truly believed in Jesus. She was a secondary wife (a concubine) and lived with the first (legal) wife and their mother-in-law. After accepting Jesus, she dared not, nor had she the right, to cast out the idols kept in the home. But she took the incense urn she formerly used in worshiping idols, brought it to the church, took it to the front, and in the presence of the congregation broke it to pieces.

People were astonished, and some were terrified lest a fearful calamity come upon her for this act of sacrilege. But God in his mercy blessed her and glorified himself when nothing untoward happened to her, and her example gave many others courage to profess their faith publicly. Mr. Zhao, a relation of Mrs. Li, was one whose faith was greatly strengthened. He went home, told his wife, and urged her to believe in Jesus. But she was a very determined person, and when she learned that both her son and husband were Christians, she scolded and cursed them, hoping to destroy their faith and hinder them in this new way of life.

After destroying her sacred urn, Mrs. Li was zealous in urging others to believe in Jesus. Even though she was poor, despised, illiterate, and not at all gifted, yet she could let her light shine. One day she took me to her home and asked me to tell her family about Jesus. Neither her husband, sons, nor daughters-in-law raised any objections.

Then she took me to visit Mrs. Zhao, who was her niece. Mrs. Zhao opened the door wide, and I entered with her and was introduced. After we had talked a while, I spoke to Mrs. Zhao about Jesus and the faith of her husband and son, pleading with her to join with them in their new faith.

Unexpectedly, she said, "I have no time to listen to this," and showed us to the door.

After a few days, Mrs. Li took me to Mr. Hong's home. He was a Mongolian and welcomed us heartily, and we had a long talk. Again she took me to see Mrs. Zhao. When Mrs. Zhao saw us coming she quickly closed the door, and even though Mrs. Li called to her many times and we tapped on the window, she turned her face away when she saw me.

Then she opened a small window and said, "Aunt, I do not approve of your going about town disturbing and confusing people's hearts about this Jesus. And don't bring this woman to me again. If you do, I shall be very impolite to you."

We were embarrassed by her discourtesy and did not go there again until she sent and asked us to come.

Jesus said to his disciples, "There is joy in the presence of the angels of God over one sinner who repents" (Luke 15:10). Mr. Zhao and his young son Deng Sheng repented and believed in Jesus. The angels in heaven rejoiced over them as they praised God for his salvation. But Satan stirred up trouble for them where there should have been peace; he sent stormy winds of opposition, hoping to destroy their faith and cause them to fall into sin. They had just entered the door of salvation and were not well established, but our Lord Jesus protected them in his own remarkable way, to save the Zhao home.

Jesus spoke these words to his disciples: "Blessed are you when they revile and persecute you, and say all kinds of evil against you falsely for my sake. Rejoice and be exceedingly glad, for great is your reward in heaven, for so they persecuted the prophets who were before you" (Matthew 5:11-12).

According to these words, Christians who are persecuted for Christ are blessed; their reward is certain; it is a promise to all; and there is no respect of persons.

The faith of Mr. Zhao and his son stirred up severe persecution on the part of his wife, first with vile words, scolding, and cursing. Then she refused to prepare meals for them at the proper time, hoping to prevent their attending meetings. They simply let her scold, saying nothing, and even went without meals in order to hear the gospel. They hoped this would touch her heart, and because of love and respect for her husband and son, calm her anger and restore peace.

But the "prince of the power of the air" continued his opposition, and Mrs. Zhao became even more harsh and hateful.

God permitted all this to come to Mr. Zhao at this time as a test of his Christian faith and life. One evening, after he and his son had gone to the church meeting, she locked the outer door to the house. This door was used by the two families who occupied the house. When they returned from the meeting and found the door locked, he rapped repeatedly, but his wife did not open it. Finally the neighbor opened it. When they came in, Mrs. Zhao was so angry she poured out her wrath on them, scolding and cursing the whole night through, vilifying the neighbor for interfering, and denouncing me for confusing her family until they believed in a strange god.

The next morning she did not prepare the morning meal, though her husband was a silversmith and had to go regularly to his work and the son had to be at school on time. Mr. Zhao, knowing his son could not endure both cold and hunger, took him to a restaurant for breakfast. This was another logical reason for scolding. When Mrs. Hong, the neighbor, chided Mrs. Zhao for refusing to open the door, she was told not to open the door again for them.

That night she again locked them out and would not listen to the pleading of her son. So Mr. Zhao tore a small hole in the paper window so that Deng Sheng could put in his hand and unlock the door. But they still could not enter the sleeping room, so they spent the night beside the low brick stove that heated the kang, adding a little fire when they became cold.

Early in the morning, Mr. Zhao prepared the breakfast, and though his wife was still angry, she had no handle on which to hang a scolding.

That evening they came to the meeting earlier than usual and Deng Sheng told me their experience of the night before. I urged them to be even more patient and to pray earnestly for her, then we knelt and made a special prayer for her. God heard our prayers and began his work of saving her.

James, the brother of Jesus, was a man of many such experiences, so when he wrote a letter, he began, "My brethren, count it all joy when you fall into various trials, knowing that the testing of your faith produces patience. But let patience have its perfect work, that you may be perfect and complete, lacking nothing" (James 1:2-4).

The persecution that Mr. Zhao and Deng Sheng were suffering was by God's permission. It was his good will, and for the blessing of the Zhao home and family. In their persecution, they learned to pray to God and to trust and rely upon him, as well as to have patience. They learned also the marvels of answered prayer.

30

When You Pray, Believe

Early one morning, Mrs. Zhao, in great anger, said, "Mei-mei is sick; now we'll see if you still believe in Jesus. Because you have sinned against the kitchen god, Lao Wang Ye, by bringing a strange god into the house, he is very angry with you."

Mei-mei was their little daughter.

Supposing she was merely looking for something more to scold about, Mr. Zhao paid no attention. He sent Deng Sheng off to school at once. As he was going out the door, he noticed that Mei-mei did not speak to him as usual, so he went to her, felt her face, and saw that she had a fever.

He loved the little girl dearly and at once carried her to a doctor, his wife going along. Strangely, the doctor did not know what disease it was, so he did not prescribe any medicine but recommended another doctor.

After examining the child, the second doctor said, "This is not a light illness. I fear it is very dangerous. I can give her some medicine, but I cannot guarantee it will heal her. I leave it to you to decide whether to give her the medicine."

Mrs. Zhao then began to weep, and her husband was in great distress. He went to the shop where he worked to ask for a leave of absence. When they returned home, his wife begged him to acknowledge his sin against *Ke-ye* (the Taoist god of the home), and to prostrate himself before his shrine, confessing his sin of forsaking him and following this Jesus.

"Pray to *Zu-xian* (ancestors) and Ke-ye to forgive you," urged his wife.

Doubts began to come into his mind: "Probably the family gods are surprised and angry that I believe in Jesus. There is just a possibility that they have made this child sick. It is to be expected. And, after all this, my wife will be very indignant at me."

While he was doubting and confused in his thinking, he suddenly recalled some former experiences. Then he asked himself: "Have I not had eleven children? And now I have only three. Now this child's illness brings doubts about my belief in Jesus. What about the eight that died? What doubts do we have about their deaths? On what did we blame that?"

Then God sent his Spirit to enlighten him. He understood clearly and said, "No, this child's illness is not because I believe in Jesus. It is because she does not yet believe in Jesus. I shall confess my sin to Jesus because I have not taught her and urged her to believe."

Then with tears he said to his wife, "This child's illness is not a thing easy to bear; if she dies, what shall we do?"

She replied, "This sickness is your fault. You brought it on her by believing in Jesus and sinning against the gods of this home, and they sent this terrible calamity on this innocent child. If you do nothing to save her, and she dies, I shall never in all my life forgive you nor regard you as my husband. Think of that, will you?"

"This sickness is not because I believe in Jesus," he said, "but because you do not believe. Why did those eight children die, for in those days I did not believe in Jesus? Why did they die? Whom did we blame for their death? I tell you, the eight died before I had my sins forgiven; this sickness is because you believe all these idols in the house. Quickly believe in Jesus, that the child may not die. And stop scolding us."

So long as the father and mother put the blame on each other, Mei-mei's sickness seemed to become more serious. Day after day she had a high fever, often wept, and none of them could sleep. The best doctors in Mingshui had seen her, but she was no better.

On the evening of the fourth day, Deng Sheng, before going to bed, went to his mother's side and looked at his sister.

"Mama," he said, "sister's sickness, is it better?"

"Mei-mei is no better. I suppose she can never be better." Mrs. Zhao wept, and Deng Sheng was very sad. Though he was very young, he had strong faith and a clearer understanding of God and his love than his father had.

"Papa," he said, "why don't we tell Jesus about Mei-mei and ask him to heal her?"

His father seemed as though just awakened from a dream, and he said, "Yes. We went everywhere looking for doctors, but I never thought to ask Jesus to come and heal her." Then, as they talked, Mr. Zhao turned to his wife and said, "Please be quiet, and we shall speak to Jesus and ask him to heal her."

Deng Sheng said, "Mama, you must not scold while we pray. If you scold, Jesus may not come."

"I'll not scold," she said. "Go ahead and invite your Jesus to come and make Mei-mei well. If he really comes and heals her, I will believe your Jesus."

"Really? Truly?" Deng Sheng said. "Will you really believe with us?"

"Truly I will," she said. "Do you think I would cheat you?"

"Come, Papa, let us pray."

The two knelt on the floor beside the kang with heads bowed low, while the mother sat holding the child. Then they both prayed.

Mr. Zhao and Deng Sheng had been believers only four months. Their knowledge and Christian experience were very little, but, according to the faith God had given them, they prayed, believing he would fulfill his promises.

The father prayed: "Lord Jesus, you are the true God, the One who saves men from sin. We ask you to hear us sinners and to save our family. Our younger daughter is sick; we pray you to heal her quickly and give faith to her mother so that we may worship you as a complete family, and be united in faith and harmony. We pray in the name of Jesus. Amen."

Then Deng Sheng prayed: "Jesus, Savior, who forgave our sins, forgive Mama's sins also; you have saved my father and me; I pray you to save Mama and Mei-mei. Mei-mei has been sick four days. You were able on earth to heal the blind and many others. I believe you can heal Mei-mei, and my mother says if you heal her, she too will believe in Jesus and not worship the gods in our home. Will you answer us? I pray in Jesus' name."

After praying, all slept, even the mother. She had watched over the child four nights and she was very weary. Suddenly, at three o'clock she awoke. The child had not cried all night. Feeling certain she must have died, she was surprised to find her breathing and the fever gone. So she slept again until morning.

At six, Mei-mei awoke, calling her mother: "I am hungry. I want some rice gruel."

The father heard her, and as he spoke to her the mother awoke and prepared the food for her. Deng Sheng was soon awake and saw Mei-mei sitting up and eating.

"Mother," he called, "Mei-mei is eating!"

"Yes, she is eating," the mother said. "Get up and wash your face."

His voice was full of joy and victory as he said, "Mother, how about you?"

"Yes, Mei-mei is well, and I believe in Jesus, just as you do. What I promised I shall certainly do."

Mr. Zhao was exceedingly happy and said, "Now our whole family believes in Jesus and is saved."

Mrs. Zhao, who for many months had not smiled, but had been cursing and scolding, was now filled with new joy and peace.

In my own experience during the years in Manchuria I came to know more deeply how God answers prayer and solves our problems as we cry to him. Once, in a particular and sudden difficulty, I was given a memorable example of this. I had received a very important and valuable letter from a Mrs. Te, which I was to keep for her, but another woman (Mrs. Hong) persuaded me to let her have it.

A friend who knew her told me that she was one who lived by deceiving and cheating others and that I had been deceived. I was greatly disturbed, so I went home and knelt to pray.

As I prayed, suddenly I heard a low voice at my side: "Get up and send a telegram to Mrs. Te at Tai An."

Supposing it was Miss Huston who spoke to me, I opened my eyes, but no one was there. I wrote a message at once, and just at that moment one of our Christians, Zhao Zi Ai, entered the room. He was a telegraph operator, so I asked him where the telegraph office was situated.

"Why? Do you want to send a message?" he asked.

I let him read it, and he went at once to send it.

It was timed exactly right. Mrs. Te received it just in time to catch the train. When she got off the train at Qiqihar, she saw Mr. and Mrs. Hong preparing to board the train. She demanded the letter they had taken by fraud; they denied having it. She showed them the telegram and threatened to call the railway police if they did not give it to her. They then produced it from an inner pocket. She came to assure me that she had received the letter, and together we had a prayer of thanksgiving and praise.

God surely answers prayer.

"Therefore I say to you, whatever things you ask when you pray, believe that you receive them, and you will have them" (Mark 11:24).

31

False Gods Burned

The Chinese have very deep faith in superstitions and firm faith in idols. The worship of *Zu-xian* (ancestors) is most important in their esteem. It is not an easy thing suddenly to reject them and cast them off. Mr. Zhao believed in Jesus, yet he did not have the courage to cast out the idols. Now that the whole family was Christian, it should not have been difficult, yet the old superstitious belief that these idols were gods held them in fear. In spite of the healing of the child, the mother hindered the father from casting off the gods.

"Isn't it enough," she said, "to believe in Jesus? Must we cast off all other gods? Why burn the gods I have worshiped for twenty-five years? How can I do such a terrible thing? Let them alone where they are."

Mr. Zhao did not dare force her to throw them out; she had not yet really heard the gospel. She was caught on the two horns of a dilemma: on the one hand were the old gods and on the other, Jesus Christ.

Deng Sheng was just then having a vacation from school and he continually urged her to cast them out. She did nothing, nor did she allow him to destroy them.

One morning the boy came to the church calling for me: "Mei-mei has been very sick. Father and I prayed for her and God healed her. Mother said that she would believe if Mei-mei were healed. But now she is afraid to cast out the idols."

After he told me this we prayed together, asking God to strengthen and establish the faith of each one and not allow faith in the old gods to ensnare them again. We asked him to help them believe, obey, and serve the God who had saved them. Then I prepared to encourage them to cast out the old gods, and I went home with Deng Sheng.

When Mrs. Zhao saw me coming she got down from the kang to show that she welcomed me. Deng Sheng went with Mei-mei to Mrs. Hong next door, while I talked with Mrs. Zhao. She told me simply and clearly how she had done all she could to hinder her husband's and son's belief.

"Then," she said, "Mei Ru, our little daughter whom we call Mei-mei, became very ill. The doctors could do nothing to heal her. My husband said, 'There is just one thing that will keep her from dying; that is for you to believe in Jesus.' We had already lost eight children by death, and I didn't want to see this child die also. My husband and son had prayed for her. So I myself prayed: 'Let me know what I should do that she may live, and I will do it.' I prayed in desperation with all my heart.

"To my surprise, the child became well. I awoke during the night thinking she was dead, she had slept so quietly. I held my hand before her nose and could feel the warm breath. I felt her head and body; the fever was gone. Before dawn she awoke and called for food; when I brought it to her she ate.

"Usually when a person recovers from illness he has no appetite for several days. I marveled that she was hungry, and wanted to eat. Now that she was well, I knew that I had not been deceived. I shall believe in Jesus as I promised.

"But if they say I must cast off and renounce the ancestral gods and Buddha, I dare not. I have worshiped them for twenty-five years. How could I do such a cruel thing as that?"

"Why do you wish to worship these gods, Buddha, and the ancestors?" I asked her.

She replied, "They are the gods of the Zhao clan, and they may cause us trouble. The family spent much money on temples; they left us an inheritance, and we paid the priests when our children died. So we are grateful to them for their grace to us, and we wish to keep them in remembrance and show our respect for them. It is not according to reason or propriety to cast them off."

"Mrs. Zhao," I said, "what you say about our ancestors is perfectly right. We should remember their virtues and show gratitude for all they have done for us. But you have worshiped only your immediate forefathers. Are you not unfair to the many generations before them? Also there is someone much more ancient than they, someone who existed before there was earth or man, the One who created the earth and man and all things. According to what you say, you are not a person without respect or gratitude. Do you know who it is that created us and all things?"

"No, I don't know," she said.

"This person who created us is none other than the true God. Almost 2,000 years ago he came to the earth, took a human body, and lived among men. His name was Jesus. He taught people to thank God for his grace and power, and to glorify him. While on earth, he healed the sick, cast out devils, and did many wonderful works, and at last he died on the cross to save sinners. Tell me, how great was his lovingkindness to us? Should you not remember him and worship him?"

She said, "I have not thought of him nor worshiped him."

"I am not surprised and do not blame you," I said, "for you didn't know of him. Besides, you are a person who has respect for those you worship, even though you worshiped the wrong one. It is as though you acknowledged the wrong people to be your father and mother. Now that you know you were mistaken, you should separate from those that are not gods and come to the true God; you should trust only the Lord Jesus as your Savior. He will forgive your sins and accept you as his child."

"I believe Jesus," she insisted. "I can believe and trust him. But if you say I must cast off the former gods, I cannot be so hard-hearted."

"But, Mrs. Zhao," I said, "our forefathers even one generation before us are already dead; their bodies are in their graves; they have no feeling, no knowledge, no life. What you are worshiping is nothing but a piece of paper on which someone has painted a picture or written characters. This paper thing cannot even move. How could it protect you? You believe it is a god. Are you not deceiving yourself?

"Even Zao Wang Ye (the ancestral god) is not a god. It is merely a picture painted with colors by some man who said, 'This is a god.' You believed him and honored it as though it were an ancestor and you made it lord of your home. In worshiping it, you make yourself of less value than a piece of paper. Is not this debasing yourself?

"I have here many pictures. If I asked you to bow to and worship one, you would say I was making a fool of you. What you have been worshiping is explained the same way as a piece of wood or paper, or perhaps gold, silver, or brass. If you burn or destroy them, there is nothing to fear. If I burn these papers of mine now will you be afraid?"

"I am not afraid. You are just burning paper things, newspaper pictures used for wrapping things," she answered.

I then burned the pictures and newspaper I had brought. Then I took from my bag a piece of white writing paper and asked if she would be afraid for me to burn it.

She said, "It is just a piece of paper. I am not afraid."

So I lit a match and burned it. Then I took a paper with a picture on it and asked if she would be afraid for me to burn it, saying, "What does the picture look like?"

"It is like Zao Wang Ye (the Zhao family god)," she said.

"Is it really like him?" I asked.

"It really is like him," she said. "Who drew it?"

"I did," I told her, "though I am not an artist. But if you say it is like him, that is all I want. Now watch me burn this Zao Wang Ye."

As I spoke I set the match to it and burned it.

Then I said, "Mrs. Zhao, were you scared when you watched me burn the god?"

"No, I wasn't afraid," she said. "I believed what you said."

"If you were not afraid when I burned a picture that I made that was like Zao Wang Ye, why be afraid of a picture someone else made? What kind of thinking is that? No matter who drew the picture, it is still just a picture. Is it sensible not to fear one and to fear the other?"

"That's true," she said. "No matter who makes the picture one should not fear."

As she said this, she got down from the kang and immediately went and tore down the picture of Buddha above the table and the picture of the ancestral god of the home from the wall and burned them. Altogether that day she destroyed nineteen such emblems while I sat and silently prayed for her.

As she gathered these together, she said, "I shall take the opportunity and use this fire to cook the noon meal."

Before I left I said, "We should take a little time for prayer. Have you any new thing you would like to tell Jesus, any difficult thing, or any hardship? You may tell him these things and he will listen. You know how they prayed for Mei-mei when she was sick, and you saw how quickly she became well. Now you should ask Jesus to forgive you for the years of worshiping idols. Also, you should ask him to guide and protect you, and teach you how to walk in his way."

After we had prayed I returned to the church.

That evening Mrs. Zhao came to the service with her whole family. During the meeting I told the people how Mrs. Zhao had destroyed the idols in their home. At once, her neighbor Mrs. Chen asked me to go to their home and help destroy her family's idols.

After Mrs. Zhao believed in Jesus she was like two persons in one; she was a very earnest, sincere Christian, in harmony with her husband. If he sang, she sang in her heart. But, as a proverb says, "Mountain and river may be changed, but it is impossible to change one's disposition." And the "old man" of her nature was not at once transformed; he often broke out and showed his power. When this occurred, Mr. Zhao would start to sing Psalm 23 to the ancient Chinese shepherd music. She would then soon forget her anger and join in the song. Instead of the scolding voice, neighbors would then hear the voice of joy and praise. Everyone marveled at this wonderful change and said, "To believe in Jesus is truly good. He changes a bad person into a good one." In May 1936 the entire Zhao family was baptized.

When I announced that the Zhao family had destroyed their idols, the Chen, Fan, and Wu families all asked me to go and help them destroy their old gods.

Mr. Fan said, "They have never blessed us. Why not cast them out? Burn them. Burn them."

All I did when I went was to pray for them. Destroying the idols was their own voluntary act because of their own faith.

Then Mrs. Song told me that she and her husband believed in Jesus, but that she, like Mrs. Zhao, was unwilling to burn the idols because she did not want to be cruel to them. She told me she had taken them to the temple, thinking they would be pleased and would not harm her in retaliation.

I said, "In loving and honoring them so much, you simply gave standing room to Satan. Now you should ask God's forgiveness for so honoring those evil objects."

I read aloud to her these words: "For there is one God and one Mediator between God and men, the Man Christ Jesus, who gave Himself a ransom for all, to be testified in due time" (1 Timothy 2:5-6). Then I read verse 4: "Who desires all men to be saved and to come to the knowledge of the truth."

"Idols," I said, "are simply senseless material things, with no life, no feeling, no power. Satan uses these things to deceive people, bind them, enslave them and make them oppose the true God. In order to escape from Satan's shackles, one must first cast off Satan's idols, showing that we belong to God and are free from Satan and victorious over him.

Mr. and Mrs. Fan began at once to take down their idols and gods, and Mrs. Song helped them.

"We trust what Teacher Li told us," they said, "that we can overcome Satan by destroying the idols. Destroy them. Burn them. Overcome Satan."

They vigorously tore down the paper gods from the walls and thrust them into the fireplace for heating the bed. Mr. and Mrs. Fan were more than sixty years of age and had served the idols several decades. Had not God's power been given to them, it would have been impossible for them to do this. As they burned the idols, we sang together a psalm of praise to God, again and again.

Then Mrs. Song led in singing, "Free, free, forever free; I shall not again be bound by sin. The precious blood has cleansed me, giving my inmost heart great peace. Trusting in Jesus, truly I am free."

After reading the Bible and praying, I went home.

On May 17, 1936, Mrs. Song and Mr. and Mrs. Fan were baptized and became members of the church.

The Three Northeast Provinces were adjacent to Outer Mongolia, so the Muslim religion influenced many people in Manchuria. Wang Tai-tai was a Mongol and believed their religion, but her husband was Chinese. In preparing for her marriage, her parents hid a Lama Buddha among her dowry to take to her new home.

This idol is an object of worship for the follower of the Lama-Muslim religion. It is also worn for protection—inside the clothing next to the body—wherever the person may go. It is made of gold, silver, brass or iron, or sometimes of semi-precious stone, and often measures less than an inch in height. Many times a day those who are held by this superstition take the idol out, hold it carefully in their two outspread hands, kiss it, pray to it, then replace it next to the heart.

Mrs. Huang's Buddha was made of pure gold, about the size of one's little fingertip, and she had worn it for many years on a gold chain about her neck. If she chose to keep it after becoming a Christian, no one would ever see it or know she had it. But when she cast off her idols and false gods, her husband said, "You should cast off your golden Buddha along with all the others. If you don't, you will naturally and from force of habit often think of it and, in your heart, worship and serve it." She then took this precious idol out of her bosom and gazed long at it. Truly it was hard to give it up. It was a valuable thing and, besides, it had been given to her by her parents as part of her dowry, so it was a precious keepsake.

Finally she gave it to me, saying, "I give it to you for a remembrance."

"But I don't want it," I said. "If its value is your reason for not giving it up, then I can find a plan to dispose of it."

I took the idol off the gold chain and returned the chain to her. Then I took a heavy hammer and beat the idol out of shape. Giving it back to her, I said, "Take it to a goldsmith and sell it to him for its full value as gold."

She was satisfied with this solution.

"For the word of God is living and powerful, and sharper than any two-edged sword, piercing even to the division of soul and spirit, and of joints and marrow, and is a discerner of the thoughts and intents of the heart" (Hebrews 4:12).

Jeanette Li (far right, first row) during her first year at the Mission School.

Reformed Presbyterian Mission buildings in Deqing, Guangdong Province.

A baby found at the orphanage gate.

Pó Yan, a messy eater at the orphanage. One of the missionaries wrote, "She liked to get up [and] walk around while she ate the last of her food—and this time came over where I was taking pictures of some—so I snapped her. Does she look guilty or just defiant? She was very very messy about her eating, but would she let anyone help? Not she!"

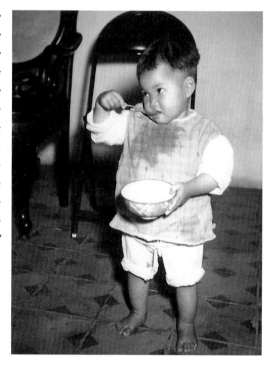

Deqing orphans with baby dolls.

Deqing altar just outside the Mission grounds.

A pagoda on the Xi River.

The schoolroom in the Deqing Mission School that Li briefly attended.

Li as a young girl soon to be married.

The workers on the field in Qiqihar, Heilongjiang Province, 1938. (Left to right) Phil Martin, Miss Li, Mr. Zhao, Li, Lillian McCracken, Mr. Gao, Rose Huston, and Mr. Zhi.

Chen Zi Xian, the store manager whose conversion is discussed in chapter 32.

Huston, unknown Chinese woman, McCracken, and Li in Qiqihar, 1934.

Written on the back of the photograph: "Enroute [from] Tai An Chan to Yi An.... Road impassable—so returned on a cart that came along." This occurrence is similar to the experiences Li had with road conditions, described in chapters 25 and 26.

Li at the entrance to the Mingshui missionary headquarters.

Li with her son, Mian Chao (Timothy), in Qiqihar, c. 1936-37.

Zhao Zi Ai, J. G. Vos, and Martin in Manchuria, February 1939.

Li in front of the home she shared with the missionaries in Qiqihar, early 1940s.

Teaching the orphans to work in Deqing, 1949.

Li on the Xi River, c. 1949.

Li operating a raft during a flood of the Xi River, c. 1949.

Presbytery arriving at Deqing, 1949.

Li at the stern of the boat, rowing Samuel E. Boyle and others to board a vessel for Canton, September 1949.

Pastor Peter Song and his family.

Last meeting of China Presbytery in Hong Kong, 1950.

Li in front of the Wong Tai Sin apartment buildings.

Li outside her 9 foot by 9 foot apartment in Wong Tai Sin.

Li's kitchen in her apartment.

Reformed Presbyterian refugees from Communist China.

Li in Jiulong (Kowloon), c. 1960-61.

Li with her son in the United States, c. 1965-66.

Huston and Li outside of the Phoenix Reformed Presbyterian Church, October 21, 1963.

Li translating from Chinese to Engish with Boyle and Charles H. Chao.

Boyle interpreting for Jeanette Li.

McCracken, Li, and Huston in the home they shared in Qiqihar.

32

Idols Become Wallpaper

Houses in the far North were quite different from those in the South. The climate in the North is cold and dry, while in the South it is warm and rainy. Most of the houses in the North were built of sun-dried mud brick, with very thick walls; the roofs were made of a very thick layer of tall grass covered with mud. The inside walls were covered with a tough white paper which was pasted on. This made the house clean and kept the sand from continually dropping down into the rooms.

Mr. Hong was a man who did little business. He carried his wares in boxes on either end of a pole and every day went from house to house in the town or out to the surrounding villages. He carried some kind of a rattle or bell to announce his approach while he called out the wares he had for sale. He carried jewelry such as rings, earrings, and bracelets, some toys; sewing materials; and also images of Buddha and kitchen idols.

It was the custom for every family, at the end of the year, to buy a new idol or paper god to replace the old one, which was first smeared with something sweet so that it would speak well of them to its successor. So Mr. Hong had prepared a great stock of gods for his New Year business in the various villages.

But before the end of the year he had received Jesus Christ as his Savior and had cast out the ancestral gods and all idols from his home. There came a day when he went with his usual load of articles for sale and called out his wares through the villages. All day not one person came to buy. In the evening he carried everything back home, discouraged. That night he came to the prayer meeting at the church. Our topic for discussion was Romans 12:2: "And do not be conformed to this world, but be transformed by the renewing of your mind, that you may prove what is that good and acceptable and perfect will of God."

Then Mr. Hong realized that the reason he had sold nothing all day was that among his wares were so many idols with which God was not pleased. He prayed a prayer of confession, and in his prayer vowed never to buy or sell such things again. The next day his business was very good. But he was faced with the problem of disposing of all those idolatrous objects. Should he burn them, or sell them? They represented his capital; they meant money.

At the year's end, everyone had an annual housecleaning in preparation for the New Year. An important part of this was putting a new layer of paper on walls and ceiling. Mr. Hong had a brilliant idea: Why not use his large stock of pictures of Buddha, and the ancestral and kitchen gods, instead of buying new wallpaper? And with the consent of his wife, that is what he did.

Buddha and other idols were painted in various colors, and Mr. Hong, having some artistic ability, pasted them on every wall and ceiling in attractive designs which were really very pleasing to the eye. Even the base of the brick kang was covered with these pictures.

Those who were not Christians said, "This is sacrilegious; it just can't be done." But the Hong family made it a powerful testimony to their faith in Jesus Christ and the true God. The New Year is an annual festival when every family visits or entertains relations and other guests, and it is a time of good fellowship. As usual, the Hongs had many relations and friends who came to visit them. When they saw Buddha and the ancient gods staring from every side, they were afraid to enter the house. If they did enter, they were afraid to sit on the kang above the gods.

Mr. Hong used this as an opportunity to introduce his relations and friends to Jesus, his Savior. But they had different ideas: "The gods will certainly send calamity on you and your family." But God truly gave him special blessings. Before he had become a Christian, he lost his only two sons to disease and death. Afterward God gave him three children to whom he gave the names Cheng Xian (Perfect Faith), Cheng Ai (Perfect Righteousness) and Cheng Jing (Perfect Uprightness).

Later Mr. Hong opened a photography shop and, with his wife's help in posing and prettying up the ladies, it became a great success. His unbelieving relations marveled and many, because of this, were led to faith in the true God. Mr. Hong and his family were baptized in December 1935.

At a meeting I usually first read a chapter from the Bible; then, as I spoke, I wrote a verse on the blackboard, or on paper, because I knew that not my spoken words alone, but the written words of God, are living and effective. As my audience saw the characters they were forced to think of their meaning.

Sometimes I wrote as I talked, with brush and ink, so that they would be more eager to get the meaning.

At that time, it was generally supposed that reading and writing were special gifts to males. I hoped to show them that a woman could have the ability to read and to write, even in the presence of men, and with God's help could move hearts to accept Jesus. And God's Holy Spirit then did a great work.

One evening I read Isaiah 57:20-21: "But the wicked are like the troubled sea, when it cannot rest, whose waters cast up mire and dirt. 'There is no peace,' says my God, 'for the wicked.'"

Then I read Psalm 1:5-6: "Therefore the ungodly shall not stand in the judgment, nor sinners in the congregation of the righteous. For the Lord knows the way of the righteous, but the way of the ungodly shall perish."

When I finished writing this, with black ink on white paper, I put it up for all to read. I read it over twice, then I gave some illustrations of those who do evil and have no peace.

As I spoke I noticed a young man whose face suddenly became pale, and drops of perspiration stood out on his forehead. At first I supposed he was ill, but actually it was the Holy Spirit doing his work as I spoke. The more I spoke, the more power he gave me, and the more earnestly the young man listened and trembled.

Then he stood up and said, "Teacher, I am the evil person you are talking about. In my heart I am a rebellious child, and I have no peace in my heart. Now what must I do to obtain peace?"

I said, "Today is the day of acceptance. Today the Lord Jesus is willing to save you. You should pray earnestly, and sincerely beg him to save you. Kneel down and pray, 'Lord Jesus, save me. I am a sinner; in my heart I have no peace. Forgive my sins, cleanse my heart and give me peace.' If you are willing to pray this prayer, he is ready and willing to forgive and save you."

He knelt at once before the audience, weeping and praying, "Lord, I am a sinner. Forgive and save me."

Mr. Zhi helped him to his feet and led him to the guest room and talked with him.

After finishing my talk, I closed the meeting and I went and talked with him. I learned that this was the first time he had ever heard the gospel message. The Holy Spirit moved his heart, and he immediately received Jesus Christ as his Savior.

This young man was Chen Zi Xian, originally from Baoding in Hebei Province. He was manager of a general store at Paichuan. After believing in Jesus, he realized that working in a shop which bought and sold idols was not the right thing for a Christian to do. He at once decided that on the fifteenth or sixteenth of the month, according to custom, he would resign.

He was very industrious and honest as a workman and had been with the firm for six years. The owner of the business trusted him absolutely. When he presented his resignation, the manager offered him much higher wages if he would remain.

But Chen Zi Xian said, "I am now a Christian. I cannot do this business in idols, incense, wine, tobacco, and such things. I do not now serve idols. No matter how much money you give me, I cannot remain at work here."

The manager smiled and said, "Mr. Chen, I respect your religion. You may follow your Jesus, and I shall continue my worship and continue to do business with idols. I hope your Jesus will bless you."

Mr. Chen left this shop and, in partnership with Mr. Lu Ci Yang and Liao Zhi Hen, he opened a business in Mingshui. This new shop was called *Xian Ai Cheng* (New Righteous Shop). They sold all kinds of food stuffs: cereals, many kinds of flour, salted vegetables, and also paper of every kind, ink, brush-pens, pencils, paste—but no wine or tobacco or objects of idolatry. Every Sabbath day they closed the shop and rested, and all the workmen attended church services together. Over the shop door they put up a sign saying, "Today is the Sabbath. We observe it as a day of rest and worship." A tenth of profits from the business were given to the Lord for the church. This shop was a wonderful testimony to God's love, for he gave them many blessings in special ways.

In the autumn of the following year, Mr. Chen left the shop and went to the Bible school in Yingkou for study. When the Japanese forced the Bible school to close, he went to the theological seminary in Tangshan in China. When the Japanese went to war with China, that seminary also was closed, and all Americans were sent home. So Mr. Chen was not able to complete his course, but he returned to Hailun in Manchuria where he was greatly used by God in his preaching until the Communists took over. After the Chinese defeat in the North, no news of him was received by the mission.

33

Mr. Tian Finds Happiness

The church at Mingshui had first used a rented building, then the following year it had moved to a building on South Street. This building was smaller, but it was on a large vacant plot of land, so the church decided to buy it in order to be able to enlarge the building as the church grew. The Christians with one heart gave generously toward the purchase of the property. They also provided whatever furnishings were needed.

The Christians now requested the mission, whose headquarters was in Qiqihar, to provide an evangelist to live in Mingshui. The mission replied that, as Jesus said, "the harvest was great but the laborers few," so they were not able to send a permanent worker at once. However, the workers who were available took turns going to Mingshui for longer or shorter periods.

But these Christians were hungering and thirsting for the Word and for spiritual help, so they sent a more urgent request for help. Therefore I was glad to go to Mingshui, even though, being subject to severe car sickness and resulting weakness, I found the trip of from ten to fifteen hours filled with intense suffering. On one such trip, Miss McCracken said to me, "Sometimes as we traveled, your face was like that of a corpse. But, thank the Lord, you lived until we arrived at Mingshui."

I had prayed, "Lord, keep me from this awful illness," but he did not remove it from me. However, his grace was sufficient for me. Every time I was ill he gave me strength to endure it.

Every time I went to Mingshui I at once gave out tracts announcing meetings. At the entrance to the chapel, we put up a poster announcing afternoon and evening meetings. The room would seat not more than fifty or sixty, so for afternoon and summer evening meetings we opened the door and windows, and put benches outside for the overflow. At the close of the afternoon service many stayed to ask questions, and that kept the meeting open an hour longer.

One day, after all had gone, I was in the kitchen preparing the evening meal, when Miss McCracken came and said, "An elderly man came in and asked me some questions, but I do not understand his dialect very well. Please go out and talk to him."

When he saw me he said, "I've seen you before. You passed through our village last year and gave me a tract that tells about happiness. Three days ago, as I came to the market, I saw many people here, so I came in to see the excitement. I recognized you, so I stood outside and listened. Yesterday and today I came again, but because of so many people, I hesitated to go in.

"But I wanted to know if the Jesus you tell about is the same as the one this tract tells about. It was given to me by a traveler when I lived in Shanghaigang. I tried to read it, but I couldn't understand it. I regarded it as something precious, so I put it in a box in the bottom of a chest. Last year when I got this other tract, I took the first one out, but I didn't understand either of them. Now, will you explain them to me?"

I recognized the one I had given him; the other was written in old-style "grass" characters. Taken together they contained excellent gospel teachings. So from these two I told him about Jesus.

Afterward I said, "Mr. Tian, who is a sinner?"

He said, "I am a sinner."

"How do you know you are a sinner?" I asked.

"I have suffered so much, and that means I have sinned and the suffering is my punishment."

"These two days," he continued, "you have said many times that if one is a sinner, he must die. So if you die, you are a sinner. I am now sixty years old. I can't say whether I shall be alive next year or not; that is to say, I am a sinner."

"Mr. Tian," I said, "what you say is exactly right; this cannot be denied. Do you know why you are a sinner?"

"I don't know why."

"Please, Mr. Tian, listen to me as I read the Bible. The Bible is like a mirror. It is able to reveal the secret things of a man's heart, things that no one but he knows.

"The first chapter of Romans tells us that from the beginning men's hearts have been wicked. That which may be known of God is manifested in the invisible things of him from the creation of the world, and by them we understand his eternal power and Godhead, so that men have no excuse. They oppose God and make themselves idols and deliberately refuse to know and acknowledge God.

Their inmost hearts are full of envy, jealousy, cruelty, hatred, deception, falsehood, pride, backbiting, and boasting; they delight in wickedness and disobey parents. They not only do these things but teach others to do them.

"Mr. Tian, do you understand this clearly? Please think about this. What sins do you have?"

"All these are my sins," he said. "Is there anything else? I can't think of any more. Everyone disobeys and dishonors their parents; everybody talks about others behind their backs; all tell lies, are cruel, proud, and boastful. All these are my sins."

"But," I said, "have you not worshiped idols and the ancestral gods? Do you not worship Buddha? You worship those that are not gods, but the true, the all-wise God and Creator you do not worship. Moreover, you have not believed in Jesus Christ as your Savior. This tract which you have had for forty years tells you about this, and yet you have refused him. This is a sin worthy of death. But God is merciful, and he has given you another opportunity to learn the way of salvation. This Jesus is the Son of God; he took men's sins upon himself and accepted the suffering and shame we deserve to suffer. He bids you sincerely and humbly to confess your sins, and he will save you and deliver you from the suffering of punishment. He will give you new life, new strength, and make you a new man. Mr. Tian, are you willing to accept him as your Lord and Savior?"

In a very low voice he replied, "I believe."

Supposing he was not quite willing, I said, "Jesus' love is so great, can you not believe?"

Then I saw that he was wiping away tears with his hand, and I knew the Holy Spirit was doing a mighty work in him, so I told him to pray to God.

Without hesitation he prayed, "Lord Jesus, I pray you to save me. How can I bear to think of allowing you to suffer such pain and bitterness for me? Your love for me is greater than the love of father and mother. If I do not believe and trust you, I am lower than a beast. Forgive me for my rebellious and hard-hearted lying, cursing, and dishonoring of parents." After he had prayed, I prayed for him. Then I gave him the four Gospels and urged him to read them, pray every day, and faithfully attend church services, where he would gradually learn more of God and his love, and have fellowship with others. Then, I told him that, at the end of his earthly road, God would receive him into the heavenly home.

He quickly asked, "When he receives me, will he also receive my life-partner?"

I replied, "If she also believes, certainly he will receive her. You must teach her and urge her to believe."

He said, "She is already dead."

"Jesus receives only those who believe. Regret is useless; to use geomancy is also useless. This is a natural result of unbelief. Now you should urge your children to believe in him, lest they too be separated from you in death."

He said nothing more, but returned home.

This elderly man, Tian Xi Qin, lived three miles from Mingshui in Liu Hao Tun (Willow Village). After this, in summer and winter, neither heat nor cold, nor rain, snow or wind hindered him from attending worship services, and he always came early.

On May 17, 1936, he was baptized and became a member of the Reformed Presbyterian church in Mingshui. Mr. Tian was a farmer, and had practically no education. God had used two small gospel tracts to lead him to salvation. His heart was a well-watered land, prepared for the seed, and when the seed was planted, it grew. God had allowed him to suffer forty years of patient digging, clearing away rocks, plowing, harrowing, sowing, and reaping. At last he was saved. This was not a natural thing; it was the work of God.

34

Activities of the Church

The saying, *Sai wai* (outside and to the west of China the grass is dry and bitter), refers to those who live outside of Shanghaigang, the Mongolians and others in the far North and West.

During winter in the North, the heavens are ice, and on the well-watered earth the frozen grass becomes bitter. For half the year one does not see the earth or anything green. In summer the night is short and the day long. Everyone knows this but wonders what causes such a change. How do the people manage a time for work and for rest? How do they care for a home and a family in such a climate? I am sure those who live in the warm zones of the South will be interested to know.

In midsummer the sun rises early, about three o'clock, and dark does not come until about ten o'clock in the evening. In the far North, summer and winter, people live by the sun; they go to work when it rises and go to rest when it sets, and this does not vary.

Some may ask, "What connection has this with Christian work? Surely it does not affect church work." But Christians are not exceptions and, no matter whether farmers, merchants, or other workers, all must be up with the sun to wash, eat, and go to work.

However, in summer after the midday meal, managers of shops and their workmen take turns for a summer nap. As for hired helpers in summer days, "the earth is their bed, the plough their pillow." Coolies, or burden bearers, when noontime comes, sleep in the shade of the north eaves of buildings until two o'clock, when they return to work. In this way the people of the North get the summer rest they need.

The first summer I was in Qiqihar I was surprised to see so many people sleeping on the streets. I criticized them for shirking their work, until I learned why it was a necessary part of their day.

Farmers usually begin spring work about the middle of May. One common test as to whether or not spring has come is to dig a hole in the ground, perhaps as deep as the frost goes, put a feather in it, and, if it floats up, spring has come and it is safe to plant. Autumn begins on the ninth day of the ninth month, when days begin to shorten and all vegetables must be harvested before they freeze. This is one of the mysteries of the Lord Creator.

Keeping the morning watch was a custom of the Christians at Mingshui. They preferred to come to the church for these devotions because there was no privacy at home. Every morning at the first crack of dawn they would come to the chapel. Before they came, of course, I had to be up and dressed and have the room tidied after the previous night's meeting. During the day I had to be on hand to receive any who might drop in for a visit. Often police came to question me. So I never got a summer nap, and naturally I lost my energy and became very weary. Even Jesus became weary and said, "You are in need of rest. Let us go aside and rest awhile."

Every evening, because of the meetings, I got to my rest very late, and due to the very short summer nights and long busy days without sleep, I became very weak; my head was dizzy, and my eyes pained me. So, in order to get the summer nap I needed, I asked a Christian who lived nearby to come before his nap and put a lock on the outside of the church, so that people would not pound on the door. After this I got a little rest, and I gradually became stronger and healthier.

A certain great singer named David asked God to forgive his sin. Then he wrote, "Blessed is he whose transgression is forgiven, whose sin is covered" (Psalm 32:1). The new Christians at Mingshui, because they knew their sins were forgiven, very happily sang this psalm and others.

So we divided the evening meeting time into three half-hour sections. The first half hour was spent in learning to sing psalms, with Mr. Lu Ci Yang as leader. Formerly he had owned a general store in Paichuan and was a member of the church there. He was not a trained musician, but God had given him an excellent voice and he had learned to sing simple music by note.

The second half hour of the meeting was spent in teaching those who did not know the Bible. I taught those who could not even read. Afterward, Mrs. Hong helped me to teach them. She was a native of Beijing; her father was a teacher in the Baoding School and her husband had a position in the government offices of Mingshui. The Hongs lived in rooms opposite Mrs. Tang.

One day Mrs. Tang returned from church saying happily, "To believe in Jesus truly is good; truly it is good. Even the blind have their eyes opened."

When Mrs. Hong heard this she said, "Since you believe that the blind who believe in Jesus have their eyes opened, why don't you go to that blind person who lives just behind us and see if his eyes can be opened?"

Mrs. Tang said, "Mrs. Hong, you know how to read. Is your learning useless? Before this, my eyes were dark; I couldn't read. After I believed in him, I learned to read. Are not my blind eyes opened? I have believed in the Lord only three or four months and I can read the Bible. Isn't this like a blind person having her eyes opened?"

Surprised, Mrs. Hong said, "Can you read the Bible? Truly, can you read? Please read some for me."

Mrs. Tang opened the New Testament at John 1:1 and read aloud: "In the beginning was the Word; and the Word was with God, and the Word was God."

"This truly is God opening blind eyes," said Mrs. Hong. "A woman over sixty years old learning to read in a few months! This truly is God's power. I shall go with you and see for myself."

She came with Mrs. Tang every day, and before long she too believed in Jesus and joined the Bible class.

In the spring of 1936, work was opened in Yi An, but because workers were too few, the work was neglected until Mr. Zheng was sent there in the spring of 1937. In the beginning the work was very difficult, so the mission sent me to help Mr. Zheng. Before I went, all American and Chinese workers held four days of special meetings for prayer for revival of the work in Yi An.

I went by train to Tai An, then by truck to Yi An. An accident and delay for repairs on the road made us two hours late, so it was dark when we arrived.

The next morning, Mr. Zheng took me to visit an elderly Christian and several others, and we asked them to come for a special meeting to pray for the church. After prayer, we all went out and handed out tracts in shops, in homes, and to people on the streets, inviting them to come and hear the good news that God loves people on earth. Every evening Mr. Zheng and others did the same, inviting people to come and hear the gospel. In the chapel I led several children in singing psalms, while two or three Christians welcomed others who came in. So all worked together harmoniously.

The first few days passed, and though the seats were filled, every heart seemed as hard as stone, determined not to believe. The seed could not enter the soil. After the meeting on the third day, we workers prayed humbly and earnestly for cleansing and for God's guidance in the work.

On the fourth evening, Mr. Zheng's voice attracted the people passing by, so they entered. The Japanese head of the *Yamen* (the office, or courthouse of local officials) had been persuaded to come, along with a number of officers, high and low. Mr. Zheng's message caused the hearts of many of them to tremble. Suddenly more than thirty people came in who had never been to a meeting before. Those who had come early gave up their seats to the newcomers; women and children filled the kitchen and bedroom. That evening five persons accepted Christ.

The next day we took out the partition to Mr. Zheng's room so that many could sit on the kang; we also opened the door that connected the chapel with a Christian neighbor's home, which gave us much more seating space.

That night an even greater number accepted Christ. After the meeting we announced that any who wished to stay and ask questions might do so. The Japanese officer and those who came with him were among those who waited.

A Japanese man asked me: "From what part of Japan did you come? And how many years have you lived in Manchukuo?"

"I am not Japanese," I replied. "I was born in Guangdong, a southern province of China. I came to the Northeast to tell the Chinese people that Jesus, the Son of God, came to earth and died on the cross to save men from sin. Whosoever believes in him shall not perish but have everlasting life."

"Ha! Ha!" the Japanese officer laughed aloud.

Afterwards, I learned that he had heard I was a Japanese person speaking the Chinese language, and he had come especially to hear me. The Lord used this false report to lead these officers to hear the Word of God.

Except for some who did not come to the meetings out of fear of the Japanese, there were no hindrances to the work. However, I did have some doubts, as I thought these Japanese army officers might have come as spies to see if I were speaking anything in opposition to the Japanese occupation of Manchukuo. Therefore, I asked God to cut off thoughts or words that might hinder the reception of the gospel. Like Paul, I wished that I might not "know anything…except Jesus Christ and him crucified" (1 Corinthians 2:2).

That evening God truly enabled me to give a message that pierced their hearts. There was no hint that any one of the officers had received Jesus into his heart, but the very least of them realized that he was a sinner, and that there was one able to save him from sin, guilt, and punishment.

Mr. Tang was head of the Chinese-Japanese city council in the district, and he, with his whole family, believed in the Lord. Afterward, he heard the Japanese saying evil things about the Christian church and was afraid to come to the meetings, but his wife and daughters were sincere Christians. His daughter later went to Yingkou Bible School, but arrived on the very day the Japanese closed it, so she returned home and later went to study in Beijing.

Mr. Feng, the head of the oil factory, and his three brothers became Christians; also Mr. Fang, his manager, and several women were converted because it was said, "Even the Japanese go to the meetings, so we'll go too." These women later became valued helpers in the church in Yi An.

The following year, Mr. Vos went to Yi An and held a baptismal service for the greatest number ever baptized in that church. God truly had stirred the hearts of those whom he had called and chosen.

That same spring Mr. Vos and a group of workers went to Daigang where God had opened a door for the gospel. Each day two meetings were held, and each time the room was filled to capacity. This aroused Satan's envy; he turned all he could to hatred and jealousy, especially the Women's Virtue Society and the Japanese officials. Among them was the Japanese district magistrate who was much displeased at the success of our work and wished to put a stop to it. But, trusting all to God, the workers continued preaching and many heard the gospel.

Once, while the gospel was being preached, several of the Japanese came for a short while, but we fearlessly continued the meeting. Later they came just at the beginning of a meeting, with an official paper commanding Mr. Vos to go to the police office.

He and one or two others willingly obeyed. The Japanese head of the police was scornful and angry when Mr. Vos insisted we had official authority to carry on religious work in Manchukuo. Trusting what he considered his authority, he tried to intimidate Mr. Vos with insulting words. Later the Japanese officer sent several police to compel us to take down the church sign and stop the work. They took down the sign board, since we refused to do so, and warned us, "If you again hold meetings we shall regard you as secretly meeting contrary to the law."

They then closed the doors and sealed them with an official red-paper seal.

We knew they were purposely persecuting the church, and we felt that it was unwise to risk our lives by "throwing eggs at a rock." So we put everything in order and returned to Qiqihar. Our work then was centered in Yi An and Lindian.

Mr. Vos had gone to the national headquarters at Shanjing, the capital, to defend the rights and privileges originally granted to us by the government to continue work in Daigang. We knew from inside news that the Japanese police officer was demoted for what he had done. In spite of this, our work in Daigang was closed for a time.

35

The Children of Daigang

In the winter of 1939, Mr. Li Feng Zao, a Christian of Daigang, came to Qiqihar and begged us to send a worker again to Daigang. Remembering the circumstances of three years earlier, and knowing that the Japanese officer who had opposed the work then had been demoted, all agreed that we should continue the work already begun. So in the spring of 1940 I was again appointed to go to Daigang.

When I arrived I did not quite know how to begin work. The Christians there knew that our former difficulties had been reported and filed with the police department; therefore we had to be especially discreet in resuming the work lest we lose the opportunity to proclaim the gospel. This time I was alone, with no pastor or fellow worker with whom to plan and decide matters, so I was forced to rely entirely on the Lord for wisdom and guidance. I had to look to him, be alert, and be constant in prayer. Because of this I was permitted to see once more God's marvelous working.

At first we did not rent a building, but I lived in a room of Mr. Li Feng Zao's home. Every day I taught his wife to read and to pray. I also had an opportunity to talk to the sick who came to Mr. Li's clinic, he being a native-trained doctor. Gradually I began going from house to house to teach the women, and as I came to know more people it was easier to expand the work.

Mr. Zhang, a friend of Mr. Li, came every day to the clinic, whether for healing or just to talk. He was the head of the Department of Education of the village, and we often had helpful conversations. But if I mentioned the name of Jesus he, with a show of authority, would point his finger at me and say, "That's enough. Don't talk to me of Jesus."

Later Dr. Li rented a house for me, and he bought the necessary articles for keeping house, as well as benches and a blackboard. Because we had no official permit, we were not supposed to publicize or hold meetings. The law was very strict about private meetings, so what should we do?

Early one morning, as I was praying, I asked the Lord to direct us. Suddenly I found myself repeating these words: "And he took a child and set him in the midst of them." I wondered why I should use these words in my prayer without thought on my part. Then I understood: God was teaching me how to begin. I thanked him and immediately prepared my morning meal.

While I swept the street before my door, I said to myself, "How shall I get the children to come?" As I turned to go into the house, I glanced across the wide street and noticed a group of children following a cartload of the long grass which people use for fuel. They followed close behind and little by little pulled out bunches of grass, then ran away and hid it. They kept coming back for more, until the driver saw them and drove them off. This went on all along the street. The thought then came to me that perhaps this was the work God was giving me to do.

So I went across the street, and followed until I came up to the cart. The driver and the owner of the grass supposed I had come to buy grass, so they stopped the cart. This was a good opportunity for the children, and as they grabbed bits of grass, the owner caught two of them and I spoke to two others. The rest fled.

I spoke to the owner and said, "Sir, I am a Christian worker who has come here to live. If you will promise not to beat them, I will pay for the grass they have stolen. Please turn them over to me. I shall take them home with me and teach them not to steal from you. Do you believe I can do this? Do you trust me?"

"Good, good," he said. "Teach them not to steal, and I'll not beat them." So I led these four eight- and nine-year-old children to my room.

They were neglected children, their faces very dirty, their hair like a hen's nest, matted and uncombed, their clothes filthy and ragged. They were the ragamuffins of the town, without manners or breeding. They were in the habit of entering people's houses to steal what they could; they pilfered food from shops or along the streets.

God wanted me to begin my work in the village by becoming a good friend to them, so I trusted him to lead me. First I heated water and had them wash their faces and hands, letting them use my wash cloths and towels. Then I combed their hair. They each had the native beauty of childhood, but the filth had completely hidden all their attractiveness. Their skin had become like the skin of an elephant. After they were washed they were like new children. As they looked at themselves in my mirror they were greatly surprised and pleased with themselves.

After they were cleaned up, I taught them to sing, told them stories, and helped them read in the Bible. When they left I told them to come every day and to bring their friends. They really obeyed, bringing their friends, and as the days went by they came with clean hands and faces, and neatly combed hair. But I kept small towels for use when needed.

I also taught them how to sew, knit, and crochet, and soon they had some handiwork to take home and show their mothers. Some parents were suspicious and came, quietly watching and listening as I taught them; sometimes people came in from the street. So my room soon became known as a school with no fees to pay, and this gave me good opportunities to speak to the parents about Jesus. Still we did not hold meetings for the public.

I had covered the walls of my room with large gospel pictures, mottoes, posters, and Bible verses. Often people would come in to look at these; then I gave the gospel message as taught by the posters. When passersby heard the children singing, they would come in to listen.

Sometimes I went with the children to their homes so that I could meet their parents. Even though they did not understand my reasons for wanting to know them, when they heard the children call, "Mama, the teacher is here," they received me courteously. Also, because they saw that their children had changed for the better, they were grateful. Thus, I was able to enter the homes with the gospel.

One day an officer came from the police department of the town. In those days, when a policeman came it was often not for a pleasant purpose. But I received him with proper respect and courtesy, for I did not know what unusual thing might have been reported about me. He sat down and said very politely, "I have come especially to thank you, because you have been a great help to me."

I did not know why he should speak such words to me, and with some fear I asked, "What has happened?"

"Recently," he said, "the children have been stealing far less than formerly. They used to sneak into houses continually, like devils in the dark, and we policemen were helpless to stop them. Now they are like different children and there is very little stealing. They have learned correct manners and good customs. Everyone says your influence is most unusual."

I replied, "Mr. Kong Qing Yue, that is not human influence; that is the power and influence of Jesus Christ to transform people. He came to earth to save sinners, whether men, women, or children, no matter how great their sins. All he asks is for them to repent, believe, and obey him. One who believes in Jesus has Jesus in his heart, and his new life and faith will be manifested. He will know he has passed from death to life; he is washed clean of his sins, just as water cleanses hands. These children now know that stealing is sin, and that Jesus is displeased with it, so they fear to steal again. That is the reason for the change in them. This change cannot be brought about by mere words, nor even by the law, as it tries to suppress them."

He said, "I believe that this is a work beyond what man can do, with all his efforts. But you have used a great deal of time and energy in teaching them."

"This is the work God gave me to do," I said. "It is my duty, and if I fail to do it, he is displeased."

36

Worship the Emperor

During the occupation of Manchuria by the Japanese, people had to walk circumspectly, do and say nothing that might stir them up, and had to treat them as victors and kings. They ruled over us by law, vigorously, and while I was in this village, they sent men with authority to watch what I did and spy on me. But because these little street urchins had been so greatly changed, they realized that in the church there was certainly a power surpassing any human power or influence. Though the policeman who had spoken to me as yet had given no sign that he believed in Jesus, yet even in the very least thing he did not oppose the church or the Christians. Moreover, in the presence of the Japanese officers, he boasted that we were doing a work with a power that made up for the weakness and inefficiency of their own efforts, especially with these children.

After this, seeing his attitude, I wished to register with the authorities, so that we could freely hold meetings for the public. Then, I hoped, I need not fear the power of the police. The Christians then would not need to worship in back rooms out of hearing and hide behind closed and locked doors. Also, perhaps the parents of these children might come to meetings and the numbers of Christians might increase.

I must explain that when the Japanese occupied Manchuria, they tried to do things in such a way as to prevent opposition. They used every possible plan to deceive the people into thinking that the Japanese were always in the right; they wanted to fool the Chinese into thinking themselves stupid and foolish, in order to make them submissive. They told people that their Chinese gods were not sufficient; they should learn of the gods of Japan, and thus be drawn closer together, and be more harmonious through religion. So they invited all the religious leaders to Japan to learn "the way of the gods" and how to worship and show proper honor. Puyi, who had been made puppet ruler, gave a commandment to this effect and gave Manchukuo a new god who had to have a temple for his worship.

The emperor of Japan also decreed that every family must have a shrine, a god-shelf, at which to worship. Those who refused to worship the Japanese gods, which included the emperor, would be dealt with severely. After this decree was made public, who would dare disobey! But, as the Japanese soon learned, no matter what the circumstances, there were always Shadrachs, Meshachs, and Abednegos willing to die for their faith in the true God.

One day, Mr. Zi Tian (Kavata Shen) came to our house especially to learn our reaction to these orders. Though he wanted to test me—and he questioned me thoroughly—he did not directly ask me if I worshiped the emperor of Japan. He began by asking if I worshiped Confucius.

"I am a Christian," I said, "and I teach and spread the gospel of Christ. I worship the three-in-one God, the only God, and I worship no other."

He asked me to explain my meaning.

I said, "This is the command of God, as written in his Word, the Holy Bible."

I then opened a Japanese Bible and asked him to read Exodus 20:1-6.

"I have a Bible," he said, "I have also read it. But to read it is one thing; to obey it is another. Now I ask you, do you worship your mother? Tell me the truth."

"I do not worship my mother," I said.

"Even your own mother you do not worship?"

"Even though she is my mother I do not worship her. She is not a god. If I worship her as a god, the Lord Jesus would not acknowledge me as his child and a Christian. My mother also was a Christian; if I worshiped her, she would not acknowledge me as her daughter. Therefore I do not worship her."

He said, "Confucius was the holy man of China. All Chinese honor, respect, and worship him. Why do you not worship him?"

"I do respect Confucius as an excellent man, for his truly good character, and for his talent as an educator. As a ruler he was sincere and faithful, and as an officer he gave the country peace. I, a teacher of the gospel, also use his teachings, but I do not worship him as a god."

He continued, "In case there comes a day when we say that you must worship our gods as well as Confucius, what will you do?"

I replied, "I will not worship any but the true God. Even though you may wish to take my head off, I still will not worship any other. As I await that day, I shall continually prepare to give you my head if you demand it."

As I said these words, I bowed my shoulders and put out my head as though ready for him to take it off.

He said, "I believe you. Goodbye."

After this, Kavata Shen's manner toward me changed, and he treated me courteously. He was head of foreign affairs in Qiqihar, and when I went to his office with Mr. Vos on church business he rose and offered Mr. Vos a chair, but not me. Mr. Vos always politely invited me to take the chair, and I politely accepted it. After this, Kavata Shen always gave me a seat, then invited Mr. Vos to be seated, and he would personally offer us cigarettes and tea. There gradually grew up between us a close fellowship, and when he was transferred to Harbin he came to bid us farewell. Later he was sent to war elsewhere and lost his life.

37

God's White Ravens

During the early 1940s, international events of great magnitude bore upon Japan's policy in Manchuria. On December 7, 1941, the Japanese Air Force, without warning, attacked the American Pacific Fleet in Pearl Harbor, the naval base of the United States in Hawaii. From that moment Japan and the United States were at war.

The Americans of the Reformed Presbyterian Church residing in Manchuria were then told that they were the enemies of Japan and that trouble awaited them.

The Mission funds were now frozen, so in a short time funds would be exhausted and salaries of workers could not be paid. Some wise workers decided to resign and seek work elsewhere. I myself was unwilling to leave the work, but I had a plan to continue making a living and to continue the education of my son. Mr. Zheng, who was in the Department of Agriculture, advised me to try raising White Leghorn chickens.

I naturally felt that I should not allow other work to hamper the continuance of the church work, so after prayer I waited until my son came for his vacation before deciding.

Timothy said to me, "Mother, you are the head of the family. If you raise chickens to help with living expenses, you can still go about the church work as usual. To raise chickens would not hinder you, and it would not bring shame to the Lord. Why do you doubt that it is right to do it?"

When he said this, it was as if he had opened a door to a clear road for the future. So I made the decision to raise chickens.

The next morning I read 1 Kings 17:2-6 over and over again and obtained comfort and strength, recalling God's call to me in the past and believing that now he would "command ravens" to support me and provide for my needs. In the beginning of February 1942, I went to Mr. Zheng and ordered little chicks of both sexes. On May 3, I received 150 newly hatched chicks.

In our small back yard in Qiqihar,[11] I built a wooden hut for the chicks. Thus began my new occupation. I had had no experience in poultry raising, but there were books on the subject. At first I did not know how to divide my time to the best advantage. I did not know how to feed the chicks without wasting feed, but I learned to save time and money, and gradually I made progress.

God taught me that I must deal rigorously with disease in the chickens. As soon as I noticed symptoms of a disease in a chick, I isolated it. If the disease was far advanced, I killed the chick and cremated the body, lest others should become infected. According to some, it was impossible to avoid or escape infection from contagious diseases in spring and autumn, and many lost their flocks. One Japanese man had a very fine modern plant for raising about 3,000 chickens every season. In one week he lost all his thousands from a contagious disease. When I heard this my heart was frightened. If one with learning and experience met with such a calamity, how could I with no experience hope to escape? But the words about God's ravens comforted me, and I lived with thankfulness in my heart.

One winter morning when I went to feed the chickens, I noticed that their combs had become pale, and the hens were not so active as usual. I recognized this as a symptom of disease. I stopped there among the hens and reminded God of his promise that the ravens would support me, and prayed to him to preserve the lives of these chickens. I was again comforted because I knew God was trustworthy and would fulfill his promises.

I went back to my room, and suddenly there came to my mind memories of how my mother had treated chickens that were sick. So I hurried to the market and bought a supply of garlic, onions, and peppers, chopped them fine and mixed it with their food. They had not been eating well, but when they saw this fresh green food they ate it greedily. I fed them with this for three days. By the fifth day they had recovered their natural healthy color and vitality. For about a month they produced only half their usual number of eggs, then they produced the normal number. Once again I was thankful for God's care and protection, and I sang praise from Psalm 36:6-8:

> O Lord, You preserve man and beast. How precious is Your lovingkindness, O God! Therefore the children of men put their trust under the shadow of Your wings. They are abundantly satisfied with the fullness of Your house, and You give them drink from the river of Your pleasures.

My business was small, for I had little capital, a very small space, no helper, and it was not easy to sell my products. At first, I personally peddled eggs throughout the city. But my percentage of profit was higher than that of others. Many bought and sold through the black market, where they got higher prices, but they also paid higher for grain for their chickens. Moreover, doing business through the black market put them in a dangerous position, because all business was government business, and to carry on secretly was against the law. Whenever this was reported to the authorities, such dealers were liable to a jail sentence.

Being a Christian and a witness to the gospel, I did not wish to tempt the law. I bought my grain from the government co-operative and sold my eggs to them, as they wanted them for hatching. This was very convenient for me. Other people thought I was stupid and pitied me, but this seemed to me a safe, dependable way, a way of peace without worry about a market.

There were many things one could not buy in the shops: cotton cloth and thread, for instance. There was no meat for sale, but I had chicken to eat. There were no eggs for sale; I could eat all I wanted. There was no milk to be bought. I had to have milk for my grandson, so I traded eggs to a Russian Christian for milk. So we, a family of five, lived through five years: I, Timothy in medical college, his wife and son with me, and a young man with tubercular spine who had been cared for by Miss Huston. God's ravens fed one man, Elijah. God also commanded the white ravens to feed five. When I was forced to leave Qiqihar in 1946, I left behind 222 laying hens.

38

Shadows of Pearl Harbor

Difficulties for the American missionaries had actually commenced a considerable time before the attack on Pearl Harbor. In October 1940, Mr. Martin[12] received a telegram ordering the Americans in Qiqihar to go to Harbin (supposedly to be repatriated). In a few hours, Miss McCracken and Miss Huston, as well as the Martins, made hasty preparation for their departure. I faithfully accepted the many responsibilities they had to transfer to me. These were an oppressive burden. They left for Harbin at three o'clock in the afternoon.

After breakfast the next morning, I had worship with Mrs. Zhao Zhi Ai. I was able to sing and read the Bible, but when it came to prayer, I could only say, "I pray…I beseech…I cry to thee…"; then I burst into tears, for the burden was too heavy for me. I wanted to cast it all on the Lord. Those who were with me at prayers joined me in weeping.

Mrs. Zhao said, "There's no use in crying," but I could not stop.

Suddenly we heard someone knocking at the outer door, and Mrs. Zhao went to open it. She came back quickly as I still knelt crying, and said into my ear, "Miss McCracken has come back!"

Still on my knees, I wept uncontrollably. Miss McCracken came in, embraced me, and tried to comfort me. While I wept on her shoulder, she said, "We have come back. Don't cry." But because of my great relief I continued to do so.

After that, when World War II burst upon us, I did not moan and cry. God gave me strength and resistance so that I could victoriously meet the responsibilities left with me. Much of the work continued as before; however, meetings in our own house and house-to-house visiting were restricted, then discontinued, and I was closely watched.

Because many Christians feared to become involved with the Japanese, they did not attend the meetings, but those who did come showed great faith and courage. One day after the service, I said to the group of brethren and sisters, "This day God has shown that he is with us."

Mr. Hao, one of the saints, said, "In the midst of fierce fire and violence, God saved Shadrach, Meshach, and Abednego from fire seven times hotter than usual. He is still able to save. What do we fear? God's Son is with us."

When I heard Mr. Hao say this I felt ashamed that I was sometimes frightened. At every service we had spies who wore ordinary clothing and sat among us. Sometimes they left without a word. At other times they questioned the Christians as to their names, businesses, addresses, and families, and tried to get their opinion of the present government administration. This simply made the Christians more firm and determined in their stand. We felt that in our present circumstances we were as Daniel amidst the lions. They were not permitted to harm us, and we were able to continue serving the Lord.

Our first hint of real trouble had come when, on the morning of December 7, 1941, two well-armed soldiers in full uniform took a stand before the gate to the compound. Trembling, I said to Miss McCracken, "I wonder why two soldiers are at our gate." Before I had finished speaking, Wang Zhong Chao rode his bicycle right to our door. His face was pale with fear and excitement, and he went to Miss Huston's room for a moment, then came out and rode away. Supposing he had some private business, I asked no questions, but Miss McCracken told me: "The Japanese have secretly bombed Pearl Harbor."

Like a three-year-old child who "knows not how high the heaven nor how deep the earth," I wanted to go out on the street to see what was happening. Miss McCracken went with me. We were stopped at the gate and fiercely asked, "Where are you going?" I passed by the first sentry, but Miss McCracken was harshly stopped and commanded to go back into the house. When I had gone as far as the next alley, I saw armed soldiers on the streets. When I returned from the vegetable market, there was a group of sturdy, armed soldiers pacing back and forth before our place.

When I had gone out, the guards had not known that I lived with the Americans, or I might not have been allowed to go. At noon two special officers came to guard us, taking turns guarding the whole household day and night. If anyone wanted to leave she had to get their permission, after first telling where and why she wished to go. Our toilet was outside and if one wished to go there, one also had to notify them. Two were not allowed to go at the same time, lest we whisper mouth to ear something important. We were required to speak in voices loud enough for them to hear. When we knelt to pray in a low voice they insisted on knowing what we said. They commanded Miss Huston to discontinue teaching the women who came to the house; of course, she had to obey. The American women were not allowed to go out on the street, and as they had no maid or cook, I had the responsibility of the marketing and other household errands. Every time I went out, spies followed me wherever I went.

At first no one realized that a spy was following me. If I met friends on the street they talked with me with no fear. But when my spies began following them and annoying them, they soon began to avoid me, or they would pass me without speaking. For a time this made me sad, but I recalled how even Jesus' own disciples forsook him and fled, and Peter said three times, "I do not know the Man!" (Matthew 26:74). Then I went about the streets unafraid, as though I were the president of a great country, with a strong guard continually about me. This was my glory and my joy.

There was yet another thing that gave me great joy: on the Lord's Day, I was necessarily the leader and the speaker, yet the Christians attended the services, as well as midweek prayer meetings, and Bible study classes. In spite of fear and some annoyance, they accepted me as leader and teacher, though they avoided me in public.

Miss Huston and Miss McCracken were prisoners under house arrest. According to international law, the Japanese should have provided the necessities of life for them, as all their funds had been frozen. I went many times to the police and to the Special Affairs Department to request money or food for them, and was promised help, but they never gave them even one grain of rice or a slice of bread.[13] I bought whatever was for sale on the street or in the market, though only a few green vegetables could be bought, and coarse grain—ground corn, millet and kaoliang. We all suffered from this starvation diet, not because of the people of Manchukuo, but because of the Japanese occupation.

39

American Missionaries Removed

On May 21, 1942, at exactly noon, the chief officer of the Japanese military police came with an important document bearing an official seal. He opened it, read it in Japanese, and had a young Russian translate it into English: "This is a command from the highest government office, that all prisoners of war must be evacuated from Qiqihar, and they must prepare to leave today at three o'clock."

At two o'clock the same officer returned with several Japanese soldiers and the interpreter. Miss Huston was told that she and the others leaving could take only as much as they could carry. All else must be left for disposal by the Japanese government.

With these officers and police to oversee the job, Miss Huston and the others packed their baggage. Promptly at three o'clock the police car came to the door; several armed police came in as though they owned the place and shouted, "Chief Officer, the police car is at the door."

The chief gave the command: "Start."

He looked as if he would have liked to send the Americans off in handcuffs. I carried part of Miss Huston's baggage and Mr. Hao carried Miss McCracken's to the police van. I asked permission to go with them to the station and was given consent. (Miss McCracken was seriously ill at the time.) So Mr. Hao, Chao Liang Yue (the tubercular boy), and I went with them. The outside of the car was black, and on the inside there was not a ray of light. As we sat there in the dark, it truly was not with the taste of freedom.

When we arrived at the station, two of the police went before the prisoners, two on each side, and two at their rear. Mr. Hao, Liang Yue, and I were pressed in between. Now the prisoners carried their own baggage, and we three Chinese were treated like the prisoners as we marched to the station platform.

Miss Huston wished to say a few words to me, but the officer barked, "If you have anything to say, say it loud enough for all to hear. To speak mouth to ear is against the law."

Miss Huston then repeated in a loud voice, "May the Lord be with you all." Then the rest of us repeated the same words to her very loudly.

The police put them and their guards on the train.

We went to call a carriage to take us home, but the Japanese officer told us to get in the police wagon. We knew well that we were simply like a piece of meat on the chopping board, so why try to escape? Even if we were to go to prison, that too was in God's plan. So, without another thought, we obeyed. They drove to the office of the military police. The Japanese entered the office, leaving the car door open while we still remained inside. After about ten minutes, as they did not return, we got out, believing we were free. We zigzagged home by back alleys, not by the main streets.

When we got home, Mr. Zheng, interpreter for the police chief, was sitting in the guest room; he smiled and said, "I came to watch the house for you, lest people come to loot your things."

I said, "Many thanks."

Even at such a time as this, one had to be courteous to those watching our every move. I felt like the deaf and mute person who was given yellow gentian, the bitterest of medicine, yet was not able to make one sound to show his dislike of it. Thank the Lord, he knew the taste of such an experience and he comforted us by saying: "These things I have spoken to you, that in me you may have peace. In the world you will have tribulation; but be of good cheer, I have overcome the world" (John 16:33).

My possessions became theirs. Mr. Zheng was the police officer sent to manage enemy property, and, though he had said pleasant words, actually he was afraid I would take possession of the property of the American prisoners.

On May 22, 1942, the day after they were taken away, the chief of the military police came and said, "I have now come by the authority of the government to receive the enemy property."

Then, with an all-inclusive sweep of his hand, he ordered his men to carry things out. This was a very important piece of business, and I did not wish to make a stupid mistake, so I invited Mr. Zheng, our interpreter, to be seated with us in the guest room. Incidentally, he could be a witness to what was said and done.

After a few polite words, I asked the officer, "Chief, are my possessions also enemy property?"

He stared at me but did not reply at once.

I continued, "I was a coworker with these two American women. We shared our work. We lived together in this house. We used the same office. Part of this furniture was theirs, part of it was purchased especially for me, and part of it I bought myself. The Americans had nothing to do with these. Now you have commanded your men to take everything away. Does any Japanese man have the right to take away the property of a citizen of Manchukuo without cause?"

"What things are yours?" he asked. "Make a list and put a mark on them."

"But you have taken everything outside. How can I know and prove it is mine? You must bring it all in and put it in its proper place. Then I can put a mark on it."

Actually, this was a small matter, as there was nothing of great value in the way of household goods. He ordered the men to carry everything back and put it in place. Then he gave me permission to mark my own things.

"Whatever was in their bedrooms was their personal property," I said. "Those you may take out, except one piece on which I have pasted a sign saying 'Miss McCracken gave this to Mrs. Hong.'"

As soon as the Americans had been placed under house arrest, all their personal funds in banks were frozen, and they had no money to buy food or clothing, nor for living expenses of any kind. The Japanese did nothing to provide for their needs. Their friend Mrs. Hong could not bear to see them on a starvation diet, so she shared her own scanty funds with them. In exchange, Miss McCracken promised her a piece of furniture, and Miss Huston gave her a portable sewing machine. These two things had already been given her. Cooking utensils we had used in common, so I claimed them. I let them take the Martin's iron cookstove. I marked all that was in my bedroom.

The military chief politely asked me to be seated, then in very severe tones said: "Now that you have no pastor or leader in the church, and no other church workers, I am willing to give you special treatment. If you will register with the government, we can regard you as an ordinary loyal citizen. But if you continue as before, then we shall regard you as nonexistent as a church. So from today you must stop entirely all church work. You may not hold religious meetings nor preach the gospel. In case you continue to hold meetings and preach, I shall count you a deliberate lawbreaker and a secret rebel."

"Suppose I hold meetings in my own home," I asked. "Will that be regarded as breaking the law?"

With some pomposity, he replied, "Any person who does not register according to the law, and get a permit from the government to hold meetings, but forms a private association, will be suppressed."

"Why then," I replied, "do the Japanese continue to worship in their homes (indicating my neighbors), burn incense morning and evening to Buddha and other idols, read their religious classics, and tinkle a bell in prayer? When they worship privately are they breaking the law? Yet you say if we worship privately in our home we break the law."

Mr. Zheng did not interpret this for the officers, but said, "You are free to worship Jesus in your own home, but you may not have a large group or congregation. You should not speak so critically to the Japanese, lest you make them angry and start something not easy to manage."

So I said no more.

Afterwards the chief of police asked me, "What property has the mission or the church?"

I said, "The church has great and precious property—Jesus Christ and the faithful hearts of Christians."

Again Mr. Zheng did not interpret what I said. He merely asked me if the church did not have church buildings and homes.

I said, "The American Mission owns no buildings. They rent only this building where the two American women and I lived and worked. They also rented the two-storied building where we held meetings, but they owned the benches, tables, chairs, stove, and other furniture, as well as the books, Bibles, and Psalm books that we use in worship."

The officer then asked me for the keys to the church.

I said, "They are in the hands of the caretaker."

He then went and looked at the building and returned the key to the owner. He also gave the house where I lived back to Mr. Ma. Many Japanese came wishing to rent the west half of the house, which I could not use, until the owner, knowing the situation, put up a sign "For the Owner's Use," and did not lease it to others. Actually I could not use the whole house, so, through the owner, that part was rented to Mr. Xu Zhai Tang, one of the Christians.

After the American missionaries were repatriated, many of the church members absented themselves from my home, though several families—twelve or fourteen people in all—came for a worship service. When they learned that the government forbade such meetings, they attended registered churches. Only Mr. Geng, Chao Liang Yue, Mr. Hao, and I met together for worship.

About that time, Mr. Kjos, pastor of the Lutheran Mission, invited me to go to their church services, as they had agreed to the Japanese demands for the registration of religious bodies. The Church of Christ also invited us to their services.

I answered, "I still have our church and the responsibility, and I cannot leave these. If I were to go to your churches, it would only bring annoyance to you and add to our mutual troubles."

Afterwards, Mr. Hao and I went to Mr. Geng's home for our worship service until I left Qiqihar.

After the war started between China and Japan, I met with the officers of the church and discussed how we could best serve. The Russian Army came in with the arrogant attitude of victors and greatly oppressed the people. Therefore, the church officers were not of one mind as to what attitude they should take.

Since the Russian Communists were in power, Dr. Liao suggested, "Wait until the Russians are ousted. Then we can be united in the work of the church. When the country is at peace, then we can make definite plans for carrying on."

This plan was adopted, but we never saw his suggestion carried out.

Originally the Russians came into the Northeast merely to prepare the way for the Chinese Communist Party, to be a vanguard until they had an opportunity to enter. The Russians set great fires as a signal to the Chinese Communists, and the Russians went out as the Chinese came in. They used the same tactics in all parts of Manchukuo. Even though the Chinese came in peaceably it was really a terrifying experience for the people. Naturally, everyone expected the Nationalist Chinese Party to resist the Communist army, and this would have been the beginning of war between the two Chinese parties.

Those who could, fled, and those who could not had to manage as well as circumstances permitted. Things seemed to be peaceful, but every heart was terrified. I believed that war was imminent, and I also fled. I took my son's wife and child to Shenyang where my son was living, so that they could be together in the event of trouble. I planned to return to Qiqihar, but in a very few days railway communication to the North was cut off, and I was unable to buy a ticket. So I lost connection with the church and could not know how they fared. To this day this distresses me.

The Reformed Presbyterian Church in Longjiang Province was like a flower that for a time bloomed profusely, then suddenly lost its strength, lost its color, withered, and was gone. Though I wished to keep in touch with the Christians there, for a long time there was no postal communication. After the way was open for mail, I wrote three times to Mr. Geng Li Ping in 1950, but never had a reply. Whether he had moved away or had met with mistreatment, I never knew. I also wrote to my former neighbor, asking for news of our Christians whom he knew, but he mentioned only Mr. Hao the carpenter, and said he had not seen the others for four years. Knowing the situation in the whole country, I gathered that the others had either fled or been liquidated.

40

Traps Laid for Me

"[He] was in all points tempted as we are, yet without sin." (Hebrews 4:15)

After the Japanese government sent Miss McCracken and Miss Huston away from Qiqihar, they sent people to spy on me, trying to trick me into some mistake. They first sent two very clever tricksters, then some worthless fellows to tempt me. Later they changed their tactics, constantly coming with suave words to lure me.

"You are now an old person with no job, no work, no money—no way to make a living," they would say, offering me money. When I refused to accept their money, they sent the highest officer of the military police.

He slapped the table, the crowning insult to an Asian, and said with a loud voice, "You stupid person, since you refused the gift and helpfulness so graciously offered you by our office, how will you manage?"

I made a deep bow and said, "I am a very lowly person who doesn't know how to live in the present conditions of the world. So I humbly bow before you, a high officer, realizing my error in failing to appreciate this gracious act. I beg you, honorable sir, to carry my apologies to the honorable officer whom I offended, and ask him to be lenient with me. I also beg you, sir, to pardon my failure to be properly respectful to you. Even though in my old age I have lost my job, the Lord whom I trust will care for me. I have often in my life met with such testing and difficult experiences, so I beg you not to be worried about me. I extend to you my sincere thanks."

After listening to me he rose and laid a ten-dollar bill on the table, saying, "Because the officer pities you in your old age he sent this to you."

He then ordered me to accept it. I saw that under the circumstances words were useless. In my heart I asked God for wisdom.

I brought a pen and paper and wrote a receipt for ten dollars:

"To the Office of Military Police: I thank you for your gracious thought of me and my need, and for the ten-dollar bill sent to me through the officer who presented it, though there was no real need for this. Our ancient wise man said, 'Do not accept gifts for which there is no reason for giving.' Therefore I do not wish to receive your gift. The wise man also said, 'To refuse a gift is disrespectful.' This truly puts me between two difficulties. But there is an easy way out. Now, I wish to ask you, sir, to take this ten-dollar note back and present it as a gift from you to the armed forces. Thus, I do not minimize your kind thought, and I also do not sin against my conscience. This is an excellent idea both from your point of view and mine. I beg you to do this with joy. Many thanks to you.

"I respectfully bow to you. Unworthy citizen, Li-Wang Wei Zhen, 14th year of *Geng Te* (ruler of Manchukuo), August 15."

Then I put the money into an envelope and gave it to the petty officer. He received it without a word and took his leave. At that time I was in the deepest financial difficulty of my life, but God made me understand that this difficulty was "poison without but sweet within" and if I could endure this distressing time, the future would be clear. This gift was "unrighteous money"; no one could know what hidden meaning might be connected with it. I feared there might be hidden danger for me if I accepted it. So I was very careful of the words I said to the officer.

A few days later the same petty officer came, and on the authority of the head of the military police asked me to go to the Military Special Affairs Office for an interview. At first, I feared they wished to put me in prison, but they offered me a job in order to win me to their side; I thanked him and very respectfully declined the offer.

Again, after a short time, the chief officer came personally to ask me to accept a position as teacher in a school.

I said, "Sir, I thank you very much for this honor; you are most kind. However, I regret that my mind does not contain the essential teachings that the students of Manchukuo require. In these pitiful circumstances, how could I be a teacher?"

He replied, "You could teach in the Roman Catholic schools."

"But the Roman Catholics would not be pleased to have a Protestant evangelist teach in their school," I said. "I would hesitate very much to do this."

"You need not fear," he assured me. "I would accompany you. They will not refuse to accept you. I know you have lived with foreigners, so you know their customs and way of living. I merely wish you to live there, not to do any work. All you need to do is to come every day and report to the Special Affairs Department what you have seen and heard."

I replied, "Sir, I thank you for your kind offer. But if you were to go with me to them, they would certainly know that I was sent by the Department of Military Special Affairs to spy on them. Naturally they would hide every important thing from me. They could do many things secretly. How could I get any real information about them? Knowing that I was an evangelist turned spy, they would despise me and would 'hold sand in the mouth and spurt it on another' (meaning it for me). Seeing me sitting about doing nothing but eat and sleep, would they not cast me out?"

He said, "Never fear. When the time comes, I shall give you instructions and guidance. Do as I say, and you will meet with no difficulties."

I said, "Officer, sir, I beg you to pardon me while I ask you one question."

"Good," he said. "Tell me what is on your mind, and it will be easier to arrange."

"Sir," I said, "I am a Christian, one who believes in Jesus Christ, one who has a commission from him to 'go into all the world and proclaim the gospel.' How can I do such things as would 'break heaven's laws and destroy earth's morals,' things that would defile my own conscience?

"Sir, put yourself, if you can, in my position. Could you promise to do what you ask me to do? If you did this in obedience to a superior officer, would not your conscience ever after reprove and condemn you? I hope you, sir, will give me a true answer."

At this critical moment he stood silent. I did not know what he was thinking, but in my heart I was praying for needful grace if sent to prison.

After a moment, the interpreter said, "Chief, sir, the time is late. Let her come another time."

The officer did not reply to my question, but rose, spoke a few words in Japanese which I did not understand, then left. This occurred in October 1942, just after schools were opening.

The Japanese evidently supposed that money was all powerful, and that it could be used to tempt and entrap me. And they wished to use their power and authority to force me to do their work. Naturally I did not wish to do anything that would bring the Roman Catholics into trouble with Japanese officials, nor did I desire to cause the Roman Catholics to hate the work of the military police. If I had not already been assured that God was with me, because of fear of hardship I might have fallen into the trap thus laid for me.

One day the petty officer, who had often come, knocked again at my door. He was wearing Chinese padded clothing, so I did not recognize him and did not open the door. He smiled and said, "Don't you recognize me?"

Then I recognized him and opened the door, saying, "How should I ever dream that one who could dress like a king would come in old ordinary Chinese padded garments?"

He remarked, "Your flower garden is so beautiful; it is more attractive than the inside of the house." Then he asked, "Have you received letters from your friends?"

"I have not. Have you received news of them? Do you know if they are well?"

He smiled and said, "Why have you not written to them?"

I replied, "I don't know where you took them; how could I send a letter? Also, the war in the Pacific is so serious that there are few ships sailing. If you have a plan to send letters I shall certainly write to them, but first I would ask you to read the letter."

Some days later, as I was working among the flowers, I heard a voice call, "Mrs Li."

I looked up, and there was the same petty police officer. He seemed very impressive, strong, and powerful in a suit of the new uniform of a soldier.

Smiling, he said, "I bring you good news. Your friends have already arrived in New York."

"Have you received a letter from them?" I asked.

"No! The news came through an official message to the Japanese government, there being no ordinary mail because of the war. The two countries had an agreement to send ships to exchange citizens and see them safely to their homeland. The ship they were on, *Gripsholm*, arrived two days ago. Now you need not be concerned for them; they have arrived home in peace and safety."

I never saw this officer again; others said he had been sent to the battlefront.

41

Still More Traps

In the summer of 1943, a strange man appeared at the door. I was not willing to open it, so he held up a card showing his credentials. Although I could not see it very clearly, I opened the door. He introduced himself as Mr. Wu, so I invited him in to be seated. He spoke the colloquial dialect of Beijing, but on the bag he carried something written in Japanese, so I knew he was a Japanese posing as a Chinese.

We had quite a long conversation, speaking first about various religions. Then the conversation turned to world affairs and finally reached the war then being waged. It soon became evident that this was a man of much experience and discretion. As he talked, I was on the alert, and in my heart prayed for God's help.

His first question was, "What do you think of the present war? What is your opinion or judgment of it?"

I knew that if I said anything displeasing to the authorities I would "receive a hat" labeling me as "rebelling against Manchukuo and opposing Japan."

I replied, "Mr. Wu, I don't pay close attention to the war. I have only the local newspaper published in Qiqihar, which gives only a very short and simple report. How can I know enough to judge? Besides, this war is the concern of government officials and the army. I have no connection with either the government or the army, and as a simple citizen I have little knowledge of such things.

"Moreover, government is a very great and important thing. Within this government there are two rulers: 'The Emperor of the Heavenly Way—the Way of the Gods' (the emperor of Japan), and *Puyi* (emperor of Manchukuo). With one heart these two agree and work and plan. They have the Emperor's ever-victorious army, so I am not concerned with all these things. As I pray, I desire strength and wisdom for the rulers and a speedy end to the war. I have no other thought beyond this, and, moreover, it is useless for me to think of it."

At once he asked, "When will the Japanese army return victorious?"

I replied, "I am not a prophet. How can I foretell things that are still in the future? I can only pray to God in heaven, and hope the Japanese army may soon return to their own land. I think you also have such hopes, do you not?"

"That is true," he said. "I also hope for this."

He inquired about my work and my plan for making a living, about my family and my husband. I answered honestly.

Then he asked, "Why don't you return to the South where your husband lives?"

I said, "Since the Japanese Army occupied Hong Kong, I have had no letter from him; now the war is entering farther into inland China. To return would be very dangerous. So, for the peace and protection of my son, now in medical school, and his family with me, I do not wish to risk the danger."

He said, "Without a doubt your husband is already dead. Why do you not seek another husband? Marry again. No one will object or hinder you."

He said this with an attitude so frivolous and suggestive that I became angry.

I rose and said, "What did you say? Why did you come here? What is your business?"

As I spoke, I faced him directly, grabbed the insignia on his shoulder and tore it off. Then I turned quickly and picked up a chair to protect myself, if necessary, and said, "Do you think I am a woman who would allow you to do anything you please? Or allow you to do as you wish to her? If you have finished what you came here to do, you are free to go. Why stay on here and babble such vile, insulting talk?"

As I held his insignia, he looked very pale and frightened. He merely bowed low again and again. I opened the door and invited him to leave, and I put his insignia on the windowsill outside. As he went out he picked it up and left.

After this, no officer from the military police ever came again to annoy me. If I had not taken the initiative in self-protection, no doubt I would have suffered further annoyance, as I knew other women had done. In a land ruled by cruel, evil-minded officers, a single woman had to be alert and ready to protect herself. By the grace of God I was spared insults and cruelty which, alone, I could not have avoided.

Even though the Japanese police no longer annoyed me, the provincial military police called me twice to go to their headquarters. Each time I felt there was no hope of my returning home. I told my daughter-in-law, Pei Deng (Rebecca), not to inquire about me in case I did not return, lest she and her son also became involved; but I prayed that I might return unharmed.

One day a certain man brought a wily conspirator to my home. As soon as he entered the door he looked all about the room as if he had come to search for something.

Finally he asked in Japanese, "Where is your radio?"

I replied, "I have no radio."

Then, speaking in Mandarin, he said, "You are lying. Many people have radios. Why don't you have one?"

"If you don't believe me," I said, "you may search the place."

He actually went all through the rooms searching every spot and took off his shoes and tramped over the kang, feeling for a radio. Of course he found none.

"Wouldn't you like to buy a radio?" he asked in alluring tones.

"I shall not buy one," I said.

"Why not?" he replied.

"I have no money, and I have no time to sit and listen to one," I said.

"Listen after you go to bed," he said. "Every night at midnight there is a broadcast from the capital, and you could get news from America. You need not be afraid to buy a radio."

I then understood his purpose in coming to see me, and said, "My work keeps me busy all day. I am too weary to listen, and I go early to rest. Since I am an elderly woman, burdened with making a living for my family, as soon as my head touches the pillow at night, I am asleep. Would it not be a waste of silver and gold to buy a radio?"

Finding nothing in his search, or in my words, to report as disloyalty or as a misdemeanor, he left. The Japanese had used every means to discover some excuse for doing me harm, but God did not permit them to find a flaw.

42

Russian Takeover

On August 14, 1945, the emperor of Japan arranged a treaty of surrender with Manchuria.[14] Then, on August 19, the local magistrate issued a proclamation commanding the people of the city to assemble just beyond the south end of the city to welcome the army that was entering—supposedly a Chinese army. I, a slave without a country for fourteen years, had seen China embattled and harassed for eight years. Recently the army had presumably been victorious and now it had an opportunity to re-enter the city and take it back. This all made me unspeakably happy. Carrying my grandson and a small flag, I followed the crowd to the southern end of the city to welcome an army from my own country.

A great crowd had assembled and stood facing the direction from which the army was to come. However, just before us stood a group of tall, fierce-looking, big-nosed, white soldiers. Every heart was bewildered with doubt and fear. When the city officer gave a command to shout a loud "Welcome!" no one uttered a sound. Then a troop of brown-skinned soldiers marched up—men from Mongolia. Supposing they were the army from China, people shouted a loud "Welcome!" It was a most striking contrast to the lack of a welcome given to the first group. Suddenly the people gazed in bewilderment at one another. The temperature of our enthusiasm dropped to below zero as we learned that these were Communist Mongols brought in under Russian command, simply to deceive the Chinese into showing a welcome.

The Russian Army voluntarily entered the war in the Three Northeast Provinces, pretending to be united with the Chinese Army, but they commanded every house to fly a Russian flag. If any had put up a Chinese flag it had to be taken down. Being a loyal citizen of China, I refused to put up a Russian flag. My neighbor, Mr. Xu, told me to obey. I said nothing, but left him to fly the flag if he chose.

When the Russians entered Qiqihar, they did exactly as they wished, obeying no orders or laws. On the third day after entering the city, a Russian soldier came to my home, led by a young White Russian with whom I was acquainted. He had formerly studied English with Miss Huston, and he had been the interpreter for the Japanese officers when they deported the Misses McCracken and Huston.

Now this young man seemed to have been transformed into an entirely different person—an official interpreter for the Soviet Army. They came this time with police officers, seemingly with authority, and boldly entered the house, saying, "We have come to search for arms or dangerous weapons."

They made a careful and thorough search but found nothing. The interpreter then asked me, "Do you have a wristwatch?" This showed me that their real purpose was also to discover if I had anything valuable that they might confiscate.

I said, "If I say I do not have a watch, you will not believe me. You should search and see for yourself whether or not I have."

They went through every shelf, drawer, and pigeonhole in my desk, not just once but three times, and found no watch. Some of the pigeonholes had small drawers which were useful only for small articles. These they drew out, and seemed to covet some things. A small clock they put back because it was too large to go into a pocket.

Actually my watch was in one of the small drawers and, though they had pulled out that drawer three times, they had not seen it.

Several days later, my son's wife, a girl neighbor, and I were spending the evening about the table, each with her handwork. Suddenly, we heard the sound of heavy army boots coming closer and closer to our door. I at once turned off the light, and told my daughter-in-law to take the baby and the girl neighbor and run to the back door, ready to escape. I quickly knelt just under the window and prayed aloud, "Lord, save us."

I heard the heavy iron hook on the door to the small entry break loose. Then men came to the house door which was a strong, heavy one, more than an inch thick. It was secured by a strong lock and a chain that allowed the door to open only a few inches. Putting forth great strength, they broke one after another. Then they entered the house.

Now there was only the thin wooden door into the room where I was. I simply crouched down, speechless, listening for their next move. The door was locked only with a small brass hook. I heard their voices—Russian, of course. After a moment, I heard their footsteps leaving.

I ran to the back door and called the others to come back, and we at once knelt and thanked God for his protection.

These men then went to the opposite side of the compound and entered the home of a Mr. Xu. His wife and daughter quickly hid in the back part of the house, while Mr. Xu treated them royally, opened two bottles of whiskey or sake and brought nuts and cakes for them, urging them to drink until they were intoxicated. They stayed all night, then left at early dawn, hoping the police would not catch them.

Mrs. Xu and her daughter had come to my house. I wanted people to know that the God I believe in sent his messengers to surround us as a garrison and save us. If he had not done so why did those wicked men not open the third door fastened only by a small, screen door hook, which they could have easily broken? Surely the Lord's hosts surrounded us and sent them away.

When these men left Mr. Xu's house in the morning, after a night of eating, drinking, and singing, they took Mr. Xu's wristwatch, two suits of clothes, blankets, and other things.

An important festival of the Chinese fell on the eighth month and fifteenth day of the lunar calendar. Whole families met together for the day, often at the father's place of business. At No. 1 Dongya Hutong, in Qiqihar, fourteen families lived in one compound. That day, twelve of the men in these homes took their wives and children out to spend the day at their places of work. Only Mrs. Hong—whose husband worked in another city—my daughter-in-law, my grandson, and I were alone in our homes. We were sitting outside the door, making cloth shoes, when suddenly we saw some young Russian soldiers, fully armed, come through the gate. I got up quickly, and closed and locked the door, while they entered a neighboring house. Soon I heard my chickens squawking. I ran to lock the back door but had got only as far as the kitchen when I heard the outer door open. Grabbing the baby, we went out at the front, around the house, and were preparing to climb the roof of a neighboring house to get over the wall to the street. Just as we were climbing on to the wall, Mr. Xu suddenly appeared and called, "Mrs. Li, don't run. I've driven them away."

So we came back. This was the second time in a month that such a thing had occurred to frighten us. This again was God's protecting care. He had caused Mr. Xu's heart to be disturbed so that he came home unexpectedly, just in time to see the Russian soldiers trying to enter our home. I recalled the words of Psalm 34, "The angel of the Lord encamps all around those who fear him," and we joyfully sang that psalm.

We had experienced eight years of China's rebellion against Japan, losing no one knows how much warm blood nor how many lives. There was war in all parts of China and, even before this time, China was divided against itself and was fighting civil wars.

During this time I was living in Qiqihar with my daughter in-law, Pei Deng, and her small son, Ch'i Chen. My son, having graduated from Shenyang Medical School, was interned in the same hospital. We were separated by about 600 miles. All railway and postal communication was interrupted by the war. I was in great fear and decided it would be best for his family to be with him in Shenyang. I hoped to find someone to accompany them on the long journey, while I remained in Qiqihar, but I failed to find anyone willing to go on this long, dangerous trip. Also, even the wind and the birds seemed to tell of fearful times to come. I could not send this young woman and her child alone with any assurance.

So I asked a man we knew well to care for my flock of chickens while I went with my relations to Shenyang. I told him I expected to return in ten days or two weeks. Actually, in the providence of God, I never saw Qiqihar nor my flock of chickens again. The guiding hand of God led me, as I will yet explain, in other paths.

43

Our Perilous Escape to Shenyang

At three o'clock on June 26, 1946, just at break of dawn in that far north country, we dressed in old worn garments and went out from our home, I carrying my grandson on my back, while Pei Deng, his mother, carried food and other things necessary for the child. We went by *droshky* (a low, four-wheeled carriage of Russian pattern) to the railway station and took the train to Angangshi, where we changed to the train to Harbin.

As we boarded the train we met two young men, one the son of Pastor Hong of the Lutheran Church and the other Mr. Chu, the fiancé of Pastor Hong's daughter. We ignored each other because on all sides were Communists, watching and listening, making every heart afraid.

The next morning in Harbin we saw them again and knew they too were refugees fleeing in the same direction. There were great crowds, largely young people wanting to go south. These people were physically strong and rushed quickly to the train, swarming in like bees. We two women could not force our way onto the train, so Mr. Hong and Mr. Chu came to help us. Finally we had to enter by way of a window. I gave the baby and our baggage to one of the men, and I pushed Pei Deng up and through the open window. They then put the child and baggage in and boosted me up. By now the train was beginning to move, but the two men climbed to the top of the train and managed to get in at the window where we were.

After many hours, the train arrived at San He (Three Rivers). Before us was the Nuoni River. Formerly there had been a great iron bridge across this river, but during the war a retreating army blew it up to prevent the enemy from pursuing them. The train had stopped three or four miles from the river, and there many horse-drawn carts waited to take the passengers. There were not enough carts for all, so we followed the crowd on foot. Since I was carrying my grandson and my daughter-in-law was several months pregnant, it was impossible for us to keep pace with the younger folk. We were soon far behind. The sun was just going down, and I feared we might get lost in this strange wilderness in the dark. I prayed aloud to God, "Lord, save us. We are not able to go any further. We must have a cart."

I had faith the Lord would provide for us, and in a short time a cart appeared. I called to the driver to come for us, but he was unwilling, saying, "My cart already has six; I can't take any more."

I said, "Sir, if you will do this kindness, I shall pray to God to give you many grandsons."

When he heard this, he stopped the cart and said, "Good. Come on—the young one at the back and you at the front. I truly hope to have many good grandsons."

We thankfully climbed on the cart.

By this time it was entirely dark. When we arrived at the river bank many people were waiting for boats on which to cross the Nuoni. We finally got a small boat that could carry only six people. The fare demanded was $400 (Manchurian) each. The boatman had promised to take us to the opposite bank of the river, but—who could know?—he took us to what seemed to be a small island, or a sandbank in the river, with water on all sides.

All began to shout, "Take us to the river bank."

The boatman said, "Don't yell, and don't light cigarettes. There are Communists hiding everywhere around here. If they hear voices or see a light, they will shoot at us. Then who would be the lucky ones?"

So all of us were quiet.

As we waited in the boat in black darkness, greatly afraid and troubled, we heard a voice say, "Come and follow me." Everybody got out of the boat and waded through the water after the guide. The further we went the deeper the water became. The river was very wide, with waves caused by a strong wind. Lightning ripped through the sky with sharp claps of thunder. All along the road we had been in danger, but how much greater seemed our danger now as we waded through the river in the darkness and storm!

God was again to show his wonderful protection and care. Pei Deng and I could hardly stand or walk. I prayed, "Lord, save our lives! I beg you to stop the wind and rain, otherwise many lives will be lost in the river. Have mercy on so many in danger!"

The Lord did answer immediately. The wind suddenly changed its course, blew against our backs and helped us get ashore.

There was no pier and the bank was high, so we were led to another place. There was such a multitude going ashore here that it was soon very slippery. We finally found a place where reeds and pussy-willows lined the shore and, with the assistance of Mr. Hong and Mr. Chu, we all got safely ashore, pulling ourselves up by the stalks of the plants. The others were far ahead by now, but these young men kindly waited to help us.

It was raining and very dark, but the Lord gave us light by frequent lightning. Soon we came to a hard road. Then I tied my grandson to my back again. The wind was now blowing strong against our faces, so it was hard to make progress. We four were alone, with the child, Mr. Hong helping me to push against the wind. We had not gone far when we could see the dim light of a house and hear the barking of dogs, so we turned in that direction and soon came to the house.

I was the last person to enter, and as I came in from the pouring rain to this dry, quiet place, I saw a great crowd huddled on the floor, for there were not enough chairs. Seeing us two lone women—the only women—the innkeeper made a place for us on the warm kang. With our rain-soaked garments, we wondered if we were being baked like bread or steamed like buns.

Altogether there were at least 200 refugees huddled in the inn. I noticed that all wore the same kind of clothing, or uniform. Perhaps it was a teacher with his pupils. After a few minutes, a person came and said, "You are people with understanding. You need not ask me anything, nor speak to me to cause me trouble. Just give me a little 'tea money,' and I shall guarantee you will have no trouble."

On hearing his words, I knew that he was a person who would steal from us, but because of so many people he dared not threaten us, and for that reason only he was using this polite approach. Everybody heard his offer, so we each gave him some money. He had given us a spot on the kang and also hot tea, so I was glad to make a contribution.

The God of peace gave us a night of rest. Before dawn we awoke to the sound of soldiers being assembled—the other refugees. I wished to be up early and leave with the group of young people, but my grandson was still asleep, and we had to feed him and eat something ourselves before leaving. Thank God, Mr. Hong and Mr. Chu also decided to wait. When the sun came up the weather was fine, though the road was muddy and slippery after 200 men had walked over it. Our two young friends themselves often fell, and my anxiety was lest my daughter-in-law fall and injure her unborn child. As we walked along, I prayed at every step that God would provide a cart for us.

At last, I prayed aloud, "Lord, it is not that we are lazy or unwilling to walk; truly we are weak and unable to walk so far. I pray thee, send a cart for us."

Mr. Hong said, "Mrs. Li, you are so earnest in prayer that you are really superstitious. In this desolate wilderness do you expect God to drop a cart out of heaven for you?"

I said, "Mr. Hong, when God does send a cart for us, will you be willing to use it? Will it not be an advantage for you? We are six traveling together; one is not a Christian; five believe in God. It would be an unheard-of thing if God would not help us. I hope that you will believe in God as we do, and trust him to care for our lives as well as to save your soul."

As we walked and talked, we did not notice that we had come to a smaller road, and that the large group was out of sight. As we stood at the crossroad we heard the sound of a cart.

We all laughed and said, "Truly God has sent a cart from heaven."

I called out, "Driver, will you take passengers?"

"Yes," he replied. "Where do you want to go?"

"We wish to go to the Te Hui railway station to get the train to Changchun."

"There are two trains a day," he said. "The first one has already gone. I have just taken some passengers to that train; you will have to wait until the train comes back from Changchun at twelve, then wait until three when it leaves. Now I must go home, feed my horses, and eat my lunch. Then I can take you at one o'clock."

"Can you be in time for the train?" I asked.

"I can," he said. "Get on the cart. I'll take you in time."

So we climbed on the cart and drove to his home. He fed his horses, then went away. We sat in the cart and, having no watch, we did not know the time and feared we would be late.

So when he returned I called out, "Driver, where did you go? Don't keep us too late. We don't want to spend the night here."

"Don't worry. I know the road and I won't delay you too long."

"Why not go at once?" I asked.

Then his son said, "Papa, why? They are so anxious to go. Why can't I take the two white horses and go at once?"

He said, "Son, we can't do that; those white horses can't haul the cart across that swift stream. Don't be so stupid."

I then realized that he was speaking the truth, so I decided to be patient.

Finally, the driver came out, jumped on the cart, and we started toward the station, the horses traveling very fast. Soon we could see in the distance a crowd of people standing together. Fearing to go closer, the driver stopped at the side of the road and sent his son ahead to get the news.

He soon came back and said, "A cart slid into the ditch."

His father said, "We must go to help them."

When we got to the place, we learned that bandits had made the ditch as a trap to catch travelers; when they fell into the ditch, they were easy to rob. If our driver had not acted according to his experience, we might have been the ones to fall into the bandit's trap.

We arrived at the Te Hui station feeling like birds escaping from a cage, happy to reach a place free from Communists. Mr. Hong and Mr. Chu then left us and went to Mr. Chu's home. In half an hour the train came, and we went on board at exactly three o'clock, arriving at Changchun on time. There was no train leaving for the South that evening, so we went to a hotel for the night.

At four o'clock the next morning I went to the station and bought tickets, then hurried back to the hotel to bring Pei Deng and the baby to the station. We boarded the train, and before we were seated the train began to move.

When we arrived at Shenyang that afternoon, we went to the medical college at Xiao He Yan (Small River Bank) where my son worked. Because of the lack of postal communication we had not notified him that we were coming, so Mr. Zheng Xu Ren went to tell him of our arrival. He was overjoyed to know that we were safe in Shenyang. He took us to his room, and the hospital later arranged for a more suitable place for the family to live. We were thankful to have escaped from the tiger's mouth.

Naturally I kept thinking about going back to Qiqihar. But God put his own mysterious hindrances in my way. I could not understand the reason for this. I had worked there for ten years; my Christian friends were there, and it was my home.

I planned to return to Qiqihar, but my design was always thwarted. I went several times to the railway station at Shenyang to buy a ticket, and on each occasion, just as I, standing in line, came to the window of the office, the window closed and no more tickets were sold. Then the father of a certain doctor went and stood in line for me, and again the window was closed before he could get a ticket. Then my son went with me and met with the same experience. At the time I could not understand why the result was always the same, but later I knew that it was the work of him who knows and rules over all that comes to pass. The ticket agent seemed to be hindering me, but instead he was really protecting me.

At first, therefore, I was discouraged and unhappy, but the Lord later gave me this message from the Scriptures: "For you shall go out with joy, and be led out with peace." Finding this promise in Isaiah 55:12, I was filled with happiness, and I ceased my anxiety about returning to Qiqihar. I took the money I would have spent on a railway ticket and bought rice for the family. So we passed the days together in peace.

At that time Shenyang was peaceful, though the prices of all commodities fluctuated several times a day. The price of thirteen pounds of rice in the morning might be doubled by afternoon. Common laborers and those on fixed salaries suffered most, as living expenses increased three- or fourfold.

In addition, the city was a critical spot in the war between the Guomindang (Chinese National Party) and the Communists; both sides took advantage of the troubled market situation.

The salary my son received was ample in normal times for himself, but, with his family suddenly increased by three, and with very high market prices, and the paper currency daily depreciating in value, he soon found his burden too heavy. But our Lord God had already made preparations for us, even before we asked.

It so happened that in 1946, an American missionary, Miss Jennie Dean, while returning to South China, met a Dr. Yin on the ship. In talking with him, she learned that he lived in Shenyang and worked in the same hospital with Dr. Li, my son. So she gave Dr. Yin $300 in US currency and asked him to give it to my son.

Thus our gracious God made provision for our needs, so that our family of five did not lack any necessary thing.

We ate the very cheapest food we could buy, such as sweet potatoes, which are called "poor man's food" in South China. I often walked for an hour to buy where things were cheap.

44

Souls Saved in Changchun Hospital

During the spring and summer of 1946, the Three Northeast Provinces were greatly disturbed. Only in South Manchuria was a railway operating. Innumerable soldiers were on the march everywhere.

In South Manchuria there were many hospitals, and in Shenyang there was one especially for wounded and disabled war victims. Long years of war had resulted in a great shortage of all kinds of medical supplies. Communicable diseases had become epidemics, and many were dying. Hospitals were forced to prepare medicines for this emergency from whatever native indigenous products could be found.

At this point in time, like an abundant stream of water to a parched desert, the United States sent great quantities of relief goods: food, medicines, clothing, and bedding. The American Relief Agency, the Red Cross Society, and other agencies sent in large quantities of food, rice, and milk powder, portions of which were allotted to doctors and nurses because of the importance of their work. But even so, all commodities were scarce.

The Scottish Presbyterian Hospital in Shenyang, the most modern and efficient hospital in Manchuria, was well prepared for such an emergency. My son accepted the responsibility for preparing serum to combat cholera and other diseases. He worked diligently day and night, preparing thousands of doses.

Later, American planes dropped great quantities of medicines, and every doctor and nurse rushed out to pick up the precious parcels, but the disease was not defeated.

During the spring of 1946, cholera swept through the country like a swift, devouring fire, and those who were preparing antitoxins were working almost round the clock, neglecting sleep and forgetting to eat.

One very hot day, as Dr. Li Mian Chao (my son, Timothy) was busy preparing serum that was urgently needed, he became thirsty and asked his "left hand" (assistant) to bring him a drink of cold water. Instead of putting it into the doctor's hand, he set it down among other cups on the table. Without looking away from his work, Dr. Li picked up a cup and thirstily gulped down its contents. He realized too late what he had done.

"I may as well regard my work as finished; this may be the last day of my life," the doctor said as he finished the work on that batch of serum. He went home an hour earlier than usual and ate the evening meal.

Then, as he left to go back to work, he turned and said, "If I don't return by midnight I fear I shall soon be going to the heavenly Father's home."

"What has happened?" his wife asked. "You speak with no head and no tail."

"Today, while absorbed in my work," he explained, "I gulped down a cup of cholera bacteria. I fear I may develop cholera. I thought I should tell you so that you will know what to do in case I suddenly die."

"Have no fear," I said. "Jesus gave this promise to his disciples: 'If you drink any deadly thing, it shall not harm you.' You believe and trust in Jesus, and while trying to save the lives of others, if you drank poison by mistake, God can overcome the effect of it. Only trust and serve him."

He made no reply but went back to finish his work.

That night at ten o'clock he came home and announced happily: "I have come home well and safe. I came home early to let you know that God protected my life again."

After a prayer of thanksgiving we went to our rest.

I had first heard the gospel as a child in a hospital, and by God's grace I was saved. I had often thought that I owed a debt to hospitals and to sick people, and God gave me an opportunity to make a return payment. While living in Shenyang without regular work, I was asked to go to Changchun and do evangelistic work among hospital patients and to help in the hospital library.

My son, Dr. M. C. Li, was preparing to go to America for further study and therefore made arrangements for his wife and children to live in Shenyang in rooms at the hospital during his absence.

I began work in the Changchun Hospital in February 1947, my work being largely among the patients. Many were outpatients who came only once or twice, so I could see little fruit from my work. However, there were some outstanding results among the inpatients. The church was next to the hospital, and I often helped the pastor with his work. One Sabbath day I attended a baptismal service and among those baptized was a young man who had been a patient in the hospital. At the evening service he gave his testimony.

"I was one," he said, "who opposed the Christian religion with all my might. I would not allow the sound of a preacher's voice in my ears. Now I have been ill for two years and in the hospital for eight months. The doctors told me I had no hope for recovery, so I waited, despondent and hopeless, for death.

"A woman Christian worker came to speak with me, and I ordered her away. A fellow patient said, 'Even if you don't want to hear her, I do. Mrs. Li, please talk to me; I will listen.'

"So I covered my head discourteously and let her talk. Strange though it may seem, I found what she had to say very interesting. The next time she came I really wanted to listen, but I turned my face to the wall as if I were bored. A few days later she came again, and her theme was this: 'And as it is appointed for men to die once, but after this the judgment' (Hebrews 9:27). Those words pierced my very heart. I hated the woman for such malicious words. But I truly began to think.

"The doctor says I must soon die. After I die, what? Would it be what the classics teach: 'The death of a man is like the light of a candle going out?' Or might it not be like that? It can't be as simple as that, or why do people fear death? Even from ancient times, many have felt that death was simply going home, so they died nobly, disinterested, and unworried about the future.

"These thoughts troubled me greatly as my strength failed daily. Death already seemed to be snatching at my life. I longed for Mrs. Li to come again. The next day she came. It was as if a close relation had come.

"She told a story of a son who rebelled against his father, left home, went to a far country, and lived a profligate life. When he began to see himself—poor, miserable, hungry, filthy, ashamed—he blamed only himself. Then, remembering his father's home, its abundance, its peace, and the sweetness of his father's love, he rose and went to his father, confessed his sin, and was joyfully received.

"Mrs. Li continued: 'There are many young people today living in sin and shame, ignoring the fact that they cannot escape death and judgment. But we have the promise: "He who believes in him is not condemned; but he who does not believe is condemned already, because he has not believed"' (John 3:18).

"When she came to this point in her talk, I shouted aloud, 'Save life! Save life!'

"She came at once to my bedside and said, 'Are you in great pain? Or is your heart not at peace?'

"'While you talked my heart became greatly disturbed,' I told her.

"'It was not my words that disturbed you; it was Jesus coming into your heart to save you. If you want him to save you, you must tell him you are a sinner and beg him to save and heal you.'

"When I begged her to say the prayer for me, she said, 'That is your personal affair; no one can take your place in this.'

"She then knelt by my bed and prayed for me until I could endure no more; then I wept and prayed, 'Lord, save me; I am a sinner.' Then I wept uncontrollably; I could not say all that was in my heart. Mrs. Li rose and comforted me and with her handkerchief wiped my tears and the perspiration from my forehead. I lost my burden and was filled with great peace.

"I lost my fear of death. My energy returned and I recovered so quickly that the doctor said, 'This is miraculous; you are healed not by a doctor or by medicine but by the grace of God.'

"This is a wonderful thing: I have come from the gates of death to this day of health and faith in God. Rejoice with me and give thanks to God."

Another day, after I had been witnessing, a well-dressed man came to me and said, "I ten-parts thank you and thank God because he used your hand to save me. My name is Liang Mao Zhang. About half a year ago, you were speaking in the chapel on Zhong Shan Road and your subject was 'Burdens.' Just then I was in great trouble and was sure my only way out was suicide. As I passed the church I heard singing, then your voice saying, 'Come to me, all you who labor and are heavy laden, and I will give you rest' (Matthew 11:28). Come to Jesus and he will take your burdens, your difficulties, and give you rest.'

"I went in and listened. Then you gave an invitation, and I took my troubles and went forward. You told us how sinners must pray, and I prayed from my heart. Suddenly I knew Jesus was there with me and was able to save me. I went home and again prayed, and God heard me and saved me from suicide. After three days my difficulties were resolved. I was a changed man and, because of this and my testimony, my family also believed, and we are soon to be baptized in Shenyang where I have found work."

As for my work in the hospital at Changchun, I was like a stranger passing through, but the final records of the church will show that it was not in vain. I was not there for long, for the influence and authority of Communists soon reached that city. For the second time I was forced to flee.

45

A Dangerous Book

In the spring of 1948, the Communist armies surrounded Changchun, and we were under siege. Many left the city. Christians, pastors, and evangelists were among the last to leave. Finally the work of the church was left to Pastor Gao and me. As my work lay in the hospital, I had only the evenings free in which to help with church services.

When the pastor was about to leave, many urged me to go with him, but I said, "If doctors and nurses and other workers are not afraid to stay and serve the sick, I too do not fear death. Though I am older and useless medically, I am willing to stay and serve until God sends me out."

Changchun, the capital of Manchukuo, was a beautiful city worthy to contain the palace of a king. The former government had erected many large buildings and homes. Business had been flourishing, and the population was growing. The Communists did not wish to destroy the magnificent government buildings in battle; they wished to save them for their own use.

So, the city was besieged in a careful and special manner, the hostile army coming closer every day. No one was allowed to enter with farm produce, so before long there was a famine. People were forced to eat leaves and the bark of trees and grass roots. Day after day, food supplies in the hospital grew less and were strictly rationed. Doctors and nurses gradually became fewer. The head of the hospital called a meeting to discuss this, and decided that those not essential to the work should go first, and that others might return to their homes. In this way, the hospital could continue a while longer. Nurses who had studied for two years or more were to be given a certificate of graduation. For all who had to leave Changchun, travel expenses were provided.

After this decision was made, the manager gave each one of us a paper on which we were asked to indicate whether we preferred to go or to stay. I wrote that I was willing to stay and do whatever was required of me. When the manager saw what I had written he called me for a special interview and urged me to leave Changchun.

I replied, "You doctors and nurses are all young and willing to remain, not fearing danger as you serve. I too am willing to share the work, the burdens, the service, the hunger, and the danger for the Lord's sake."

He then explained the crucial situation of the hospital and surrounding community and urged me to leave.

Finally he said, "When your son left for America, he asked me to take responsibility for you. Now that the country is at war, I must assume that responsibility. But I have a wife and children, and under the circumstances I could not care for you also. Besides, you are an elderly woman. I fear you may not be able to endure hardship and suffering like a young person. So I urge you to return to your own home."

I went at once to my room and, after praying, I decided to return to Shenyang to live with my daughter-in-law and grandchildren.

Even before the Communists had overcome the Northeast, there was very severe fighting between the Chinese Nationalists and the Communists. Nearly all railways and bridges had been destroyed. When I left Changchun there were no trains running, and of course no airplanes. The pastors, doctors, nurses, and others who had already left the hospital had hired horse-drawn carts in which to travel. They had taken very little baggage. Their Bibles had been sent by the post office. I decided that if I left my clothing behind, I had no money to buy a new outfit, and if I did not carry my Bible I would have nothing for a Christian testimony. What should I do? Again I inquired of the Lord.

I knew of a nurse, Miss Sun, who wished to leave, and also Mr. Wei, a laundryman. Mrs. Gao, wife of a pastor, wished to go with her five children. We decided to pool our money and to buy a cart and two ponies. Each could take baggage; but Bibles were to be left behind.

I said, "I must take my Bible. The Bible was given to us by God for our protection and help in days of trouble, and to oppose the evil that is in the world. It is the sword of the Spirit. If we do not have it, how shall we be safe?"

Mrs. Gao said, "I fear if we take a Bible it may be very troublesome. None of the pastors who have gone has carried a Bible."

I said, "They are afraid to carry a Bible because they are pastors. I am not a pastor, and I am not afraid to carry mine. I must have it with me. If it brings trouble, the Lord will take the responsibility."

Mrs. Gao was opposed to my taking my Bible, and did not wish me to travel with them. But Miss Sun, the nurse, and the laundryman agreed to let me go with them and take it. "The Bible is hers," they said, "and she carries it on her body. If she is not afraid, let her take it."

Even as we got on the cart, Mrs. Gao urged me not to take it.

"It is already in my bag," I said.

The bag I carried was not an ordinary handbag, but one I had made to carry by a strap over my shoulder. In it I had packed toilet articles, some medicines, and my Bible. My Bible was of large size with large characters, leather-bound and gilt-edged, but I did not fear any trouble because of it.

We left the hospital about eleven o'clock on May 3, 1948. At six that evening we arrived at Fanjia village, about twenty miles from Changchun. This was a place infested by many bandits. The group of pastors who had gone earlier had been robbed there. But he who kept Israel kept us safe, and we spent the night in peace.

When we went into the inn at Fanjia, we noticed that the innkeeper was careful not to let it be known that we were there. He talked in low tones to us and had us eat our meals in our room. Because the man in our party had to guard the ponies lest they be stolen, he slept in the empty cart out in the courtyard.

Next morning we started on our journey, glad to escape safely from this robbers' nest. By evening we arrived at Gongzhuling, the first outpost of the Communist army. This was an important city, a great business center, and an important point on the travel routes from south to north. Therefore the Communists had a large force stationed there.

As we entered the east gate of the city, the first person we met was a very stern soldier on guard. He looked at my passport, and when he saw that I was a native of Guangdong Province in the far South, his suspicion was aroused. He presumed I was a member of the Nationalist Party, probably a follower of the army.

Naturally, I gave a good account of myself, acknowledged that I came from Guangdong, but I said, "Not all citizens of Guangdong belong to the National Army, just as not all northerners are members of the Northern Army.

"The National Army came only last year to the North. I have lived in the North for sixteen years, so that I speak the Northern language fairly well. Also, that army was one of young men. Can you imagine that an army of young men would permit an old woman to follow them to make a living?"

He had no answer, but he was not ready to free me. He opened my baggage to examine it. I had a khaki-colored blanket such as is ordinarily used by soldiers. This made him all the more suspicious, so he detained me further.

I told him, "This truly has been an army blanket. When the Japanese were forced out of Manchuria, they opened a market on the street and sold many things that they could not take with them. I bought this blanket for five dollars local currency. Because it was lightweight yet warm, I did not wish to leave it in Qiqihar, so I carried it with me. If you do not believe me, you may open it up and you will see the Japanese characters on it."

But he said he had to take me to the superior judge's office. So I went with him, taking my shoulder bag with me.

Mrs. Gao called out, "Throw out your Bible quickly, so it won't get us into trouble and hinder our getting away."

But I paid no attention to her words, as I went to the office of Special Affairs.

This officer, after looking at my passport, asked, "What is your occupation and where do you come from?"

I told him, "I have been a Christian worker in the hospital at Changchun."

He then asked. "What proof do you have that you have been a Christian worker?"

"I have a Bible which is my credential," I replied, as I took my Bible out of my bag. I opened it at John 3:16 and asked him to read it. Then I said, "This verse contains the heart of the Bible and its teaching."

He said, "Can you speak just for me to hear?"

"I can," I replied. "All men are sinners; the wages of sin is death and after death the judgment. But the gift of God is eternal life. I urge people to believe in God, and in Jesus Christ, God's Son, confess they are sinners, to leave their evil ways and follow the good, and they will be saved."

Then I took from my Bible a tract on which was the picture of a face. There were two ways of looking at it. In one view it was a kind, smiling attractive face; turn it upside down and it was a fierce, cruel, unhappy face.

"How do you explain this?" he asked.

"The picture represents two different kinds of people. The attractive, happy one is a Christian, happy because he knows his sins are forgiven. His heart is at peace and he has hope. The other picture is one who does not believe in Jesus. The thoughts of his heart are all evil, hatred, jealousy, fighting, murder, and all other sins. The evil in his heart shows in his face. Just as our ancient classics say: 'Whatever is in the heart shows on the outside.'"

As I kept turning the picture about, those who listened to me could not conceal that their feelings had been stirred by the picture.

Then the officer rose and said, "It is getting late. You should go to the inn to rest. The inn nearby is not too expensive—two dollars per day. If you need anything, come and let me know." Then he courteously showed me to the door.

This inn was convenient for them to examine the baggage of travelers. Mrs. Gao and the others were waiting for me at the door, so we went to the inn.

Mrs. Gao said again, "Throw away your Bible before it gets us into trouble."

I said, "This trouble is not because of my Bible; it is because I came from Guangdong. My Bible is proof that I am a gospel worker and a Christian, as my passport says. Also, having my Bible, I have an opportunity to tell those men about Jesus. It is the Lord's command, and it is also my joy. If I had not had my Bible, I fear he would not have believed that I am a gospel worker, and he would not have permitted me to speak of Jesus."

Mrs. Gao had nothing more to say.

That night, before we slept, the woman in charge of the inn said, "Here we lack many things, especially toilet articles, such as soap, towels, anything of cotton, toothbrushes, combs and many other things. If you have any extra things, you could sell them at a very high price."

I went through my baggage and took out things I did not need. I took the blanket that had caused me trouble, folded it, put it inside a feather-filled quilt, and covered it with a piece of pink cloth with a white lining, making it like the bedding the northerners use.

With thankful hearts, we went to rest.

46

Our Passport—My Bible!

On May 5, 1948, we left Gongzhuling and continued our journey south. About noon it began to rain hard, and we on the cart were soon like wet chickens. When we came to Guojia village we stopped, as it was impossible to travel further. We lodged in a place near the Red Army camp. We were soon recognized as educated people, so they allowed us to stay and even promised to give us good positions if we would remain there. Thanks be to God for giving us wisdom to meet such experiences and for his protection. Because of the heavy rain, we stayed there two days and three nights, though we were in great fear. All the guests at the inn were there to escape the rain; and everyone was apprehensive. There was one man; the others were all women and children. All were lonely refugees. We had a good opportunity to tell them of Jesus.

At early dawn onn May 9, 1948, everyone was glad to leave Guo Family village, though the road was very wet and muddy. We in our cart were so many and had so much baggage that we were an hour or two late in getting started. After three or four hours of travel, we came to Siping. This was a large city, a prosperous business center and an important junction of travel routes between the South and the North. Because of its importance as an army base, many battles had been fought there in the past. There had been battles between the Nationalist Chinese army and the Japanese, between the Japanese and the Communists. The latest battle had taken place during that very spring when the fighting was in the city and in outlying villages. The casualties were so many that doctors and nurses went from every hospital in the country to care for them.

We arrived at Siping expecting to be able to buy food there, but the Communist army had guards everywhere, and no travelers were allowed to enter the city. Before long we noticed a foul smell which we soon discovered came from the carcasses and skeletons of horses and men killed in the battle a few weeks earlier. Holding our noses and lashing our ponies, we hurried past this terrible scene. Directed by the army guards, we were soon far out in the unknown and trackless country. As far as the eye could see there were unending fields of half-grown kaoliang, with no sign of life or homes.

This was the seventh day since we had left Changchun, and our food supply was gone. We had not prepared food at the last place where we stayed because we had expected to buy food at Siping. As we had not been allowed to enter that city and instead had been driven farther and farther until we lost our way, we had no idea how far it was to the next town. The children became hungry and cried for food, but we had nothing to give them.

I thought of the Israelites when they left Egypt to go through the wilderness, and I told the children these stories of how hungry and tired and thirsty the Israelites were, how they came to water springs and found the water bitter. What did they do?

As I told these stories and compared ourselves to the Israelites, the children forgot their hunger and thirst for a time. Then, as I was praying for God's help, the little seven-year-old shouted, "I hear someone calling! She is saying, 'Big corn cakes for sale! Big corn cakes for sale!'" As I continued my prayer, he punched me and said it again, and as I finished my prayer, all the children were shouting.

Listening carefully I could hear a girl's voice. They wanted to run and buy, but I said, "We should first give thanks to God," so they waited until I gave thanks to God for hearing in heaven and sending food.

We asked the driver to call out that we wanted to buy. The girl heard and said, "I'm coming." We stopped the cart, got off, and ran through the kaoliang to meet a fourteen- or fifteen-year-old girl, her head just showing over the kaoliang, carrying cornmeal cakes in large oil tins which were on a carrying pole across her shoulders.

"Was it you who wanted to buy cakes?" she asked.

These cakes were the food largely eaten by people in the far North, just as we in the far South ate white rice. When the children had eaten their fill, they played happily about while the horses rested and ate kaoliang stalks.

This girl directed us, and we were soon on our way. As we entered a small village about sunset and decided to spend the night there, several men rushed out and kindly offered to feed and care for our horses. I had some doubts about the kind actions of these men; they were too eager to help. Perhaps they wanted to examine our horses.

That night, the head man at the inn where we stayed told us: "On the road you must take, there are people who want to trade horses." But he added, "If you get safely by that place, you will have no further trouble on the way to Shenyang. But I fear you will have trouble, for you have good horses."

We discussed what to do, and the head man said, "You should hire a local 'fast-horse cart' and separate your good horses, putting one on the local cart and keeping the other on your own cart. Let Mrs. Gao and the five children take your cart, and hope that the horse traders will refrain from taking the good horse for the sake of the children."

We found we had not enough money to pay for hiring this "fast cart," so we sold some of our belongings to the lady who owned the inn. Our driver was a merchant who did business in many towns and villages and also was often in Shenyang, so he knew the roads and the conditions of the country. He was also eyes and ears for the Communists as he went about and reported to them.

This merchant woke us before daylight next morning and started us on the road. When we had gone a few miles, he suddenly told us not to talk, while he kept beating the horses to go faster. We had gone a short distance when we heard someone coming, and we turned into a side road. Our driver knew that that road would lead us to where the horse traders did business, so he hurried us on lest the Communists commandeer our good horse. We soon came to a village where we rested the horses, having arranged to wait there for Mrs. Gao.

We arrived at 10 a.m. and waited until 3:30 p.m., when Mrs. Gao and her cart finally arrived. We soon saw that the Communists had traded a half-blind horse for the good one, but she was a good bargainer and had persuaded them to give her sixty dollars as well. Our merchant driver felt sure that one of her horses would not be able to get to Shenyang, so he had his son put in one of his own horses. It turned out that this man owned horses from the army with a special mark on them, so the army allowed them to pass, and we passed through the horse trader's area safely. As we started south we did not wait for Mrs. Gao, as she had to feed her horses and rest them.

On May 11, the driver roused us up before daylight for an early start so that we could get to Kaiyuan before six o'clock that evening. In peaceful times we could have made this entire journey by train from Changchun to Shenyang in fourteen hours. Now we were in our eighth day, and everyone was wearied with the trip, but we got up at once and boarded our cart. About four o'clock that afternoon we entered the North Gate of Kaiyuan.

This was the last outpost of the Communists, and the guard who stopped us was especially careful and severe in examining our baggage. He noticed that, besides toilet articles and such things, I had a Bible in my bag.

"What book is this?" he asked.

"It is a Holy Bible," I said. "It is the book that teaches salvation through Jesus Christ. It tells of the God who created heaven and earth. He sent his Son Jesus to earth to die for sinners."

"Such a book you should throw away at once," he snarled.

I said, "Even if I were to throw away everything else, I would never throw away this book."

He opened it and held it in his outspread hands, but upside down. So I knew that he could not read, but I said nothing.

Our driver said, "Never mind. We shall have to be examined in the city."

The guard said, "This book is so big and thick. It certainly contains many things which I must examine carefully."

I said, "This book tells you how to be saved; it is the best book you could read. If you turn it the right side up it will be easier to read and understand."

As I spoke I turned it around and put it back into his hand.

"I have no time to read," he said. "Go on and find an inn."

Then he put down the Bible and left us.

We then entered the city and went to the office where baggage was examined, but they had closed for the night.

The driver said, "We need not be afraid to enter the city now. In case you are awakened during the night and quizzed, just tell who you are and where you came from."

We prayed to the God who neither slumbers nor sleeps to protect us, and we slept undisturbed.

At seven o'clock next morning, we went to the south gate to be examined. We were the first to arrive and were first in line for examination. But the man in charge for some unexplained reason put us at the end of the line, and kept us there in the hot sun from 7 a.m. to 3:30 p.m. By that time, all were tired and hungry, the children were crying, and I had fever and a headache. Our driver begged the officer to examine us at once, but he refused; so our driver went out and bought food for us.

I had two travel permits, or passports; one was given me by the hospital regarding my work. The other was a certificate of citizenship from the National Government of China.

While we waited at the end of the line, several young women came who, I judged by their dialect, were from Guangdong and probably had some connection with the New First Army. They insisted on getting in line ahead of us, but when they came out of the office they were weeping. I heard whispers that it was because of their passports, and the officers had been insulting. Then I thought of my two passports, so I took out the one given me by the National Government in Changchun. What could I expect if the Communists saw that? I went at once to the toilet, tore the passport to small pieces, threw it into the open toilet, and covered it with a brick. I came out and was immediately called for examination.

The officer asked my name, address, and occupation. I said, "I am an evangelist; I have been teaching the patients in the hospital in Changchun."

He asked, "What is the number of your passport?"

"I cannot remember the number," I replied.

"An evangelist and you cannot remember the number of your passport?" he questioned. "What did you teach the sick people?"

I said, "I taught them about the God who created heaven and earth and all things. That he is owner and ruler of all. Though men do evil, he loves them and sent his Son to die on the cross to save them."

He said, "Do you live according to what you teach?"

"I teach what the Bible tells me and what I have personally experienced," I replied.

He asked, "Let me see your Bible." I took it out of the bag on my shoulder and handed it to him.

He took it and said, "Up to this time many men have passed through here and claimed to be pastors, but they had no Bibles. You are the first Christian to carry a Bible. I believe you really are a Christian teacher. We don't need to examine your baggage. How many are with you?"

When I told him, he at once wrote a paper permitting us to travel.

All along the way I depended on my Bible to testify for me and to be, under God, my guardian. After receiving back my permit, I told the others to get on the cart, and we went on to a further gate of the city where we met another examining officer.

They asked for our passports and I showed them, and they noticed that all were included in one. He asked, "Who is Wang Wei Zhen?"

I said, "I am she."

He looked at the permit, gave it back and waved us on, telling the driver to go quickly so that we would pass through a certain village before dark, because neither Communists nor Nationalists were guarding the place and the bandits were dangerous.

The driver obeyed his instructions, and we passed the village safely and arrived at Tiehling. At last we were in a city where we need not fear anything. Again we had escaped from the tiger's mouth.

Thanks to God who cares for sparrows; we who were bought by his Son were of more value than many sparrows. If we had been allowed to have first place in the line for examination, the examiner would have looked carefully because then he had time, and he would certainly have discovered my Nationalist passport. Then I might have been subjected to unexpected problems. The officer showed partiality in not permitting us to keep first place in the line. At the time I was dissatisfied, but in the end I knew it was the good purpose of God. I had been warned by what others suffered and had destroyed my unfavorable passport and thus escaped trouble.

47

Back to Deqing Again

The last stage of our journey was by train. We arrived at Shenyang railway station on May 13, 1948, at 10 a.m. Later that morning, my traveling companions and I reached the compound where the doctors of the Scottish Presbyterian Hospital lived. We went to the house where my daughter-in-law was living with my grandchildren while my son was in the United States studying. My traveling companions stayed with us for a night, then found a place for themselves.

At Shenyang I found that Pei Deng was preparing to go south and was waiting for me. The way by sea was already closed, so we were forced to depend on the airplane *St. Paul* sent north by the Lutheran Missions. It came to bring food and medicines to the hospital. They had no passengers for the return trip, and therefore many people from the Lutheran Missions and from the YMCA. arranged to go to Beijing with the pilot. Naturally, he was glad to take them as it brought in a lot of money. He permitted missionaries and their families to buy tickets.

My son, though now in America, had formerly been a physician in the hospital, and as I was an evangelist, I expected to have no difficulty in getting tickets, and seats on the plane. We were not acquainted with the pilot, but a young man who had known my son in school offered to ask his father to buy our tickets. On May 28, 1948, we were ready to board the plane, but God's time was not yet. At the time advertised for us to board the plane, it was announced that the plane could not go for a week.

After a week, the YMCA. sent a telephone message telling the date and time of the flight. Again, we went to the airport only to discover that we had not taken our tickets with us. Fortunately, Dr. Zheng stopped to see if we had gone from the house, and there he noticed the passports and the tickets. He took them, called a droshky, and hurried to the airport where he found us, and we boarded the plane.

In every period of my life, I have found God sufficient for my every need, for my help in every weakness. At this time if we had not met with these delays and disappointments, we should have been on a plane that wrecked; all forty-seven passengers were killed.

It was June 5, 1948, when we left Shenyang by the *St Paul.* Dr. and Mrs. Leng of Qiqihar were also on the plane going to Beijing. We stayed two days in their home, then went to Tientsin by train and stayed in the home of Mrs. Leng's father for a month. Then we went by boat to Shanghai, where we stayed for two months in a special lodging place for travelers. On September 5, 1948, we arrived at my home city in Guangdong. We had been on the journey for three months.

I had been away from my native land sixteen years. During eight of these years, I had experienced war against Japan, then the war against the Communists. All this time I had no communication from my husband, nor from any of his friends or relatives. What were their circumstances? There was no way of my knowing.

What should I do on arriving? My plan was to go to a hotel and leave my family there, then go alone to learn the situation of my relatives. Later I could make plans, and decide whether to live in the ancestral home or to find a separate place. Of course, I had a rightful inheritance to a place to live in the ancestral Li clan home.

We traveled on a small towboat up the Xi River, and, as we neared Deqing, my heart was anxious, though I sat quietly.

I said, "Lord, the next step before me I can't yet see. What place You have for me, I don't know." Then a word from the Bible came to mind: "He went out not knowing where he went" (regarding Abraham, Hebrews 11:8). This phrase came again and again into my mind, and I felt it was God comforting me.

I said, "Lord, why should I be anxious? I believe thou hast planned my way, and it is a good way. Help me to follow thee like a blind person who cannot see one step ahead."

When the towboat stopped at Deqing, I led my family across the gangplank to the public boat landing on the shore. At that moment, I saw a girl I had known in school. She brought her boat close to me and called out, "Teacher Yin, these many years I have not seen you. Where have you been?"

I replied, "For fifteen years I have been in the Three Northeast Provinces, Manchuria. I am happy to see you again. Have you any passengers?"

"None," she said. "Get into my boat." We did so.

"Where are you going?" she asked. "To the city or to the foreign houses?"

"Who is at the foreign houses now?" I asked.

She named them one by one, and I decided to go there.

When she moored at the shore in front of the foreign buildings, I asked her to care for Pei Deng and her children while I went to find Miss Stewart. Soon I met the teacher of the Hebron Orphanage, who directed me. When I entered the gate, her old servant saw me, recognized me, and called Miss Stewart.

"Miss Stewart has said many times that you would come, and here you are."

He gladly took me to her door, opened it, and said, "Yin Wei Jie is here."

She came out and welcomed me most heartily. After the greeting, I told her that my family and baggage were at the river. She called several women who went to help with the baggage. They took us to the former home of Mr. Kempf and prepared rooms for us there, telling the cook to prepare food for us. My grandchildren were sick, so she sent for the doctor.

God had opened a good road for me. I thanked God and the Christian friends who welcomed me. I understood more clearly the words of Jesus: "Therefore do not worry about tomorrow, for tomorrow will worry about its own things" (Matthew 6:34).

48

New Work: The Orphanage

When I went back to the old home, I found many relations, and all were surrounded by many sons and daughters. They had two things, children and wealth. One of my relations was an old man with white hair and whiskers. It was good to see them all again.

My husband lived in another place where he taught school, so they sent word to him that I had returned, and during his vacation he came. We had been separated for twenty years, and now we were grandparents. No communication had passed between us for eight years, and when we met it was hard to know whether to laugh or to weep. This was especially so because he had been a husband who wandered after women, and the state of my heart was such that I could not write of it nor speak of it to others.

I had been in Deqing only a few days when Miss Stewart said to me, "Miss Dean has written saying she would like to ask if you would go to help in the work at Luoding. Mr. Boyle also wrote that they needed help in the work in Canton. If you wish to go to either place, please let them know so that they can prepare a place for you to live. However, we here in Deqing have the first right to ask you to help in the work here. What is your desire?"

I replied, "What God leads me to do, that I shall do." But I gave no definite answer.

Later when she asked for my decision, I said, "This is my native home. My people, my family and friends are here. They need the gospel, and I am willing to stay here for their sakes."

In October 1948, I began work, and during the first three months I went with a pastor to Mahui, Geliang, Liupo, Ducheng and Fengcun when he held communions. In January 1949, I went to Ducheng to do evangelistic work there.

My daughter-in-law and her children stayed at Deqing, living in the building used as a home for aged women. They did not understand the local dialect (Cantonese) so they met with difficulties, and I was anxious about them. But, as the ancient proverb says, "First come public affairs, then that which is private."

Should I quit gospel work, which I loved, and work for the orphanage? By that time the conditions throughout the country were very unsettled. Officers in the Nationalist Government were going to Taiwan, leaving a wide opening for the Communists to come in. Hearts everywhere were frightened. If people had families, they wished to be together for help and comfort in times of such distress. About the middle of April, Miss Stewart asked me to return to Deqing to discuss important matters.

I returned the next day, and she told me of the desire of Mrs. Zheng, the manager of the orphanage, to return to Luoding.

I was mystified and said, "This is strange. Why ask me to discuss this matter that does not concern me?"

Miss Stewart replied, "If I do not release Mrs. Zheng to return home, when the Communists come they may accuse me of separating families."

I said, "There are many people in Deqing that you may find suitable for the work."

But she said, "We have discussed this, and all agree that you are the most suitable person we know. I realize that you prefer evangelistic work, but I wish you to come and take the management of the orphanage."

"Why not ask Ze Lai Man to take over this work?" I asked. "She has been connected with the orphanage for a long time. She is a native of the city and knows the people. She keeps well informed of the conditions of the country and the activities of the Communists. She has been in the orphanage since its beginning, so by the rules of logic she is the right one to take charge."

Miss Stewart said, "We have thought of her already. She has a loving heart, and her work has been satisfactory and good. But she has not a strong, courageous disposition and, if there came sudden danger, she would give up quickly. I fear that if we foreigners should have to leave, she would desert the orphans altogether. That is my greatest fear."

"As for this aspect of her character," I said, "I do not know her so well. Even though we were in school together, I was younger than she and did not understand such things."

Afterward I saw Wang Mao Chen, Zhang Min Fu and Zhang Man Fu. They said, "We did not say that there were no people with ability in Deqing. We did say, "There is no suitable person in Deqing." If you can promise to accept this position, we shall propose you for this work at the church council meeting next month."

"Let me have a week to think about it," I replied.

"That is good, very good," they agreed.

After a week I returned from Ducheng and went first to consult about it with Pei Deng. She heartily approved of my accepting the position.

When I spoke to Miss Stewart about it, she said, "We have been praying especially about this for two weeks, and all are agreed that you are the most suitable person we know. We ask you not to decline."

I said, "Miss Stewart, I fear that I may not be able to carry so great a responsibility alone. You must remember that sooner or later you foreigners may not be here, and all this burden and all the difficulties will fall upon me. It will not be like Mrs. Zheng's work at present, with you to carry all the responsibility. I fear that when trouble comes I may become weak and fearful and desert my responsibilities."

She replied, "I believe you would never do that."

"Good," I said. "If you believe that I would not fail in face of difficulties, then I am willing to trust the Lord who gives me strength, and I will accept this work. But of course I shall depend on you to pray for me and to lead and instruct me."

"Naturally I shall do that," she said.

"Then with this one word I am finished," I said. "When Mrs. Zheng leaves I shall take over the work. I shall live and eat even as these homeless children do, and I trust we shall not suffer any hardship. For, 'A bruised reed he will not break, and smoking flax he will not quench' (Isaiah 42:3), and in his name shall we trust. How much more shall he be sure not to cast off and desert his little ones!"

After accepting this work, my heart was exceedingly happy, and this joy was proof to me that it was God's plan. After two days I returned to Ducheng. Late in May I received notice that Mrs. Zheng would be leaving and that I should return on June 15 to receive the management of the orphanage from the church council. So I resigned from the work at Ducheng.

Mrs. Zheng finally left on June 20, and on June 21, I, quietly and silently, in the presence of the Lord, accepted the general management of the orphanage. I knew well that many difficulties awaited me, but I fully trusted that the faith God had given me would sustain me. I also depended on the words of the ancients: "We who are old respect the aged as though our own; we who are young respect young ones as though our own." I took a Chinese brush-pen and wrote this proverb in large characters, putting one up in the children's general room where they could see it, and one in my office as a motto.

49

The Story of a Gun

I remained in charge of the Deqing Orphanage from June 21, 1949, until January 4, 1952, when the Communists put me in prison. During this period I met with not a few difficulties. Some of these were from without. Half a month after I took charge, the Xi River overflowed its banks, and the land where our buildings stood was entirely inundated. Deep water invaded even the buildings on high land, so that everything had to be moved from the ground floors to the second and third floors. When the flood receded, the silt and mud had to be cleared from both the buildings and the grounds.

Just at this time, the church council and presbytery held its annual meeting in the orphanage, because the church and other buildings were flooded. I acted as hostess. Those connected with the government were confused; their hearts were filled with fear. "The sound of wind (rumor) was very fierce; people feared ambush in every tree and tuft of grass."

In September 1949, all foreigners were evacuated to Hong Kong from Luoding and Deqing. The night before the Communists entered Deqing, all city officials and soldiers fled. As a precaution, in case we were attacked, I called all workers together and urged them to stand firm. I divided the work of protecting the children and carrying water in case of fire. The one man we had was to patrol the walls of the compound; I myself would go to the roof where I could see on all sides if the enemy approached. There was never a moment that I was not praying to God for his care and protection; my one thought was for the safety of the orphan children. There was danger not simply from the oncoming army but also from bandits who might seize the opportunity to enrich themselves before the soldiers entered the helpless town.

During the night I heard sounds like scattered shots from rifles, and gradually those sounds came closer. I went to the roof and saw on the opposite bank of the river a long line of torches moving from the west, following the mountainside that seemed to be ablaze. Suddenly there was a sound as of incessant firecrackers, and within an hour the city was covered with dense smoke.

Early next morning, I went to the city to learn what had occurred. Every street was littered with papers from exploded firecrackers. Some said they had been set off to welcome the Nationalist army; others said the noise had been to welcome the Communist army. On every street the doors were closed and every heart was filled with fear. Then at four o'clock that afternoon the Red Army entered the city and took possession.

The soldiers immediately began to try to quiet the people's fears. The next day merchants began to open their doors for business as usual. Then we learned that the firecrackers set off on the previous night had been a deception intended to mislead the bandits into thinking that the Red Army had already entered the town and that the crackers were announcing a welcome. It was a successful plan. If the bandits had crossed the river that night, the whole city would have been looted and destroyed as by an overflowing flood. In that case, we at the orphanage would have had great difficulty trying to make an escape. As it was, Deqing was taken over without a shot being fired.

God had given wisdom to the merchants and city leaders to use the sound of firecrackers to frighten away the bandits. This combination of ancient and modern methods had thus made it possible to avoid a dangerous situation. My thought was, "Jehovah, how great is thy name in all the earth!"

The morning after the bandits had been frightened by the firecrackers, when I returned from my tour of inspection in the city, Mr. Xu, manager of the Hebron Orphanage (which was housed in our former hospital and chapel buildings) came and asked, "Were you frightened last night?"

"It isn't necessary to ask," I said. "And you? You are right on the river bank, and I am sure you could see everything better than I could, as you have no trees or buildings to interfere with your view."

He said, "I saw a long line of burning torches following the base of the mountains, coming from west to east, so that the whole mountainside was bright. Probably it was a band of bandits ready to come and loot the city. I heard that part of the group had already crossed the river and were at the city pier, but they fled when they heard the firecrackers, supposing it was a welcome to the Reds. Using their torches to send messages, they retreated back up river. If they should learn that they fled unnecessarily, fooled by the firecrackers, they may come back tonight. You should get out your gun and be ready to protect yourselves; or lend the gun to us, as we are in front of you and can act as the outer wall of protection."

I said, "Mr. Xu, we have no gun."

Then he said, "You just fear to lend it to us."

"No," I said, "We do not fear to lend it to you; we simply have no gun."

"I understand that you personally have no gun," he insisted. "But that liaison officer had a gun. Everyone knows that."

"That is true," I said. "But up to this time I have never seen his gun. Shall I tell you the story of that gun? During the war between China and Japan, the Rev. J. C. Mitchel was sent here by the church in America, and he traveled everywhere along the Xi River. That area was then occupied by the Japanese, and he was encouraging Chinese Christians and refugees. There were United States soldiers in Kwangsi Province to the west, and as Mr. Mitchel acted as a liaison officer, they provided him with a gun and some ammunition. This gun he carried on his body for his protection.

"After the Japanese retreated, this man returned to Deqing, with the gun. Everybody knew he had the gun, and the reason he had it. When Mr. Mitchel returned to America, he left the gun in the Kempf house, Mr. Kempf having returned to America. When Mr. Boyle came, he heard the gun was there and, having a good understanding of world affairs, he knew that there might be trouble. He did not wish to carry the gun to Canton, so he asked the Consul what he should do with it. He was advised to take it all to pieces and throw it into a deep part of the river.

"In July 1949, Mr. Boyle came to Deqing for the annual meeting of the church council. While there, he took the gun apart, and with Qin Gang and Jiu Lan, he rowed out to a deep, swift spot in the river and threw it overboard. So it is buried deep at the bottom of the river. This story was told to me, and Miss Stewart was also witness to it."

When I had finished, I asked Qin Gang and Jiu Lan to come in.

I asked them, "When Mr. Boyle was here, and you went with him to row the boat, did you see him throw something into the river?"

"Yes, we did," they both said.

Qin Gang continued, "We rowed to a place out in front of the Roman Catholic buildings, out almost to the middle of the river. The water was very high and swift, being in flood.

"Mr. Boyle asked us, 'Do you know what I threw in the river?'

"'No, I don't know,' I said.

"Then in a low voice he said, 'I threw that officer's gun in the river.' So I knew he threw the gun away."

"Now, Mr. Xu, do you believe the church has no gun?"

But he insisted, "I heard that there were two guns, a long one and a short one. Merchants up the street always said he carried two guns."

I said, "I never heard that."

Qin Gang added, "My grandmother said that Pastor Song carried one to Canton."

So I called his grandmother.

"Ah Poh," I said, "did the officer that was here have two guns?"

"Yes," she said, "a long one and a short one. The short one Mr. Song took away when he left, and one he left in the Kempf house. Hou Zhen Gei knows about that."

So I asked Hou Zhen Gei to come.

"How many guns did that officer have?" I asked her.

"How many he had I don't know, but I know he left one in Mr. Kempf's house. I saw it. But the last time Mr. Boyle was here, he took the gun, took it all apart and sawed the handle into three pieces. Miss Stewart gave them to the children to play with."

"Please excuse me a few minutes," I said, "while I go and get these pieces from the children's playthings."

So I brought the three pieces of fine polished wood, all one color, and fitted together.

Zhen Gei said, "Those are the three pieces of the handle of the gun."

At last I was believed when I said the church had no gun. Soon after the Red Army took over the city they put out notices calling all who possessed guns to report them to the authorities. Then Huang Mo Jing and Hao Zhuo Man told me that I should report that gun, and once again I related the story of the gun.

After I was imprisoned, an officer asked me why I had not reported the gun and registered it with the government. So I repeated the story to the judge of the court. I have no doubt he quizzed those who knew about it, for the matter was never mentioned to me again.

Our all-wise God knew beforehand all that was to befall me, and he arranged every detail. If Mr. Xu had not spoken to me about the gun, when in prison I could not have answered those who interrogated me, and the Communists certainly would have accused me of secretly keeping a weapon. Then I should have been condemned.

50

Dissension at the Orphanage

Some of my difficulties at the orphanage were from within. In the orphanage there were both girls and boys, from the age of a few months old to fourteen or fifteen years. I believed that a boy wishes to be like his father, and a girl, when in any difficulty, longs for her mother; therefore the orphanage should have at least one man to teach, to provide discipline, and to fill up the lack in the lives of the boys.

In the summer of 1950, I mentioned this to the managing board of the orphanage and they agreed. Mr. Zheng, the evangelist, recommended a certain Mr. Lin for this position, though he was not a Christian. I noted that he was very thin, his face sallow, and he seemed physically weak. I was not in favor of hiring him, partly because I feared he might have some disease that would be transmitted to the children, and also because he did not have sufficient strength. But the board decided to try him for half a year with the understanding that if he still were not in a healthy condition, the contract would be ended. All agreed to this. After six months, during which he had sufficient food, he seemed stronger, so I made no objection to his staying. This was not a wise decision.

The Bible says, "The heart is deceitful above all things, and desperately wicked; who can know it?" (Jeremiah 17:9). I was too simple-minded to see through his wicked heart and deceitful plans. The board again asked him to teach, and not one objected (openly). But Mr. Lin, having some knowledge of communism, knew that, according to Communist laws, we had no power to dismiss him for any reason whatsoever. During 1951, this and other matters were fermenting. When I gave him the new contract, after a glance, he slammed it down on the table and said, "You renew my contract, but do not advance my salary."

I replied, "The board of managers did not suggest a rise. Therefore I cannot give one. Moreover, not one of the other workers has an increase in salary."

He said, "If you do not increase my salary, I shall oppose you and fight against you until I force you out."

"Mr. Lin," I said, "I also am a paid worker, and all are treated the same. I am not the head of a great organization."

"You are the head of this institution," he insisted.

I saw that he was being unreasonable so I said nothing, but went on with my usual inspection of the children, their food, and clothing.

Mr. Lin immediately began to incite the others to revolt, but only one, the man Jiu Lan, paid any attention to him, though the others became confused and split into cliques, opposing one another and me. I then began to realize that Mr. Lin was using the tactics of the Communists.

I was driven to prayer and said, "Lord, what am I? No more than a grasshopper, a worm. You entrusted this work to me. Without is confusion and trouble, within is dissension and distress. Mr. Lin is not willing to be under the authority of a woman. What do you wish me to do?"

Then I remembered Paul's suffering and dying for Christ (see 2 Corinthians 4:8-12) and I read this many times while praying, "Lord, even as thou didst with Paul, give me this spirit of courage and even more, that in these distressing circumstances, I may show in my body the marks of the death of Jesus, that his life may be in me in this, my weak helplessness."

On February 2, 1951, I went with two other representatives of the orphanage board to a meeting of the church council and presbytery in Hong Kong. Representing the orphanage, I reported everything that concerned the orphanage as follows:

1. I explained the government situation, both world and national, including the growing hatred towards the USA.
2. Since my 1950 report to Miss Stewart, former head of the orphanage, the mission had been considering abandoning the work and letting Miss Stewart resign. Miss Stewart, as treasurer, then delivered all orphanage and church funds to me.
3. Because of the bitter enmity of the Reds for the USA, they would not permit me to receive US funds given for relief work among the poor.
4. I reported these funds deposited in the bank in Hong Kong and the interest on same; I reported the cloth, yarn, garments, food, milk powder, and other things already on hand in Hong Kong.

5. I reported that supplies of food, clothing, bedding, and medical supplies remaining at the orphanage would not last more than six months with seventy-six people to feed and clothe.
6. The children were young and small, unable to work or earn money. No one could know when the day of peace would come. It was certain that our American friends could no longer send help for these children. As the proverb said, "When you are anxious about something in the far distant future, you should face it now."

"Since it is impossible simply to sit and wait for the year to pass," I said, "I asked for this meeting to be held, first so that all might learn the circumstances of the orphanage, take responsibility for it, and pray. We must do our duty and prepare for these troubles before they come upon us, so that these little ones will not be left to starve. Therefore, I ask you to discuss these matters, and advise as to our future road."

On hearing this, all at the meeting made suggestions: be more economical, be frugal, save, plant gardens on the mission land. But not one could tell me how to be more frugal, what to plant, how to save. Then I mentioned some ways:

1. We cannot save on food; children must be well fed in order to grow. But we can avoid wasting food; we can eat all, and throw nothing away. We can also find a way to destroy the rats. I obtained some good cats, but the Communists stole them, killed, and ate them. They told me to "cry as though for your father," when they saw my distress at what they did.
2. We can make salaries uniform for all, beginning with me; each teacher to receive $20 monthly or the equivalent in rice; other workers to receive $10, I to receive $20 per month, one-half of my former pay.
3. If any teacher or worker wishes to resign and find other employment, she is free to do so and will receive two months' pay on leaving. Those who are willing to stay and eat whatever comes, of bitter or of sweet, will be welcomed.

"Then, how can you increase the income?"
I suggested:

1. We can make use of the mission land, including that at the north of the buildings. We can plant things that can be used for food: rice, corn, sweet potatoes, beans, and melons.

2. We can raise animals: water buffaloes for farming, chickens, and rabbits.

I asked others to express their opinions. The first to object was Ze Lai Man, because her salary had already been cut by a third. Some members of the Board of Directors urged her not to object, and they advised me not to deny myself by such a large deduction from my own salary.

I replied, "Did not Jesus deny himself far more in his dying for me? Even if God's plan did not grant me a salary, I would still be glad to work and care for these children."

Back in the orphanage, Mr. Lin also raised objections. And when he failed to win a rise of salary, he put up posters and slogans, both in the school rooms and on the outside walls: "Beat down the foul Capitalists," and others that were definitely against me.

Chi Zhang, the oldest boy in the orphanage, demanded that I hand over all accounts and funds.

I said, "Chi Zhang, do you take responsibility for this, or do you have others to help?"

He said, "I shall ask Mr. Lin to help."

"Is this your own idea," I asked, "or did Mr. Lin tell you to do it?"

"Mr. Lin said I was the oldest boy in school, and I ought to be responsible for an adult's work."

I said, "Chi Zhang, now is the time for you to be diligent in getting an education. You have no time and no ability to carry this responsibility. If you study diligently now, you need not fear bad times in the future. But if you neglect study now, you will greatly regret misusing your opportunities, as you will not be fitted for anything."

He said nothing but bowed his head and went out. He was a fifteen-year-old boy in second class of the upper primary and had been very obedient.

At once I brought out my account books, showing the month's expenses and the food needed, put them with the key to the food storeroom into a box, took them to Mr. Lin, and very courteously asked him to help bear the heavy burdens. He gladly accepted my request, so this affair passed peacefully. Actually he wished me to hand over the banking business as well, but I did not agree to this. After two months he found this business too troublesome and returned it to me. Thereafter the institution had a short period of peace.

Afterwards we learned that the Communists wanted to take over both our orphanage and the Hebron Orphanage, which had purchased two of our Mission buildings. They persuaded the teachers and workers to demand that

I hand over both institutions and everything connected with them, including finances.

I refused to do this.

They said, "Do you think that because you are in charge of all these things you may escape being put in prison?"

I replied, "I would rather die because I was honest and faithful in all things. I am not willing to neglect what God gave me to do, and I am not anxious. If the government takes over I need not worry about it."

My present responsibility was to be "both father and mother." For instance, children from nine to twelve are sometimes disobedient, lazy, destructive, or sick. If one child does something wrong and is not disciplined, others in the same class imitate him and will not confess who did it.

I divided the children into four grades: infants, kindergarteners, and older children with boys and girls separated. Each group had a separate room with an older person in charge. With ages ranging from six months to fifteen years, there were in all sixty-four children, besides eight workers and teachers, making seventy-two living at the orphanage. In addition there were three elderly people in the Home for the Aged, which had formerly been the School for Women.

51

Hazardous Journeys to Hong Kong

I was first arrested by the Communists on a Sabbath morning in mid-October of 1949.

A Yong, the water carrier for the Hebron Orphanage, called me and said, "There are some people looking everywhere for you."

"Why do they want to see me?" I asked.

"I don't know."

Now, why did A Yong come especially to tell me this? I asked myself. Probably it was a hint to me to hide away.

But I knew that whatever came to me it was in God's plan, and there was no possible way to escape even if I wanted to. So I went as usual to teach my Bible class at the church. On my way I came face-to-face with two men in police uniform. They did not know me, and I paid no attention to them.

Just as I started the church service these two men came into the church and called out, "Which person here is Wen Wei Zhen?"

I said, "I am Wen Wei Zhen. What is it you want?"

"We have some business," one said. "Please come with us to the Yamen."

"Must I go at once? We are just beginning our service."

"Yes, you are to go at once."

I asked Mrs. Zheng to take my class, and I went out with them. Then I thought I should have my Bible and psalter, so I said, "Please wait a minute while I get something I need."

Of course they did not let me go alone, lest I run away.

They followed me back and watched while I put the books in my bag.

At the Yamen, Judge Li An courteously asked me to be seated. Then he, his secretary, and another officer questioned me until twelve o'clock. Two of them went out, leaving me with the third. I took out my psalter and began to sing.

"What are you doing?" the Secretary-guard said.

"I am singing praise to God," I said. "This is our worship day, and while the Christians are worshiping at the church, I also wish to sing praises."

The secretary then said, "Don't you recognize me? My name is Ze Zhu Cheng."

"I thought I recognized your face. Now I remember. You once studied in our theological school. But you seem so much older. Of course, thirty years have passed."

Then he brought out his Bible and handed it to me. On the front page was written, "This book was used by Ze Zhu Cheng." I added the character *lata*, meaning "you got loose" (a backslider).

The judge returned and questioned me again. Then I was sure they had arrested me because of the four wounded soldiers Miss Stewart had allowed to live in an old house on the Mission property.

One of these soldiers had entered the Yamen and announced, "I want to kill the magistrate."

Supposing him to be a spy sent to assassinate the officer, the officials arrested, bound, and questioned him. As he mentioned my name they supposed I was using him as a tool. Now that I had guessed the reason for my arrest, I explained.

"When the Guomindang (Nationalist) Army retreated, four wounded soldiers who were unable to march with the troops stopped at the hospital for healing and were permitted to live in the old house. This was before I returned to Deqing, but I know it was out of compassion they were allowed to stay there. Among these four was one whose mind was weak, and it was probably he that caused this trouble."

After hearing my explanation, the judge went to question the man and became convinced I had told the truth.

At nine o'clock that night the judge came to me and said, "If you can secure a guarantor, you may go home, but if you are called back you must come at once."

I asked for Dr. Ze Chi Ying at our hospital and he came at once. I was back at the orphanage at 10:40 p.m.

We learned later that the guard surreptitiously annoyed the man so that he kept calling out all night, and he was pronounced insane next morning. Thereupon, all were released, and we were assured there would be no more trouble. I requested the People's Government to return them to their native homes. This they did, providing them travel permits and free passes on the railway, one to Manchuria, two to Hunan, and one to Guangxi. They received no allowance for food, so I gave them each $50 local currency. Two had become Christians while with us, and they sent letters of appreciation for all we had done for them and expressed thanks to God for his mercy.

Two years later, when I was in prison, the Communists continually brought up this matter and cursed me, saying that I had once harbored their enemies. How many times I was cursed for this I have no idea. In my heart I said, "Lord, you know all this, but great will be the joy when these soldiers go to thy home."

At this time there were no fast steamships available. Travel was limited to sailboats, junks towed by small launches, and slow trains. All that would have been tiresome under any circumstances, but where there was no freedom and much to annoy and frighten, we had a truly bitter experience.

After the Communists took over the country, everyone had to register with the government and get a permit to travel anywhere; even in going to a country village one had to be searched. A trip to Hong Kong (about 150 miles from Deqing) was as troublesome as a trip to the South Pole would have been and as difficult as flying to heaven. During 1949 and 1950, I made six trips to Hong Kong, and on every trip I met fright and danger, but God let me know his presence and I felt protected.

At the time of my first journey to Hong Kong, when the Communists had been in power in the land for four-and-a-half months, the foreign workers had been away from Deqing for half a year. Letters frequently passed between us; in particular the treasurer of the mission wrote to me. In reply I gave news of the Christians, of the orphans, and of the general situation, but of course I could not be specific about financial matters.

There was no bank in the city where I could deposit funds, so I kept money hidden in small parcels here and there about my room. When I discovered an error in my accounts that I could not solve, I decided, after much prayer, that I must go to Hong Kong and compare my account with Miss Stewart's. I was fearful of going alone, so I persuaded a young Christian man to go with me.

On February 4, 1950, we boarded a small towboat, and I was surprised to find that A Jin, a distant relative, was part owner of the boat. I was treated very courteously and was warned before we passed a point where there might be an attack by bandits, or where loyal Guomindang soldiers might fire on us, or where Communist guards might search us. I was instructed how to prepare to meet each of these contingencies. From Jiang Men (Kong Moon), where the towboat stopped, I asked my relative to go with me to Hong Kong, and so he did.

Once in Hong Kong, the treasurer soon found the error in my accounts, and my burden of several months was lifted.

More than a month later I received a letter asking me to go to Hong Kong to receive five large parcels of clothing for the orphanage. On April 4, I secured a permit to travel to Canton. Mr. Hou Zhuo Man also had business there, and we went to Hong Kong together. Because of an enlarged thyroid and a slight heart disturbance I stayed a week for medical treatment. Before I left, Miss Stewart put into my hands $3,000 Hong Kong currency for the orphanage. At that time local Chinese currency was very unstable, and no one wanted to accept it, preferring rice as payment. Besides, the People's Government tried to ban the currency of Hong Kong or in fact any other currency. Banks in Hong Kong were not dealing in the currency of Red China, so exporters and importers had their private plans for carrying on business without exchanging cash. Formerly, when I had funds to receive, my relative of the towboat took it in the form of goods to Jiang Men and the funds were then delivered to me safely in Deqing.

Mr. Hou had a medicine shop in Deqing and wished to obtain supplies from Hong Kong but failed to get permission. However, the Hong Kong firm accepted the money, and their Canton branch supplied the medicines.

Now I obtained a receipt for $3,000 Hong Kong currency, and the Canton firm delivered to me $2,500 in the same currency, and the balance in local money. I opened one of the five parcels of used clothing and, after praying for guidance, put the whole amount into the sleeve of a child's sweater. I repacked the parcel and fastened it as before. We put the parcels on the boat as baggage on our two tickets.

We had passed one station on the river, and as we approached the second I heard a voice calling, "Who is Yin Wei Jie? Be ready for examination by the police."

I went calmly to where the inspector stood. He looked at my declaration and found it in order.

"What is your occupation?" he asked.

"I am manager of the orphanage at Deqing," I told him.

"What was your business in Canton?"

"I went to receive some parcels of worn clothing for the orphanage."

"Bring them out. I must examine them," he said.

The parcels had been stowed under the bunks on a shelf two-and-a-half feet high.

"I have five large parcels," I said. "They contain secondhand clothes sent from America."

He ordered his men to haul them out and told me to open them for inspection. It was difficult to open them, as they were bound with wire and I had no tools, but he sternly insisted.

One of his men said, "If she opens them, she won't be able to close them, and we'll have to do it, and it will delay us. Why not inspect one and see what sort of things she has, and, if only clothes, why bother?" So the inspector consented and chose the parcel to be opened.

He chose the one that had the $2,500 Hong Kong dollars in it. One of the sailors had an iron bar, and I asked him to let me use it. I had become nervous and was not able to open it.

Another passenger said, "That is not easy. Let me help you."

He opened it quickly. The inspector then took out the garments one by one and shook them to be sure there was nothing harmful packed with them. All the while I was praying, "Lord, still my heart; keep me in peace."

And the Lord did a wonderful thing. The inspector failed to see the money in the sleeve of the small sweater.

When he had finished the inspection, I folded each garment carefully and put all back into the carton. When binding it up I cut my hand on the steel wire just as I said, "Lord, I thank Thee."

A bystander said, "What did you say?"

I said, "I was giving thanks to my God."

They saw my bleeding hand and said among themselves that I was thankful the cut was not serious. But they did not know all that was in my heart.

I went back to where I had been sitting. Mr. Hou's face was very pale, and perspiration covered his forehead.

"Why are you looking like this?" I said.

"I was afraid for you," he said.

"Do you think I am a piece of wood with no feelings or fear? In my heart I kept saying 'What shall I fear? The Lord is at my side,' so I was able to go through this calmly because he was protecting me."

"God is our refuge and strength, a very present help in trouble" (Psalm 46:1).

52

Annihilate the Christian Church

In April 1950, the People's Government of Communist China made clear their laws regarding citizens' privileges and their purpose to suppress all churches. As they claimed that there is no God, they were unwilling to permit people to believe in God, so they put out notices requiring every church to register and to obey the regulations. It was as if the church was being forced to stick its neck into the noose for its hanging.

On May 1, 1950, I received a letter from Pastor Song, chairman of the church council, asking me to call a meeting of church leaders in all districts to discuss the new conditions. Representatives were also to be chosen to meet later in Canton. I at once did as he asked.

When Miss Stewart had left Deqing in 1949, she had asked me to be responsible for the church work she had been doing, that is, Bible classes, meetings, and business affairs. She had given me the church minute books, account books, and all deeds for church land and properties. In 1950, I was appointed secretary of the church council, and all official books and papers of the churches were put into my hands. At the time Pastor Song wrote to ask me to call a meeting, the Communists were in the act of taking over in Deqing.

On June 1, 1950, a meeting of the church council was held at the orphanage, leaders from all outstations being present. After the usual reports, they discussed the matter of registering with the government, and it was decided to hold another meeting with the church leaders in Canton. Again they could make no decision, so they went to Hong Kong to discuss the issue with the American missionaries. I went with them.

This meeting was held at Tai Po Road, Jiulong,[15] with Rev. Peter Song as chairman. Officers were elected for the coming year, and the law about registering churches was discussed, with the unanimous decision that our churches should not register with the government.

Then the future work of the church was discussed: what could be done and how to do it under the new regime. Finally Mr. Boyle summarized the difficulties, possibilities, and suggestions:

1. In case public meetings are forbidden, visit in the homes of Christians; do "little business" (peddling) from house to house; pray with Christians.
2. Visit Christians of other churches, encourage and strengthen faith; spread church news quietly.
3. If one church meets persecution, pray for them; inform other churches, the church council, and missionaries if possible; unite in trying to help those in distress.

As a church secretary, I recorded these things, but I hesitated to carry the minutes on my person, so I sent them by first-class mail.[16]

All delegates stayed in Hong Kong for a week of refreshment and sightseeing, while I was advised by the doctor to rest. At my request, the mission treasurer paid each pastor and evangelist a half-year's salary in advance, so that each could take the responsibility for getting it into Red China and thus lighten my burden. I left orphanage funds in the Bank of China in Hong Kong, which afterwards had become Communist owned. They agreed to transfer it to Deqing. Realizing that Communists are enemies of the church and of individual Christians also, the leaders nevertheless resolved to carry out their aims.

In July 1950, I was not in good health, so I decided to visit Hong Kong again for treatment. I also wanted to bid farewell to some who were going to begin work in Japan. After the tiresome trip by boat and train, I had to spend a night at Shumchun, the entrance to Hong Kong. Inspectors came four times to examine my baggage. Before dawn I went out to stand in line at the entrance gate, but there were so many "little business" men crowding in that in three hours I had not moved forward one step. By pushing my way and standing my ground I was near enough to the gate where the British police kept people in line, and I was again in free British territory.

It was suggested that I should go to Japan with those who had already arranged to work there, but I was not willing.

"Is it because I asked you to be responsible for the orphanage?" Miss Stewart asked.

"Not only that," I replied. "I choose to stay because God gave me the work of being a shepherd for his little lambs. It is not your responsibility if harm comes to me. God will take the responsibility. Put your mind at rest."

I consulted my doctor and he advised an operation on a gland in my neck, but I had to postpone that because I had not prepared to stay away from my work for a sufficiently long period. He urged me to return in September, and I did so in company with Pastor Huang.

The doctor was happy to find my trouble gone and said, "But you must continue the medicine."

I replied, "God must have some work for this worn-out unworthy person to do for him."

I was constantly under the watchful eye of the Communists, and as they became more severe and secretive, I did not wish to go to Hong Kong again.

However, at noon on December 29, 1950, Wan Sao said to me, "Are you going to Hong Kong to see Miss Stewart? The manager of Hebron has just told me that she is soon going to America."

I had barely time to pack. I said to Wan Sao, "Please prepare some food for me. I shall go at five o'clock."

Again God did a wonderful thing for me; the boat arrived at Canton almost four hours earlier than usual, and I went to Pastor Song's home. But he had gone to the station to see his wife off to Hong Kong, so I hurried to the station. While I was standing in line, a friend bought a ticket for me. Otherwise I could not have gone that day and would not have had time to consult with Miss Stewart.

She gave me $20,000 Hong Kong currency for the churches, the orphanage, and for some other people, and I planned to have it transferred by the Bank of China as before. But I learned that certain funds sent that way had been frozen, so I had to find another plan through Pastor Song and my friend in Canton. When we were short of funds Mr. Song forwarded it in small amounts, so that by October 1951, when the Communists took over the orphanage, we had had the entire amount.

On January 1, 1951, both Mrs. Song and I had gone to Hong Kong and I had returned to Canton when, three days later, the wife of Mr. Zhang Min Fu came to the Song home searching for me. The Communists had sent Mr. Zhang to Zhao Qing as a prisoner, and she wanted me to try to have him released.

There was no boat that day, so I went with Pastor Song to a meeting at the YWCA, supposedly to hear a certain pastor from Lingnan University. Pastors, church leaders, and men from the YMCA were there, and also some Communist agitators. It was an accusation meeting against a Mr. Lockwood, a former YMCA. worker, and the Communists shouted at him many a vile epithet and false accusation.

I was so agitated by this meeting that I was too weak to walk, so I went to a friend who was a doctor, and he gave me a sedative that enabled me to sleep from 3 p.m. to 9 a.m. the next day. I awoke refreshed and as strong as ever, then went to see Mrs. Zhang to discuss what we might do to save her husband.

On December 30, Ya Zhong, one of the Christians, had seen Mr. Zhang on the road, bound between two armed soldiers. Ya Zhong ran quickly to tell Mrs. Zhang, and she ran out to the river, but the soldiers with their prisoner had already entered a boat. She did not see her husband nor learn where or why they were taking him.

Early in January, when I had returned from Hong Kong to Canton, Mrs. Zhang came there to find me. She went hither and thither over the city to find a way to save her husband, while I rested a day or two. Then I attended a meeting of pastors and church leaders, for I wished to learn of their experiences and their plans for continuing church work.

I learned that the Communists had occupied practically all churches in Canton, and that their chief aim was to annihilate the Christian church. After they had confiscated all churches for their own use, a certain Pastor Chen spoke against this. As reported in *The Heavenly Wind*, a Red magazine, it was "as if he had dug up his own ancestors," a most despicable thing.

A new law, even more severe, decreed that all religions of whatever faith, had to be united in one organization. All leaders were to meet together in the largest, most magnificent church building in the city for worship. Pastors were to take turns preaching, each one perhaps once a year, while pastors rendered idle were to engage in hard labor, with vacated churches at the disposal of the Communists.

For instance, Miss Song, then a worker in our church in Canton, was sent out with only hand tools to break up land that had not been farmed for years. The church building was then used as a nursery or home for children whose parents were sent out to labor, often separated, on farms, in factories, or in mines. Many children never saw their parents again but were brought up as wards of the government and trained as Communists.

The church building in Deqing was used as a health and sanitation office and maternity hospital; Luoding church premises became a match factory; at another place, the pastor was expelled and the buildings used for accusation meetings.

Throughout the entire country churches were treated in this way.

According to Communist law, there was to be freedom of religion for all. In public they declared: "We don't interfere with your church nor hinder its working. You have religious freedom." At the same time they occupied church buildings, prevented the holding of regular church meetings, and even tried to prevent the private gatherings of Christians for prayer.

When visitors came from abroad, a guide showed them the great Union Church and expounded the law of religious freedom, but tourists did not see the inside of the church with a few courageous and devout elderly people at worship with a spy looking on. How then could anyone outside China know how hypocritical the Communists were (and are) on the subject of religion?

53

Red Army Domination

When the 13th Route Army of the People's Communist Government first occupied Deqing some months after my return there, everyone from government officials and army officers to private soldiers wished to live in the homes of the people. Because space was limited they also decided that our church and other buildings were eminently suitable for their accommodation.

Opposite our church door lived two Christian women, mother and daughter. Their home was roomy, clean, and in good condition. It became headquarters for government and army officers, and every time we gathered for worship in the church they came to spy on us.

Before long, they announced: "We are at liberty to enter as we wish, and to take over and use the building as we wish. We shall tell you what to think, and what your attitude and behavior must be."

For obvious reasons, we kept the large main door closed and used a small side door. One day, officers came through the small door and opened the main door, saying, "We want to use this building," and, without waiting for permission, soldiers came marching in.

When the minister spoke of this with the chief officer, he was told, "We are obeying the orders of our chief, Mao Zedong. We shall use this for a dining hall, but we need not disturb your meetings." But we could not meet regularly, and each day we had to clean up after them before we could hold a meeting.

Many weeks passed, and I spoke to the chief officers about how their use of our church building inconvenienced us in our worship. I also said our churches were dedicated to the worship of our holy God, and should not be used for secular things. He replied: "I know that Buddhists do not allow outsiders to eat in their temples or places of worship on their holy days because they believe that those who eat pork are unclean and would defile their holy place. Does the Jesus church have the same custom?"

"The God of the Christian church is truly a holy God, and we are even more strict than the Buddhists in many ways."

He said nothing but went away, and they did not use the church as an eating place for some time. For that we were thankful.

Some time later they came again and merely announced, "We need this building for a study room. We shall not hinder or inconvenience you."

This seemed better than to use it as a public eating place; in any event it was useless to object. They covered the church walls with Communist notices, placards and slogans, as well as large pictures of Lenin, Stalin, and Mao Zedong.

I went to see the higher officer about this and waited a long time for him. The petty officers and secret service men did not want me to hear their conversation, so they forced me to leave. With tears of distress I prayed to God, "Help us to get these things out of our place of worship."

Afterwards, I asked the petty officers to remove their slogans and pictures after their meeting and before ours. They promised to do so but did not. Psalm 137 was a true picture of our situation. How could we sing the Lord's songs surrounded by these God-denying slogans? So we sat "by Babylon's river" for half a year, hoping for an opportunity to plead for the return of our church building to us.

Finally Mr. Zhang and I went in without permission, near the end of one of their study periods, and begged for the return of the building to us before the Christmas season. The officer promised to let us use it from the evening of December 24 to the morning of the 26th. We begged for a longer time while we made preparations, and afterward for our charitable work to the poor. But they refused any longer time.

"We have business and meetings much more important than your meetings."

"But the law says clearly that we all have freedom of religion. Are we not allowed to worship our God in our own building?"

"We do not prevent you from worshiping on your worship day."

So saying he turned and left. A private soldier standing nearby scolded and cursed me so vilely that I did not wait to listen but returned to the orphanage.

Just as I got back, Mr. Zhang's eldest son came looking for me.

"Soldiers from the 13th Route Army have taken my father away. Go quickly and see him."

I hurried back to the office, but the guards would not allow me to enter, nor would they take a message. So I stood on the other side of the street for a long time. Finally a private came and spoke to me.

"That man Zhang whom you wish to see is in jail at the Yamen. Perhaps you may see him there."

"I am not waiting to see him," I said. "I must see your commanding officer."

"He has gone away. Won't be back for three days."

So I went to the Yamen and asked to see the magistrate. He received me courteously and said, "You may return home. Our law makes right and just judgments. It does not treat innocent people unfairly."

I then returned home.

That same evening at nine o'clock Mr. Zhang returned home and came to tell me all that he had endured after his arrest. When the soldier had cursed me that morning, Mr. Zhang reproved him by quoting the orders of the high command that soldiers must not curse others. So Mr. Zhang was arrested because he had "exposed the offense" of the soldier. He was falsely accused of cursing a soldier and of vilifying the picture of Mao Zedong.

Because the 13th Route Army had no authority to arrest a man for such an offense, the magistrate freed Mr. Zhang and sent him home. We now supposed that the storm was over and that we might live in peace. But the soldier opposed the magistrate and demanded that Mr. Zhang be arrested again. Because of this we suffered many things. Next morning the magistrate ordered his arrest, and he was sentenced to forty days in jail.

After his arrest the army did not occupy the church building for a time, so we cleaned it thoroughly and whitewashed the walls that they had covered with posters and slogans. For a while we worshiped God in freedom and great joy. Because Mr. Zhang was in jail, every church responsibility and difficulty fell upon me. We held no special meeting on Christmas day but distributed the gifts prepared for the poor.

While in Canton, Mrs, Zhang asked a friend to write a letter telling in detail the reasons for Mr. Zhang's arrest. She took a copy to the army headquarters and delivered it in person to the chief officer. After she returned to Deqing, I went to the magistrate and inquired about Mr. Zhang.

"He has been sent to Zhao Qing," was all I learned.

I asked Dr. Ze, his physician, to get permission to send warm clothing and bedding to him, but this was refused. I then took a part of Mrs. Zhang's letter and sent it to the commanding officer of the army in Deqing. The next day I took Mrs. Zhang and her seven children with me to the army headquarters. I usually asked to see a petty officer or the secretary, but now I said, "I wish to see the commanding officer."

After waiting seventy minutes, we were admitted to his office. "Commander," I said, "these are the children of Mr. Zhang. They continually ask their mother for their father, and she comes every day begging me to try to find him. Early this morning this whole family came with their mother, crying and begging me to get their father freed. I can only lead them to you."

When the children heard this, they began to cry, "I want my papa. Where is my papa?"

Soon all were crying uncontrollably, and I could not hold back my own tears. The longing of these children for their dearly loved father seemed to touch the fatherly feelings of this man who had the power of life and death over their father—a good, innocent man.

Suddenly he said, "Don't cry. Don't cry. I'll find your father. Go back home now, and tomorrow I shall tell you."

I tried to hush their crying and said, "Did you hear what the officer said? He promised to find your father. Don't cry. Bow at once to the officer and thank him for his kindness."

They stifled their sobs, wiped away their tears and bowed politely, while their faces looked like the face of a calico cat.

We had gone only a short distance when the officer called me back.

"Tomorrow I want you to come alone. Don't bring all those seven children."

Next morning I went again, and the commander spoke very harshly: "Why do you come here? That man Zhang is not here."

"You said you would give an answer to those children if I came alone. Here I am, and alone."

"Zhang is not here," he said angrily. "Go and ask the magistrate."

I went, and the magistrate said, "Go and ask the commander of the 13th Route Army."

"But why do they pass the responsibility to you and you pass it back to them?" I asked.

"This trouble was worked up by the army. When they say 'Put a man in jail,' how can I free him?" he answered.

"If you cannot reverse their orders, how can I?" I said.

I went back to the army commander and said the magistrate had sent me back to him.

He very angrily said, "I told you, he is not here. If you bring this matter up again I shall jail you."

"It doesn't matter if you do put me in jail. Shall I tell those children that you have deceived them? I know there is a law of Mao Zedong that children must not be mistreated; they are the hope of communism."

In fiery tones he called: "Someone is coming to see me."

I took that as my dismissal, so I left and did not go again.

I went back to the Zhang home and said, "I believe God will hear our prayers and that your father will soon return."

A few days later I was in the market buying vegetables when someone came up behind me and grabbed my arm. I turned quickly and faced a policeman. I felt chilled all over.

"What does this mean?" I asked shakily.

"That man Zhang that you went every day to the Yamen to ask about, has come back. Go to the Yamen and ask about him."

"Thank you," I said.

But as I walked with him to the Yamen I said, half laughing, half in earnest, "How should a person feel when she is grabbed from behind by a policeman?"

I returned with Mr. Zhang in a small boat, and the children ran joyfully to meet us. The next day we invited Mr. Zhang for lunch and afterwards had a meeting for thanksgiving, the children choosing psalm after psalm to sing, expressing their joy and faith and love for Jesus in freeing their good friend.

54

Communist Infiltrations

"Before one calamity passes, another falls," says an ancient proverb.

Less than three months after Mr. Zhang was freed, a document came from the head of the Provincial Government saying that they wished to use our church buildings permanently and that we should vacate them before May 5, 1950.

The church leaders agreed that we had to obey. Dr. Ze Chi Ying suggested that we use some vacant rooms at the hospital. The army had wanted to use those rooms but had been persuaded that it would hinder the hospital work.

A week after we had moved to these rooms, just as we started our worship service, officers came from the army and made Dr. Ze order us out. We moved out as soon as the service ended. The only place left for us was a dilapidated, old house that termites had made unsafe for a dwelling. Only the outer walls and a verandah were fairly good. With mats of bamboo and palm leaves to keep sun and rain out, we used the verandah for our meetings.

Through these troublesome times the faith of the Christians became more earnest and active; their love for God greatly increased. It was difficult to raise money for Mr. Zhang's salary, so they helped by planting and caring for a garden for him and his family.

They said, "Even if we didn't have this veranda, we could worship under the big tree in the yard." In fact, we had our next Christmas meeting there, and at times had a church dinner on the grass.[17]

A few months after the Communists occupied the hospital rooms, the hospital was ordered to move out as the Communists needed the whole building. So the church lost two of its most important buildings to the Communists.

They utterly hated and despised every department of the church work and social service. They tried to overthrow everything by false reports and slander, saying that all Christians were evil conspirators, their teachings mental cruelty and poison. There was even a proclamation that all affairs of the Chinese people should be managed by the new People's Government, and their plan was to take over all the activities of churches—hospitals, schools, orphanages, leper hospitals, and industrial work. They claimed that the work of these institutions would then be carried out more efficiently.

In April 1951, two officers of the Executive Committee of Communist Affairs were sent to live in the buildings of the Hebron Orphanage and several others to live in our orphanage, to investigate the doings of our workers. They kept a very close watch on us, and thoroughly examined everything about the place, whether public or private. They received and read all mail that came to me. I sometimes went to the post office and asked for my mail, but only one clerk dared give it to me.

Whenever I was to be away even for a short while, I locked my private room, for it was my office as well as my sleeping room. Yet they somehow got into it, and I could always be sure they had tampered with my things. Once I locked the drawers to my desk as well as my room and set off for the market, then suddenly decided to go back for something I had forgotten. I opened my door and saw all the drawers open and books, papers and other things scattered over the floor.

I shouted, "A thief! A thief! Help catch him!"

Mrs. Huang, one of the Communist spies, showed herself and said, "It is I. I wanted your picture, and I was just looking for one."

"Excuse me, please," I said most politely. "I didn't know it was you. I've never had such a thing happen before, so I yelled for help to catch the thief. I bought three dogs just to protect us from such things. Please take whatever it is you want."

Zheng Ai, another spy, was more open about such things.

She would say, "Yun Xian Shang, come and open these doors, unlock the drawers and trunks." She openly taught the children Communist songs. She forbade them to pray, told them to disobey the former workers and to obey only the new ones, and to shout *Wan Sui!* (10,000 years) to communism. In the following years they thoroughly indoctrinated the children with communism.

Beginning October 20, we saw well-armed police or soldiers pacing back and forth outside the orphanage walls. About ten o'clock on the night of October 23 there was an urgent battering at the gate, and a voice called, "Open the gate."

Wan Sao said, "Who is there?"

From outside, the same harsh voice said, "Household inspection."

"Wait a minute, while I get a key," she called, and took the opportunity to run upstairs and tell me. We had learned from past experience that when a Red officer came to "inspect a household" he usually came with an order and authority to arrest someone. Wan Sao was so much frightened that she could only stammer "K-k-k-k-ai M-m-m-m-en" (Open the door).

I told her not to be afraid, and went down to take the responsibility for what might happen, all the while praying "Lord, this may be the time; thy will be done in me." Though I had told her not to fear, my own legs suddenly became as weak as though my bones were water, and I could hardly stand. I prayed for strength, and his word came, "Fear not; I am with thee." So I opened the gate.

"Comrade," I said, "have you come to check the people who live here? The children are already in bed asleep, and the workers are also asleep."

"Call them all to get up," he said roughly.

"I can call the adults to get up, but how can these small children get out of bed? We don't have enough helpers to carry so many. May I not bring the book with all their names and take you through all the rooms to check?"

He then said, "Who is here besides the workers?"

"Only Huang Zheng Ai and Qian Rui Chen," I said.

"We want to see these two and speak with them," he said.

I led him to where Zheng Ai was. She came out and invited them into her room, and I returned to my own room. Actually this was the working out of a plan of the local government with Zheng Ai. They were afraid we would try to escape and had soldiers stationed at every door and stairway.

Zheng Ai led these men all over the place, then said, "These men wish to spend the night here. Prepare a place for them to sleep."

So I obeyed, and by the time all were settled it was midnight. I took my lamp into the bathroom and prepared for a bath. Seeing no light in my room, these men began beating on my door and calling my name, fearing I had escaped. I opened the bathroom door a crack and called out, "I am here. It is very late; rest in peace until morning."

After I had gone to bed, they again flashed a light into my room to make sure I was there. Except for God's grace, I fear I should have been too worried to sleep, but like the psalmist I quieted myself like a child in his mother's arms.

55

Robbery by Daylight

Exactly at nine o'clock in the morning on October 24, 1951, Huang Min Fang, secretary to the governor of the district, and Feng Jian Xiong, secretary to the Deqing magistrate, led a large group of men from the city. Half of them entered the Hebron Orphanage, and the rest came to the Reformed Presbyterian Orphanage of which I was in charge. Though I did not know the exact number, as I saw them divided into small groups for various duties, I estimated there were more than sixty on our premises, many of whom I recognized.

I was working in the garden at the time. Huang Min Fang called me and demanded that I give him the keys to all the rooms, chests, desks, trunks, and boxes, as well as those of my private room and desk. After about an hour, he ordered me to indicate where each key belonged and to label each with a small piece of wood. I did as he ordered, and then saw that they had numbered each door and sealed each with a paper bearing the official seal. Across some, boards had been nailed. When I had finished this work for them, I delivered all keys to the officer. Huang Min Fang then told me to order the cook to prepare our midday lunch an hour earlier.

While we were eating, Huang came to the dining room and said, "At twelve noon exactly, all those connected with this orphanage—children, manager, teachers, and workers—will go to the Hebron Orphanage for a meeting."

We hurriedly ate, cleaned up, and at the appointed time I led the way to the Hebron building. The doors there were guarded by fully-armed soldiers. The Hebron group were already seated, with many people standing about. Officer Huang rose and read the official decree of the District Magistrate. As I now recall, it was approximately as follows:

At exactly noon of the 24th day of the tenth month of the year 1951, the People's Government of China is taking over the Hebron Orphanage and the Reformed Presbyterian Orphanage. Hereafter these two will be united into one institution, and will belong to the Deqing District of the People's Government of China. It will be under the jurisdiction of the Deqing District Magistrate's special officer, Huang Min Fang. All employees of the former regime will be retained, and will be assigned to their various duties as before. This is by order of the aforesaid District Magistrate."

As soon as Huang had made this announcement, Zheng Ai made a speech of acceptance, saying, "In accordance with the magistrate's decree of the People's Government of China, I accept the management of this orphanage. And now, all employees should accept their responsibilities and promise obedience to the new regime and earnestly perform the duties assigned to them, in obedience to the new People's Government."

Feng Jian Xiong then spoke. His speech was in praise of Mao Zedong and of the policies of the Communist Government. He said, for instance, that "the industries and factories of the country will now expand greatly; agriculture will produce much greater harvests; business will prosper, and financially all will be equal and prosperous. In our contact with foreign countries, we shall gain a victory; new China will become a great country instead of being poor and despised. Its standing will be exalted in every way."

On the other hand, he reviled all that foreign countries had done in China; all had been Imperialists and opposed to all that was just and right. Foreigners had mistreated these poor orphans. In their education they had poisoned their minds; they had taught them harmful things, and treated all as "running dogs" and lowest slaves.

At the end he spoke these very comforting words: "Heretofore you have suffered greatly under the old regime. Now that is all ended, and all will now be pleasant. There will be no more cruel mistreatment."

Then he began to speak venomous words to fan the flame of hate against the former workers and the church. He stirred up the children to hate and disobey the former workers. He urged them to despise forever the former manager, teachers and church people.

After this speech, he divided the children, managers, teachers, and helpers into four groups and appointed four leaders to instruct these groups in separate rooms. Our group was under the instruction of Xie Lu Yuan, a nephew of Xie Lai Min, a teacher in the orphanage.

He first gave a long talk on the war situation in China. Then he spat out the vilest of language, repeating the words he had been taught to say. He reviled and defamed all who were enemies of communism, hoping to impress us with these brave words and also to prove his loyalty to the Communist Party. He urged us to follow his good example, and to realize from what a miserable existence we had been rescued. He vehemently urged us to confess our former sins in refusing to accept communism.

But we were all like cicadas when cold weather comes; we uttered not one word.

He named me especially, and urged me to act like a wise person who understood great matters and to take this step forward at once.

"Mr. Xie," I said, "as for the aims and policies of the Communist Party, I have not yet made a deep study of them. I do not fully understand all you have just said, certainly not well enough to accept it and speak about it. How could I blindly do as you suggest?"

After this reaction to his important official instructions, he seemed chagrined, perhaps humbled. He said nothing but glared at me with a very black expression on his face. Quickly recovering his arrogance, he gave us to understand clearly that he was there to instruct us and to persuade us to change our ways and remain in orphanage employ.

This meeting had been called simply to keep us all penned up while the Reds "received" all they could pilfer and steal, without interference. When those sixty or more men had had time to do this, our meeting for instruction was ended. And the clock struck five.

As we left the classrooms and walked back to the orphanage, I was certain that before me lay the fires of testing and tribulation, and not for me only, but for all these little children, the teachers, and the helpers. I longed to go to my own room and tell it all to the Lord.

I found my door locked and sealed with the official seal. Of course I could not enter, so I went to my office. That also was locked and sealed. I looked for Zheng Ai, the new manager, but she was nowhere to be found. The new crew had all gone to the district magistrate to report "Mission Accomplished."

I simply sat on the stairs and recalled the proverb, "A dog whose home and his master are gone is homeless with no place to go." In addition to locking all private rooms and my office, they had locked and sealed all supply and storage rooms, so no one could open them except an official. I later learned why the doors were sealed: they had stolen everything, even my personal belongings. (My daughter-in-law later saw a man wearing my watch and bravely insisted on getting it back. It is now a prized possession.)

All I could do was to call the church leaders together and announce: "The orphanage which was owned, managed, and supported by the church, and all persons, property and furnishings connected with it, were confiscated on October 24, 1951, by the Communist People's Government under the Magistrate of Deqing District."

This method of taking over the orphanage and church property had not been in accord with the decree put out in Beijing for the regulation of religious bodies. In 1951, Mao Zedong had called a meeting of leaders of all religions and sects, with representatives of the People's Government, and declared religious liberty for all. But these government people utterly disregarded the regulations and, probably because of ignorance, acted stupidly, but they felt they had done very well and boasted of it.

Instead of employing former workers at the orphanage, they brought in six Communists. They distributed the children as they wished. Older ones were put out to beg and act as spies in villages; some were put out for adoption; the blind were sent to another city. Others were assigned rooms at the convenience of the new masters.

It was impossible to escape from all this, and it was hard to endure it patiently. Then the words of Revelation 2:10 came to me: "Do not fear any of those things which you are about to suffer. Indeed, the devil is about to throw some of you into prison, that you may be tested, and you will have tribulation ten days. Be faithful until death, and I will give you the crown of life."

"Amen," I said. "Thy will be done."

As I sat resting on the stairs, I heard the bell ring so I went to the dining room. The place was filled with people and every thing was in disorder and confusion. The Hebron orphans were older than ours, mainly thirteen- to fifteen-year-olds. They rushed in, got their food, and soon filled the tables. For a long time that orphanage had been short of funds and had insufficient food, and that explained their actions. Our children were smaller and accustomed to being orderly. When they saw others rushing in and grabbing food, they stood and stared. The new manager had planned nothing beforehand, so it was a case of everyone for himself. There was not enough rice; bowls and chopsticks were too few; latecomers had to wash bowls, then came back to find the food all gone. Since I had no authority to speak, I gave over all my responsibilities to the new management.

For two days this confusion lasted, and those who went hungry were our orphans and helpers. The third day some wanted a second helping, but there was no food, and they stood crying with empty bowls.

I said to the person in charge, "After three days when children have been crying with hunger, you still don't know how much rice to cook? You didn't notice they were crying? In the end, you will let them die of starvation."

Manager Zheng Ai finally came back and called a meeting of all workers, both former and present, and asked if tales of children crying with hunger were true. We said it was true, especially of the smaller ones. I wanted to add that as my room was locked and sealed I had no place to sleep, no bedding or clothes, no towel, washcloth, or toothbrush, but I kept silent.

A night or two later I noticed there was a light in my room after twelve o'clock. The next morning I knocked at my door. Huang Min Fang answered and ordered me to come back at nine o'clock. After breakfast, I knocked again, and Huang opened the door. "Why do you come looking for me?" he asked.

"I didn't come looking for you," I said. "I came to my room to rest. Since you sealed my room three days ago, I have had no place to sleep or rest. I have no bedding, no clothing, not even a washcloth or toothbrush. Winter is now coming, and evenings and mornings are cold. I have no warm clothing, and I have caught cold, developed fever, and have swollen glands on my neck. So I must return to my room to rest."

"But others are already living in this room," he said.

"Why is this?" I asked.

"This is the plan of Superintendent Zheng Ai."

"How can she move all my things out and put other people in my room?"

"You may take your toilet things and anything else you need. As for the rest, speak to Zheng Ai."

"Why?" said I. "Why can't I use my own things? Why must I let others use my room, my bed, and other things?"

"In Communist countries," he said, "nothing is privately owned. All is for all."

"Already?" I said in surprise. "Even though we have not yet attained to that ideal and perfect society which you proclaim? If it is here now, should I not also have enough for my own use? You take my personal property and give me nothing, not even a place to sleep. I should have my own bed to sleep on as my portion of what you have taken for common use. Should I not have enough of my own garments to have a change occasionally? Moreover, this is not in accord with the laws of the ideal society of the new People's Government: 'all for each, each for all, without partiality.'"

He was embarrassed and said, "Please wait until Zheng Ai comes and tell her these things. This is her business." I had just taken an extra suit of clothes and my toilet articles from my room, including a wash basin.

"Now, where shall I put these things?" I asked. "And where shall I find a place where I can use them?"

He had no answer, so I said, "Excuse me. I must go to work." I left them on the floor outside the door and said, "When you assign a place for me to wash and sleep, let me know and I shall come and take these things away."

Zheng Ai had just then come and was displeased and said angrily, "Don't leave your things here. I'll not look after them." But I paid no attention to her and went away to my work.

After the Communists took over the running of the orphanage, they looked on me with growing envy and hatred. They felt that the sooner they got rid of me the happier they would be. So they trumped up charges against me. They taught the children to call me *Fa Yun Kai* (Dizzy Chicken), hoping thus to incite me to be so angry that I would scold and beat them. They used every possible way to open the door to prison for me.

I could see the reason for all this, but I knew these little children were too small to understand and were being used as a cat's paw to make trouble for me. Though they used the children to trouble me, I ignored it and prayed God to give me strength and patience to endure it all for his glory.

Another day, I heard Hou Xu Chuan call, "Fa Yun Kai! Fa Yun Kai!" I paid no attention and did not answer. She came up to me and said, "You Fa Yun Kai, why don't you answer when I call you? Why do you always oppose us?"

I said, "Miss Overseer, of course I did not answer to another person's name; I would not risk such a thing. Didn't you call Fa Yun Kai? That is not my name. You are an important person—an official placed over my head. How would I dare not answer when you called me? If you called me, would I not answer at once?"

She was very angry and said, "You hope for a long life, do you? When the right time comes, we shall take care of you by cutting off your head." She left in anger.

At one time it might have been possible for me to leave because of their unlawful acts, but now under the cruel authority of these people, I knew very well that if I left I would be accused of rebellion against the People's Government. I was constantly in prayer to God, lest I sin against him or against these people who were over me.

"Instruct and discipline me," I prayed, "and may thy will be done in me, in my heart and my body."

Postscript to Chapter 55

A list of things known to have been confiscated by the People's Government or stolen by the managers whom they installed:

1. Six substantial brick buildings and between ten and fifteen acres of land which the Reformed Presbyterian Mission had left to the Chinese Church and Orphanage.
2. Foreseeing future need, Mrs. Li and other helpers had often labored in the fields with the older orphans. They raised corn, beans, sweet potatoes, melons, and other vegetables sufficient for six months.
3. They had five water buffalo and three calves; about forty small pigs, many hens, 240 pigeons, and many rabbits to provide meat. The Communists even took fifty pigeons from their nests, leaving unhatched birds to die. Two fine watchdogs were killed for a feast.
4. The money Mrs. Li had brought from Hong Kong was illegal by 1949, so she had bought rice, oil, and salt sufficient for a year. The balance she had converted ito gold and silver bullion—a very old Chinese custom. In the then-current Communist scale, this was worth $274,600,000. Some private funds she had made into rings and bracelets.
5. In addition, Mrs. Li had provided twenty-four bolts of cotton cloth for clothing; twenty bolts coarse cotton cloth for bedding; 240 pounds cotton batting; three boxes of soap. Five large boxes of used clothing and blankets from America had not yet been opened. There was also winter bedding and clothing for orphans locked in boxes for the summer—all this disappeared.
All this was confiscated.

Copied from notes I made while I was with Mrs. Li in Hong Kong in 1958 and 1960.

—Rose A. Huston

56

Prayer and Praise in Prison

As the body depends on food for nourishment and growth; as air is necessary for purifying the body, cleansing and nourishing the blood; in much the same way the spirit of Christians also depends on Bible reading and prayer for life and growth. Therefore Jesus said to Satan, "Man shall not live by bread alone, but by every word that proceeds from the mouth of God" (Matthew 4:4).

After the Provincial Government took over the orphanage, the new official gave orders for us to cease singing praise to God and forbade our praying to him. The children had been taught the importance of prayer, and they continued to pray as usual.

On one occasion, as the children were being served their rice, Zheng Ai did not allow them to pray. But they prayed in spite of her, so they were not given their rice. It was a plan to persecute them with hunger. Zheng Ai then called the new helpers and told them not to allow the children to pray anymore. Soon, of course, the children changed color; they became Reds, and sat down and ate without prayer. Also they were not allowed to pray morning and night as we had taught them to do.

Afterward Zheng Ai ordered those of us who formerly had been in charge, to eat with the new workers. Her idea was to see if we insisted on praying and also to find a "handle" for accusing us. God was with me and I had no fear, so I continued to pray as usual.

Lu Jing Cheng said to me, "You are too obstinate."

One day Huang Min Fang called me to go to him for an interview.

He said, "You are too stubborn. Lu Jing Cheng has advised and warned you twice. Jia Su has also instructed you about the present situation and urged you to take special note of this. But you insist on praying as you formerly did. You still want to lead those little children back into the old ideas of imperialism. You must be careful lest you bring trouble on yourself and stir up trouble for others."

"For many decades," I said, "prayer has been a very important thing in my life. Were I to lose this one thing my whole life would gradually yield to black darkness and fear."

He was angry and said, "Do you mean to say that we who do not pray are in darkness and you are in the light? Your convictions are entirely too rigid. You are so set in your ways that you will yet eat the fruit of your stubbornness. Your old ideas will keep you in the dark."

"Does not the law of this new government say that all citizens have religious freedom?" I asked. "Why then should I ever be troubled for praying to my God? Why is it stubborn to pray? Why should trouble be the fruit of prayer?"

He was too angry to speak and, seeing his attitude toward me and prayer, I said, "It is time for me to go to work," so I left him.

On January 4, 1952, I was at my work cleaning out the cow stall. Lu Jing Cheng came and said, "Wen Wei Zhen, Huang Min Fang requires you to go to the meeting hall." His attitude was quite unusual, as though something had amused him.

I was not pleased about this, but it was a command, and I had to obey. I put down my tools and went to the meeting hall. There I saw Huang and several police and some men in civilian clothes. The other former managers were already there. While I found a seat, Huang said, "They are all here now."

Feng Jian Xiong, Secretary to the municipal Judge, at once made an announcement: "The chief in command says, 'In accord with the command of the judge of the court, I have come to arrest Wen Wei Zhen, Zheng Shi, Wu Liao, and Li Qi. These four persons are now in my custody.'" As I had just entered I did not catch the first name, so I said, "Officer Feng, who is the fourth person? I caught only three names."

He shouted loudly, "Wen Wei Zhen, Zheng Shi, Wu Liao, and Li Qi,[18] these four. Now these four may pack up a few simple necessities and prepare to go to the Judgment Hall with us. There they will receive further information."

When I heard this announcement, I knew what was in store for me. The Word of God had been given me as a warning to comfort and protect me: "Do not fear any of those things which you are about to suffer. Indeed, the devil is about to throw some of you into prison, that you may be tested, and you will have tribulation ten days. Be faithful until death, and I will give you the crown of life" (Revelation 2:10).

I laid fast hold of those words of God, stood up, and went to prepare the things I should take with me. Officer Feng then ordered the police in civilian dress to escort the four of us, one to each prisoner. When I had gathered together what I thought I should need, I returned to the meeting place. Officer Feng accompanied us to the Yamen, each carrying her baggage on her back.

Even before this, rumors and talk of war and fighting had affected the nerves of my stomach, and now there seemed to be something within me causing me great pain and distress. I was now over fifty years of age; the other three were younger and stronger than I. I was not able to walk at their pace, so my guard called out to the leader, "Don't walk so fast." Then I was able to keep up with them.

When we entered the Yamen, the judge came out and looked at us. Then they escorted us to the jail. There an officer inspected our baggage, and we four were put into separate cells. They thoroughly searched me and my baggage before thrusting me into the cell. They took away my Bible, pen, paper, and about fifteen dollars, allowing me to keep one piece of cotton padded bedding, a towel, a washcloth, comb and toothbrush, and an oiled sheet in which I had wrapped my bedding and which proved to be very precious and useful.

They took down my hair, searched through it carefully for anything I might have hidden in it. They kept all my hairpins and the ornament I used to keep the roll of hair in place. They even took away the strong tape we Chinese women use to keep our trousers in place. I had no mirror so never knew what my personal appearance was, nor what a sight I must have been.

At first, I supposed that in a few days "the water would have dripped away," my case settled, and I would be free to go home to the orphanage. Buoyed up by hope, I had strength to endure any bitter affliction. But day after day passed; day after day, they added troubles and annoyances. I had no Bible for encouragement, so my mind and spirit were famished, strength and energy were gone. Then I remembered how Paul and Silas had sung praises at midnight, and I rebuked myself for not rejoicing as they did.

A worker at the Hebron Orphanage was arrested at the same time as myself, and was put into the room adjoining my own. We were not allowed to see each other or speak, even when we were taken to the outside toilet. By standing on a bed, I could reach a small opening a few inches square and see into the next cell where my friend was, and when the guard was away we might speak a few words.

Of course speaking to her was against the rules, and if we were discovered by the guard it would add greatly to our crimes. But we two had one idea, and through this opening in the wall we agreed to pray with one heart and mind in the early morning, at noon, and at night.

We had no watch or clock, so we watched for the shadows made by the sun, as our ancestors had done. Whoever first saw the shadow began to sing, and the other would stop whatever she was doing. Together we sang, "Morning, noon, and at night I'll pray, and may the Lord draw nigh and hear." After singing we would pray; if either had heard any news, she would pray about it, hoping the other would hear. Sometimes we would write a message on a slip of paper, wrap it around a bit of earth to make it heavy and toss it through the hole. So for some months in this way we had fellowship in prayer and praise, and in the midst of grueling afflictions we had peace in heart and mind.

On Sabbath days we were not able to worship with other Christians, but when we knew by the sun that it was time for the worship service we sang praises and repeated verses from the Bible. Though we had no Bibles, and no pastor to preach to us, we had our memories, and with what we had we worshiped God.

Then we were put into other cells, and for seven or eight months we had no fellowship through the hole in the wall. But we continued our regular times of prayer and praise.

When we first began to sing and pray, my cellmates ridiculed me. One of them had heard only the poisonous teachings of communism so she strenuously opposed me. But the Spirit of the Lord was working, and before long they had no words to oppose me. Gradually their attitude changed, and they would say, "Venerable Wen, please pray again for God to save us from this place—and soon."

I prayed together with them, and God did let them see his work, for they were released before me.

57

The Sighing of the Prisoner

Seventeen months cannot always be called a long time. If one were having an enjoyable time, seventeen months would seem all too short. But in jail, half starved, weak and ill through many hardships, besides being continually cursed and reviled and threatened with death or worse, then it is much too long. So I wish to speak now of physical life in prison.

Clothing, food, a place to live and some degree of activity are essential in any human life. While in prison I was not able to add to my small stock of clothing, and for all seventeen months I had only the one outfit I wore when I entered prison, besides a long padded garment and some extra garments my daughter-in-law succeeded in getting to me, so that I could change and wash the clothing I had worn for so long.

The long padded garment I divided into two parts. The upper part I kept for myself; the lower part I made into a short jacket for a young woman who was sentenced to jail for fifteen years, and who had no warm clothing. Her home was in Yun Fu. She was imprisoned for being a landowner, and had no one in Deqing to visit her or provide for her. She was made to do hard labor outdoors, although she had only one thin suit. The guards and overseers had no mercy on her.

Part of her work was to carry the food and water to other prisoners. One day when she brought our food to us she was shivering with cold and her lips were purple, so I secretly slipped this garment to her. Soon she risked danger coming back to thank me. She quoted a proverb, "In all the world how many poor are there who can give to the rich? How much less do people in prison show kindness to other prisoners!" With feelings of true sympathy and affection, tears streamed from her eyes and from mine.

I said, "I hope you will believe in Jesus and be saved."

She answered, "You believe in Jesus. Why are you here? Why does he not save you from this place?"

It was hard to answer her, but I finally said, "This is a world of suffering, and I must accept and endure whatever he permits."

Each day we were given two meals. Each meal consisted of one small bowl of rice. We had no green vegetables; still less did we have meat of any kind. To go with the rice, we had only a few bits of salted and sun-dried greens, or a few salted black beans. We ate all they gave us but were never fully satisfied. We were always hungry but not hungry enough to die.

While the United States of America was at war with North Korea, the Communists began to agitate for the helping of Communist Korea and the opposing of America, so they cut down our ration of food an ounce more or less each meal. We were given one cup of water for drinking in the morning and another cup in the evening, and two cups a day for cleansing purposes.

My fellow prisoners all had body lice and seemed to accept them as unavoidable. Of course I got them too; then began my war with lice and I spent much time catching them. I finally persuaded an old lady who had once been wealthy to remove the cover off her infested bedding, take it outside, and shake off all she could—under guard, of course—then try to capture any that were left. Then I unraveled the top of my hose to get thread to sew up her bed cover.

The first three nights in jail I slept on the damp floor of earth, and was thankful for my oiled sheet. My spot was directly opposite the doorway, the door being simply several large upright posts set in sockets, barred on the outside, with wide cracks between the posts. At first my bedding was warm enough, but when the time called the "Great Cold" came, the winter wind was so cold it was like a sharp file scraping at my flesh.

My three cellmates had made themselves better beds. They urged me not to sleep on the cold, damp ground.

I said, "How can I manage? Do you mean to say I should bring a bed from my home?"

They said, "Out beside the toilet there is a pile of boards from an old house. When you are allowed to go to the toilet, just steal a few boards and slip them in."

"But," I said, "I am a Christian. How can I steal things?" They said, "We'll steal them for you, and you can use them until they give you a bed. Tomorrow when we go to the toilet we'll each bring in a board for you."

"That won't do," I said. "If you steal for me, it is the same as if I stole them. That is against the rules, and it would just add to my crimes."

At once, they each took a board from their own beds and gave them to me to sleep on. Even though not wide enough nor long enough, it was much better than sleeping on the ground. Next day when they came in from the toilet each one had a piece of board under her clothes. I still did not wish to accept them lest it get them into trouble.

After many days one of the younger prisoners was compelled to go out to hard labor as part of her punishment. When she came back she brought a very good board that had been given to her. She used it for her own bed and gave her old boards to me. So I built a foundation with a few brick-bats, two boards across them and two lengthwise, and with the other boards laid on the foundation I had a comfortable bed which I used for most of the seventeen months. I was moved to other cells five times, as the Communists were suspicious of small groups who were together long enough to become friendly. But I took my complete bed with me except once when the new cell had a crude bed in it.

At set times every morning, the door was opened, and we were called to go to the outdoor toilet, under the watchful eye of the guard. This was used by both men and women. A vessel was also provided for use in the cell, which was very necessary when anyone was ill; it was our job to empty it.

About the fourth or fifth month after I was imprisoned, I got a severe cold with high fever. After a few days the fever subsided, but the glands below the right ear, extending to the shoulder, swelled to the size of two eggs, and a row of eight smaller ones like beads such as officials used to wear, appeared across my neck and chest. Though not too painful, the right side of my body was very uncomfortable.

Because of my high fever I grew weaker with no desire to eat or to talk. There was no doctor to be had, and I had no medicine. I wondered if sulphadiazine might help, so I wrote this name on a paper and gave it with five dollars to the guard and asked him to buy it for me at the hospital.

He yelled at me with vile curses and said, "Who is willing to be your slave? Who would go to such trouble to buy medicine for you? We ought to have killed you long ago."

At that he tore the paper to bits and threw the money back through the narrow slits between the doorposts. I began to cry aloud, not because of pain but for emotional weakness. I cried much for several days, and my fever remained high. Then I realized that I had allowed my troubles and my suffering to overwhelm me and hedge me in.

I cried to God and said, "Forgive my lack of trust. How can I allow myself to be defeated by the cruel cursing of this evil person? Heal my body and my spirit, and make me to praise thee with all my heart."

After I had prayed, I rose and ate my food. Though it was very poor it gave me a little strength. Into the cell where I now was, the sun shone for a little while, so I sat with the sunshine on my neck. I feared the swollen glands would become ulcerated. Thanks to God this did not happen, though they did not entirely heal at that time.

After the intense heat of the summer of 1952, an epidemic of dysentery broke out and spread rapidly among the prisoners. More than one hundred died. I also became ill again with high fever and intense pain. My earnest prayer was, "Lord, I don't want to die in this place, lest they gloat over my death and say 'The death of this stubborn person will be a warning to a hundred of her followers and make them afraid to say they are Christians'; thus thy name would be dishonored. Let me have one day of freedom, then I will die gladly."

The illness was so severe that my intestines hemorrhaged continually, and for five days I ate nothing. I drank two cups of water daily, which they were kind enough to heat. Then for some days I had water in which rice had been cooked, and after ten days more I had unpolished rice, which gave me some energy.

In prison, like Robinson Crusoe, I had no calendar to mark time. Time dragged wearily by. We did not know the day or the month, I had no news of the world, I knew nothing of my family. One of my cellmates could tell the day of the lunar month by the moon, so I took some of my history paper and marked twelve squares for a year, each square divided for days. I made one calendar for the lunar year and one for the Western calendar. In this way I knew when the Sabbath came, when my fellow Christians would be worshiping God, and I observed the day as best I could.

Inside, the cell was dark and damp, a most appropriate dwelling for mosquitoes. They came in swarms with continual buzzing, not loud but very annoying. Many were anopheles that do not buzz but are the carriers of that dread disease, malaria, and the more dangerous because noiseless. All our homes had mosquito nets over their beds, but it was not so in prison. So I took half the cover of my bedding pad and made a sort of tent. My cellmates did the same and we slept in peace—for a while.

However, when the guard came in at midnight to call me for brainwashing, he saw our bednets and angrily tore them down. So I could only pray God to close the mouths of these enemies, even as he closed the mouths of lions in Daniel's day, and make this a wonder to people. (Later, I was restored from this hopeless despair and given my freedom, I went to a hospital for a thorough examination. I asked the doctor to examine my blood for malaria germs, which he did and found no trace of that disease. I marveled, rejoicing and praising God.)

At one period during my long-drawn-out trial, I feared that, while sitting in jail, my body would lose its strength, so I began to take regular exercises. Soon my cellmates said, "She doesn't just 'sit jail' (Chinese idiom); she dances jail." It helped to keep me warm in winter, so they soon joined me. Before long the guard caught us at it and yelled at us like a lioness that had lost her cub. He so frightened the prisoners that they sat down in the proper manner. One of them said to me, "You have been in prison more than a year. Do you insist on taking exercises in the hope of shortening your life in jail?"

I said, "I must keep my body strong."

My time in jail was divided into three periods: the first ten months was a time of loathing and discontent, trials, investigation, brainwashing. During the day, I had to write a history of my life—frank and open like the white of an egg. At night, I could not sleep because I was continually called out for brainwashing at midnight or the third watch, so that I had no energy, lost heart, and was always ready to drop to the ground.

Then came a time when I was required to do handwork for the police and soldiers. Though I disliked doing this work, it was better than to be idle. One day, seeing I was capable, the magistrate said, "If we were to open an industrial school here, would you be willing to act as manager or director?"

I replied, "I can't say that I could manage such a school, but the clothes I am wearing I made, and you know the work you require me to do."

Even though they did not start such a school in the jail, they brought me all kinds of work to do. I made clothes, mended old garments, sewed cloth feet in their socks, mended cloth shoes, and made cloth soles for shoes.

Then they brought me old sweaters to rip up and re-knit. They gave me no knitting needles, so I found a piece of bamboo and whittled out a pair with bits of broken glass. Altogether I knitted five sweaters, two pairs of trousers, two pairs of socks, and two of gloves, besides mending many others. When the judge asked me to do this work, I told him I could not see to do it, as they had taken my glasses away. He took off his own and said, "See if you can see with these." I could see very well, and he gave them to me to keep as he could get another pair.

Near the end of my imprisonment, after the judge had completed the many details of examining my case, he ordered the guard not to lock me up, and I was treated with more leniency. I was to go out and in at will, as he was sure I would not try to escape. Then I was given outside work, carrying water, laundry, and garden work. During this time I was permitted water for a bath since I carried it for myself—a great luxury after months without a bath.

Postscript to Chapter 57

Just as we were translating this portion of her narrative Mrs. Li complained of sudden pain in her head, of failing eyesight, and of dizziness. The emotional strain of reliving these experiences caused cerebral hemorrhage. She soon passed into a coma, and died in the hospital in a few hours. With some help from her friend Mrs. Yue, I completed the translation from her Chinese manuscript.

Not long before this, an incident occurred which she did not include in her manuscript. I copy from notes I made as she told me when in Hong Kong:

> A woman of seventy-five years from the Shen village was believed to have some gold. She was brought to the jail and put in the same room with Mrs. Li. The Communists demanded gold. She said. "I have none." They took her out and beat her with clubs until she produced some gold. This was not enough, and they demanded more. She denied having more. They took her out for another beating, taking Mrs. Li and certain others out to see it as a warning. After another beating, another denial. Then they continued beating, calling for confession and beating until the woman died.
>
> "This is what may happen to you if you do not confess your sins against the People's Government," they said to Mrs. Li.
>
> "After this," she told me, "in every prayer, I said, 'Lord, when it comes to my time to die, let them shoot me or cut off my head, but please do not let them beat me to death.'"

—*Rose A. Huston*

58

Brainwashing

The greatest fear of the Communists is secret meetings of small groups, and they are very severe in suppressing them if discovered. Immediately prior to my imprisonment the authorities had learned that four members of the orphanage staff, including myself, as I wished to buy Leghorn chickens for the orphanage, wished to go to Canton at the same time. They supposed, therefore, that we had planned a secret meeting, probably with others in Canton, to oppose the Reds.

So they had no alternative but to arrest us and upset all our "evil plans" by putting us in jail. This would also frustrate the plans of any others expecting us. All through these events, and also at other times, we often heard their slogan: "Da dao! Da dao!" (Beat down! Knock over!)

We four belonged to the Lord. We were to be the objects of the hatred of the world. Now this was perfectly evident and logical. We were happy to accept this status.

Up to this time the Communists had nothing whatever for which to accuse me or to punish me. They had not one shred of testimony of any misdemeanor or breach of the law against me. From the lips of those called to witness against me, they found it impossible to frame a charge. When they wanted to learn the truth of anything, they called me to them; then after questioning and cross-examining, I was taken back to the cell.

Everyone who came to brainwash me was young, not yet twenty. They were ill-fitted for this responsibility; they perhaps knew only a half of what they ought to have known. They were uneducated young men who did not even know how to write the Chinese characters for their reports.

Sometimes they came during the day, but more often they sent for me when

I was asleep. Often at midnight I would be awakened by someone rudely shouting my name, ordering me to come out. By that time I was not in good health. I was nervous and easily disturbed, so that a sudden shout caused my heart to beat furiously. Then I would become dizzy.

About four o'clock on the day I was taken to jail, the jailer led me out to a small room. In this room was a young person, less than twenty years old, who asked my name, age, and occupation. He was crude, coarse, and discourteous. I soon saw that he had little education and was not at all expert in writing Chinese characters.

"I have come to ask you in what ways you have broken the law," he said. "Just tell me this. I know you have broken laws. I am not a stupid brute. Tell me."

He did not speak very clearly, so I did not know how to answer him. (*Fan ge ming*, "counter-revolution," in poorly spoken Mandarin could be mistaken for "breaking all laws.")

Then he said, "You tell me, and I'll listen."

"But I don't know what you mean by 'breaking every law,' so I can't tell you anything."

"What you have done you certainly know. Just tell that, and it will be satisfactory."

So I said, "I have cared for children, cooked for them, made clothes and mended them; I have taught school as well as telling about Jesus Christ."

He was very angry and said, "You truly are as stupid and stubborn as a pig. People say that one who opposes the revolution will never admit it. This is absolutely true. Now will you talk or not?"

"I repeat, I do not understand what you mean when you say I am a *fan ge ming*. Please explain to me. Just what is the meaning of *fan ge ming*?"

"*Fan ge ming*," he said, "is reaction or opposition to the Communist revolution. All who are sitting in jail are guilty of opposing the Communist revolution."

"Surely not," I insisted.

"Why not? A murderer is a counter-revolutionary. [They had accused me of killing many babies.] To destroy the social order of communism is counter-revolutionary; to oppose communism is counter-revolutionary. Think seriously about yourself. Haven't you resisted the laws of the People's Republic?"

"Now that you have explained," I said, "I positively deny being a reactionary. I have not committed murder. I have not destroyed the People's Republic, nor have I opposed or broken their social customs."

Gloating, he said, "If you are not a reactionary, why were you arrested and put in prison?"

I replied, "I have not revolted against the revolution. Neither do I know why I was arrested and imprisoned."

He slapped the table angrily and said, "You stubborn, rebellious person! You keep insisting you have broken no laws. You ought to sit in jail. Sit there until you die."

He then called the warden to come and take me back to my cell.

Several days passed. Again a young fellow came and called me out. He ordered me to tell him how the Christian church came into China.

"I am not able to tell you this," I said. "I have never heard how the Christian church first came into China."

He was very indignant and said, "Everyone says you are a most stubborn person and refuse to talk. No mistake about that! You are a Chinese and you are a Christian. Do you mean to say that you do not know how the church and imperialism came into China?"

"But those are two different things," I said. "They cannot possibly be classed as one and the same thing."

"The church is imperialism; imperialism is the church," he insisted.

With some spirit I said, "You are mistaken."

He glared fiercely at me with wide-open eyes when I said this, but he said nothing, so I continued, "The church is the church. Imperialism is imperialism. They are entirely different things, so how can you say that the church is imperialism and imperialism is the church?"

"How not connected—why not the same?" he insisted. "Everybody says the Imperialists used the church to gain entrance to China."

I said, "Please pay strict attention to this saying: the words *li yong* (to use for your own advantage) do not apply to this matter. That imperialism sent or forced the church into China for its own advantage is not true. The very center and heart of the church is Jesus Christ and not greed for power or wealth. If people use the name of the church in a bad cause they are not true representatives of the church. If you are willing to learn more about the Christian church, I shall be glad to teach you. Jesus Christ is the founder of the Christian church."

He shouted angrily: "Nonsense! Don't talk rubbish to me!" It was as though I had thrown filth on him. He then called the prison guard to take me back to my cell.

Another time, the night guard suddenly called me from my sleep and led me out through the darkness to a room with several tables used for instruction classes.

A young man sitting there said, "I have been sent here by the Yun Fu magistrate especially to learn from you just what you have done. Wang Ming Yuan (the pastor at Luoding) has been killed. Jin Yong Heng has been imprisoned in Dong An (another name for Yun Fu). They have charged you with acting with them, ordering them to be faithful to the Imperialists."

I said nothing, then he urged me to speak. At last I said, "Tong Zhi (Comrade)…"

"I am not your Comrade. You are a *fan ge ming*. How can you call me Comrade?" Again I said nothing.

"You don't need to call me by any title. Just tell me how you have been faithful to imperialism."

I said, "It is the middle of the night. When a person is rudely awakened from sound sleep by loud shouting, her soul and spirit seem to leave her, and she seems to be in a bad dream. How can you expect me to discuss such important things? How can one be calm and composed?"

Then he said, "I will give you a few minutes to calm yourself and think a little."

When he called me again I said, "Jesus told his disciples to be faithful to him and to his gospel and he would give them a crown of life. I continually encourage myself and other fellow workers and Christians to do this. I do not fear or hesitate to labor or suffer for the gospel, so wherever I have been I have proclaimed the gospel of the true God. I have urged people to believe in Jesus as their Savior."

"You don't need to tell me those things. I simply want to know in what ways you were faithful to imperialism. Why do you not make even the slightest mention of that?"

I said, "Because of him who saved me from death by dying on the cross. I am faithful to him, and beside this aim I have no other. Everyone must die. And after death…"

There he cut me off and said, "I did not call you to preach the gospel to me. Now I ask you, what special business did the Imperialists give you to do? How were you to accomplish what they wanted done? This is what I want to know. Tell me this, and it will be satisfactory."

"But I do not know what imperialism is; nor do I know any Imperialist. Tell me what to say."

"You really make me angry enough to kill. You pretend to be stupid. You act like…All right, I'll tell you. What important responsibilities and instructions did they give you, such as ways to oppose communism; and how do you go about doing it?"

I said, "When Miss Stewart was preparing to leave Deqing she put that group of orphans into my care, to teach and instruct them well. She gave into my hands some money and articles to be used in caring for them. She also gave me some responsibilities in managing the church organization of Deqing. The session of the Deqing Church also asked me to help with the testimony of the gospel and the arrangements pertaining to it. So in addition to managing the orphanage, I did some of the church work. I went to the hospital and talked to the patients and endeavored to teach the prisoners at the jail about Jesus."

He said, "I don't want to talk about that. I want you to tell me what the American Imperialists commanded you to do for them."

I thought a moment, then said, "I do not recall anything they asked me to do for them personally."

He very quietly said, "Jin Yong Heng said that you told him that the American Imperialists said he must be an enemy to communism even unto death. You are simply the hidden wise person, the power behind them, giving them orders as to what they should do."

I said, "If the Americans told Jin Yong Heng to oppose communism, you should ask him. He will tell you the truth. The Americans gave no instructions of this kind to me. Therefore I cannot speak of it."

"You are the wise one. Why don't you tell what you know?"

I said, "I had the responsibility of sending the evangelists to the various places, and sent their salaries to them at the proper time. The evangelists simply preached the gospel that Jesus gave his own life to save others. Jesus commands us to be faithful in proclaiming his Word. He did not command us to be faithful in those things that oppose the doctrines he taught. Therefore, we must be very careful to differentiate in these matters."

He said, "You stubborn, deluded person. You don't know the severity of the Communist Party. You must be taught how severe they are."

As he spoke, he strode out of the room, while I sat waiting to meet some of the severity of the Reds. But I did not see him again. The guard then took me back to the cell. It was eight o'clock in the morning.

59

My Furnace of Affliction

How very many times I endured such examinations and brainwashing during the year 1952 I cannot say. One day at 3 p.m. the guard took me out of my cell, and I was met by a young fellow whom I had never seen.

He said, "I have been sent here from the Hai Jian magistrate. Lu Yuan Bao of Fengcun has been arrested. He testified that you often went to Hong Kong to meet with Americans. Now you must willingly admit this, otherwise we must kill you. I was sent to ask, Why did you go to Hong Kong? When were you there? Whom did you see? What instructions or responsibilities did they give you? When you returned to Deqing, how did you carry out their orders?"

They continued this questioning until the next afternoon at three o'clock. All that time I had nothing to eat. All they asked me were very simple questions. If they had believed me, it could all have been finished in half an hour. They said I was lying, hiding important things, that I was stupid and crafty; that I told only unimportant things and refused to tell what was important, that I did not have enough courage. They decided that I was worthy of death and that I could not hope for clemency or forgiveness.

Afterward, he changed his manner and said, "If you are not willing to answer these questions orally, you may write your replies on paper."

So he brought a table, pen and paper, and I wrote in full detail all that had occurred on my six trips to Hong Kong, and all in chronological order. Again, he declared it was not right, and he certainly could not accept it.

He accusingly pointed his finger at me and said, "You are a person in great danger. You went to Hong Kong and were deluded with imperialistic ideas. You have turned against the Communist Party and have concocted a plan to oppose us. And you have actually begun to carry out those plans by disobeying the laws. But you do not even mention such things. I shall give you one more opportunity; think well and seriously about this. You must not omit the least thing. Everything must be confessed satisfactorily. Otherwise you need not think that you will ever get out of jail; without a doubt you will be killed."

I sat there and thought and thought again. I really could not recall one thing I had done to break their laws. I did recall some things that had occurred to me at odd times, so I took the pen and wrote again.

While I was writing he sat and kept saying things to ridicule and frighten me, trying to get me confused. He wanted to trouble me and weary my spirit, to disturb me so that I would make mistakes and unintentionally confess that I had rebelled against the Communist regime. He also insinuated that I had indulged in exceedingly improper and immoral conduct.

As I kept writing very carefully I was also praying, but he still supposed that I had *bu gou tan bai* (not enough egg white, that is, frankness). He said again and again that I was stubborn and was purposely writing all this in rebellion against the Communists. Though he really was very angry, he kept his self-control, in order to compel me to tell what he wanted to hear.

So he said, "Wen Wei Zhen, your stubbornness will do you no good. It will merely add to your troubles with the Communist government. By this time you should begin to realize how very broad and magnanimous and how patient the Communists have been with you, to give you one more chance to change your attitude and confession. But I tell you, you must not write again the same things you have written."

Having said this he went away.

I closed my eyes and quietly thought, but I could not remember one thing I had said or done to oppose them. When he came in again, he noticed me sitting with closed eyes.

He took a stick and beat on the table and said, "Why are you not writing?"

I did not answer.

"Write quickly and finish, then you may go and sleep," he said. Again I said nothing.

Then he gave me a push, saying, "What are you doing? I told you to write."

I said very fiercely, "Don't you know how men should treat women? Why did you push me?"

"I was afraid you were asleep and I wanted to wake you," he said. "I told you freely to admit, without delay, what you have done. Then you may soon rest and sleep."

"I will not write," I said. "You already want to kill me. Why should I write again? You have made up your mind to kill me. Why weary myself to write any more, since you do not believe me? What I have written is absolutely true and according to facts, and I have not held back anything. And, besides, I must speak with Jesus, and pray him to receive my soul when you kill me, and to receive me in peace into heaven where I shall never again suffer your ill treatment and persecution."

Then I bowed my head and closed my eyes.

"Let me give you something to read," he said. "Perhaps it will help you to recall the things you did in Hong Kong."

"I will not look at it," I said. "And I will not write any more. If you want something to read, then read what I have written."

But he took a sheet of paper and stuck it before my face.

"I must give you something to read from your church monthly magazine. It is true."

I repeated what I said before, that I would not read it. In this paper was written the testimony of Wang Ming Yuan, also about the prayer of Song Pei De. In my heart I wanted to read it, because they were Chinese in our church and they were the president and vice president of our church council, including both Chinese and Americans.

Again he said, "You need not be afraid to read it; it has nothing in it to harm you."

So I opened my eyes and took the paper. It told of a meeting in Hong Kong in which Pastor Song had prayed that President Chiang[19] might be blessed with restored health and restored to his own land. It was used by Wang Ming Yuan as testimony against Song. It was a very short sentence, yet it was regarded as intensely rebellious against the People's Republic of China.

He commanded me to write in the same way about what had occurred in Hong Kong. Then it suddenly dawned on me that no matter what was said or done, it must be viewed through Communist-colored glasses and heard through their special hearing aids. So with this new idea, I thought of what I should write. I thought of the prayer of Song Pei De. At that time such a prayer was the duty of every Christian in praying for his country's leader. I had no idea at that time that it could be construed as a rebellious thought or act. So it was not surprising that I was accused of hiding certain facts and not being frank and open.

I sat and thought a while. I had already written all this at least twice. Perhaps I should write it in this new vein, adding Pastor Song's prayer as though seen through Communist eyes. So I wrote again of the meetings of our Chinese-American Church Council to discuss the registration of our churches with the government and continued thus:

"The Rev. Peter Song opened the meeting in Jiulong, Hong Kong, with prayer, in which he asked God to bless Generalissimo Chiang Kai-shek with restored health; that he might be able to return soon to his native land, and that the people might be blessed with peace.

"When he prayed thus, I felt he was praying for our native land, which is our duty as Christians. I did not regard it as being in rebellion against the People's Republic, though in the Communist view it might be so regarded.

"During the discussion we naturally spoke of the possible future of churches as planned by the new government. For instance, Communists proclaim materialism; they say there is no God. But we believe there is a God; we love, serve and worship God and proclaim the gospel of Jesus Christ.

"In regard to registering with the government, there are important principles that Christians must remember: God is Creator of heaven and earth and all things, and Jesus Christ is the only Savior from sin. We should pray for the grace of God to keep all Christians faithful to him.

"The Church on earth cannot acknowledge the authority of earthly kingdoms over it in spiritual things; nor should we register under the atheistic People's Republic.

"In case the Communists forcibly take over church properties, pastors might engage in some legitimate business and keep in touch with the Christians and encourage them. Christians should show a spirit of love and friendliness, and pray for those who may be in trouble."

I wrote all in detail and gave it to the one in charge of me at the time. He admitted that what I had written was satisfactory, then led me back to my cell. I had gone through twelve long hours of weariness and hunger, contempt and persecution, reviling, and cursing. My fellow prisoner—and fellow sufferer because she was a landowner—had not slept, but sat up and waited until I came back. She was weeping for joy as she said, "Now my heart is at peace."

On another night the guard yelled, "Wen Wei Zhen, come out!" and led me to where we met the court judge and a woman inspector, Liu Wen Xiao. I knew Liu because she came every day and stood just outside our door to torment us by talking as if to herself: "Yesterday we killed so-and-so; tomorrow such-and-such a prisoner will be killed," and on and on with gruesome details until we were utterly weary of her and her harangue. When she came this time she began to speak in a natural voice, and utter dislike rose up in me.

When the judge saw me, he said: "Wen Wei Zhen, old as you are, you still rebel, break laws, and join the band of revolutionaries. Now you should tell us what other persons were with you in this rebel band; tell us who are your officers and leaders, and what things the group has done."

"I am not a revolutionary," I said. "And I am not a member of any revolutionary party. I am simply a person who believes in Jesus Christ and bears witness as his follower. My work is for the Christian church."

The officer then said, "You are a cunning, deceitful, and stubborn rebel. Unless we give you a chance to observe very severe, rigorous treatment on others, you are too stubborn and clever to tell us the truth. Without such treatment as Mao Zedong advises for such women, you will not speak. Or should we be very indulgent and benevolent and give you another opportunity to tell us everything? Act like a wise person, then we can point you away from these rebellious ideas toward…"

"But I have never been a traitor to my own country, so why do you call me a rebel?"

"This is not your country," he said, "and we cannot allow you to sell this country. Taiwan is your country. No, no, no! Taiwan is not your country. There is coming a day when we shall liberate Taiwan. Then we shall see where you will go."

I asked my own heart for the truth, then said, "I have never been a rebel against my own country. Since I believe in Jesus, it certainly is my duty to love and serve him who died to save me and all who believe on him. He told his followers, 'Fear not them which can kill the body but are not able to kill the soul.'"

The officer interrupted me and said, "Every time we call you for an interview you begin to talk about the doctrines and teachings of the church. I can see that you do not speak with white of egg (frankness)."

"The words that I speak are from the Holy Bible," I said, "and they are most important. The Bible tells of God's holiness, power, justice, goodness, and truth. It tells us of the very important relationship between God and man, and between man and man. It teaches that we should love even our enemies and pray for those who persecute us. We may not worship any but the one true God. Also, if men forbid us to worship the God we love and Jesus our Savior, we must act as did Daniel and his three friends, who did not fear the king's command, so were thrown into a fiery furnace rather than worship an image the king had made."

Suddenly the officer ran to me and tried to burn my hand with a lighted cigarette. I instinctively drew back my hand, and he said, "You say those men did not fear the fire. Why did you draw back your hand?"

"It was involuntary," I replied. "My nerves felt the pain and instinctively drew back, not by any thought of fear."

"Can't you understand," he said, "that when you teach these things you are simply trying to influence others against communism? Such talk will tear communism to pieces and stir up the people to oppose us. This is clearly revolutionary propaganda and conduct. It is rebellion against the government. You must be wise, you must look at your own mistakes, you must face your sins. Be sincere and frankly confess. Don't be so self-willed and obstinate, and you may not suffer so much bitterness. For us to take your life is nothing, merely like blowing off a speck of dust. You come out here with the idea that one sentence of yours can overthrow a hundred words of our teachings. We only hope you will change your thinking, move yourself, do something. Wen Wei Zhen, you are not a stupid person. Think!"

When he had finished his speech he called the woman officer to take me back to the cell. It was the dark period just before the break of dawn. Very weary, I lay down and tried to sleep. The following afternoon the woman Liu came, stood at the door of my cell, and yelled, "Wen Wei Zhen, are you on your knees praying? You should be praying to your Jesus to come and take down the bars of your cell door."

She came every day to chatter offensively at our door, so I said nothing.

"Wen Wei Zhen!" she yelled again. "Come to the door; I have something to ask you." So I went obediently.

"Why were you praying to Jesus to come and break down the bars and let you go home?"

I said nothing.

"Why don't you speak?"

"Yesterday the judge told me not to be stubborn, so I will not contradict you or argue."

"I command you to pray right now and ask Jesus to come and let you out. I want to see if he really can open your iron cage."

I replied, "The Bible tells us about two men, Paul and Silas, who were beaten and put into prison; at midnight they prayed and praised God, so that all in the prison heard them. Suddenly an earthquake opened the prison doors and the prisoners were freed. But I shall not pray for that kind of thing. If I were to pray in the presence of God's enemies just to please them, God would not hear me. If someone were to break the bars of the door and escape, you would suspect me of doing it by prayer and you would certainly kill me. I may be stupid, but not so stupid as that."

Liu shouted, "I'd like to kill you. I want to kill you and your God together."

"God is a living God and has power to punish your sin," I replied.

"I'd like to kill you right now," she shouted angrily.

"You are at liberty to kill me if you wish," I said. Then I sang, "Lord, Thy power to protect is everlasting."

I sang so loud and long that my cellmates laughed heartily. Liu was furious, shook her finger at me, and shouted, "You're crazy! You're crazy!" and went away angry.

60

A Proselyte Communist Judge

One day the judge had me called out for another interview. He brought a chair and asked me to sit down, saying he wished to have a talk.

"Judge," I said, "will you please permit me to answer you in the Mandarin language?"

"Certainly," he said. "That will be more convenient." So without an interpreter I was much more at ease.

He wished to give me a psychological explanation of the first and second chapters of Genesis and said, "I have explained this to many Roman Catholic nuns and persuaded them to reform." He hoped to reform me in the same way and change my faith.

"Before Chairman Mao found me, I believed as you do and thought I was right. I have been changed for three or four years. I hope you will not be so obstinate. Think earnestly about your problems; then your future should be good and very prosperous."

I sat and listened "with clean open ears" for a whole hour without arguing or antagonizing him. As he left, he handed me a letter from my daughter-in-law. She urged me to confess my faults and get the favor of the officers so that affairs might be settled satisfactorily. In the letter she had enclosed five dollars. I had been in prison for a year and had no money. When I read the letter and saw the money I wept, for I lacked many necessary things.

After about ten days the judge told Liu to bring me out to him again. This time she was not so abusive and impudent as before but spoke in very courteous ladylike tones.

"Wen Wei Zhen," she said, "your language is that of a highly educated person, but unfortunately you have gone off on the wrong road and entered the wrong door. Even now, however, it is not too late to reform."

When the judge saw me he said, "Have you thought things through clearly? According to the directives of Chairman Mao I shall not kill you. We shall give you another chance to reform and come over to our side as soon as you clear up your mistakes. You have been our enemy. Now get rid of your problems and we can free you at once."

"Judge," I said, "I have written my whole life history honestly and frankly from the time I was five years old. I have wasted much time, paper, and money writing it several times, fifteen or more pages on each occasion. You never once accepted it, but instead I was cursed and reviled. I have no heart to waste my energy by writing it all again. I have fully prepared myself for execution. You may kill me at your convenience."

"But I already told you we would not kill you; and I didn't command you to write it again. All I want is to talk with you."

In a very friendly manner he then talked with me for several hours, asking questions about my whole life, and I answered all frankly. At last he said, "You are standing here, according to what you have said, on the side of imperialism. Now, if you will just stand over on the other side, in the light of communism, can you not see that you were wrong in all you did? You certainly cannot deny that you were a counter-revolutionary and an enemy to the People's Republic and its laws. In all the life history you have written, in all the letters you wrote and in what you have told me today, in all these things you have been a rebel and a law-breaker.

"But at the time you didn't realize it. You didn't know. You were always ready to object and resisted stubbornly. You acted as though we had arrested and imprisoned you illegally; as though we should free you and send you home with firecrackers and a band playing. I speak truthfully; you resisted too strongly, like tea too strong to drink. Your words and even your thoughts were against communism. At every opportunity you rebelled and held to your old beliefs.

"Now I shall give you a few minutes to meditate quietly. Then if you think I have spoken the truth, we shall continue the conversation."

This said, he went out.

When he came in again, he carried a roll of paper in his hand. He sat down and said, "Have you thought things through?"

I said, "I have not thought things through. I don't quite know whether it is because I am too stupid and slow to think this through, or because you have tried to use your law to put me in jeopardy, like a boomerang."

"Again you talk the same way," he said.

I said, "It is clearly written in your laws that citizens have freedom of religion. But you insinuate that I should not believe as I do. You urge me to cast off and forsake my faith, to cover it up, to bury it. But if one does not have a clear-cut definite faith, then nothing will be clear or logical."

"Yes, that is true," he said. "We do have laws for religious freedom and we observe these laws. If we did not, we should have killed you long ago. We have not forbidden nor hindered your religious activities. Is not that proof that we permit freedom of religion?"

I wanted to say, "You Communists occupied our churches and other property and you imprisoned and killed our evangelists and pastors," but I decided that since these things were in the past it was useless to mention them. So I said nothing.

He assumed the attitude of a cat torturing a rat and proceeded to ask about what I had suffered and what things were hard to bear while in prison. I simply "sewed up my mouth."

Seeing that I was not talking, he got up greatly agitated, and paced back and forth before me with hands behind his back. Finally he sat down and began again to speak to me.

"Wen Wei Zhen," he said soothingly, "we are not surprised at the things you did in the past. You simply did not know or understand the aims of the American Imperialists. Now if you will simply acknowledge those mistakes, the People's Communist Republic will treat you with great benevolence. I myself was once just as you are now. Those who would work for the new regime must go through these experiences. There are no born Communists. There are no Chinese-born Communists. All are proselytes. And there is not one who has not made mistakes. You need have no fear. Simply imagine yourself in the position of a Communist and look at your former life and actions with Communist-colored eyes. Cast off and bury your former anti-Communist ideas; frankly and fully confess past wrongs, both your own and those of others; write them all with your own hand and give it to me."

As he spoke he gave the roll of paper to me and told Liu Wen Xiao to take me back to my cell.

Back in my cell I recalled that Wang Ming Yuan had reported in his confessions that the prayer of Rev. Peter Song for Generalissimo Chiang was an act with revolutionary intent. Today the judge had reproved me for "agitating, and encouraging Christians to oppose communism" and said that that was revolutionary. In sending letters to American friends he said I was acting as a special secret agent, being a traitor to my country, telling secrets and important news of China, giving them reasons for being anti-Communist.

I thought of the police who came from Yun Fu and said, "Jin Yong Heng testified that in sending him out to preach you were acting against the government." And the police from Hai Jian reported, "Mr. Lu Wen Bao said you frequently went to Hong Kong to consort with foreigners, to form a revolutionary group."

Now the judge was urging me to look at these things as a loyal Communist sees them; as if in looking at the West with Communist glasses the scene would automatically change color.

At last I tried to stand in the position of a Communist and to view affairs through Red-tinted glasses; to see things as they see them; to use the rude language they always used when scolding me as I described my own actions "before I understood the goodness and greatness of communism or saw the evils of imperialism and of my own religious beliefs."

I tried to imagine my real enemies as my friends. Admit "my father was a robber" (a local proverb), and I, a traitor, opening the door of my own country to the enemy? In writing letters to Americans was I acting as a secret agent, giving aid to the enemy? Instead of using the currency of my own country I used foreign currency, Hong Kong or American, and also used rice instead of local money in barter when at the orphanage. In these ways was I destroying the social economy of New China, lessening the value of its currency? Was I simply an underground agent, a rebel?

I had objected to Communist soldiers coming and taking orphans away for a walk without permission, and I had taught the children not to follow them. I did object to the Reds coming in and taking authority that was not rightfully theirs. They accused me of acting as though I were ruler at the orphanage, and so I had done, because it was my duty and responsibility. I had been accused of belonging to the wealthy class and classed with former officers of the old government, all of whom were killed.

So in this way I acknowledged their right to condemn me for lack of loyalty to the People's Republic of China. When he came for me again I gave it to him as I had written it.

61

Testimony and Release

After several days the judge came again and asked me about some things I had not mentioned. He said he was satisfied with what I had written, and that after my case was completed and I had been acquitted, I could be set free. However, he said there were still many small things that might be brought up against me, such as my involvement with certain personal friends in the past, the fact that my son was studying in America, and my failure to write certain things about my family and relations. All of these matters they considered very important. Fortunately I had no property, and my family were of the working class. God knew that I would come to this day and he had given me this special advantage, a thing that turned out in my favor. The judge did not again bring up the subject of my religious faith.

One day an executive officer came and escorted me out of my cell, and this time he spoke to me very courteously.

"Your case has been finished. I have called you out in order to ask you some questions about religion and your faith. Do not think that I am against freedom of religion or against your particular faith. I wish merely to have a friendly conversation."

When we were outside he said, "Look. There are people planting vegetables."

"Yes, I see them," I said.

"From this it is quite clear that man produces vegetation. Why do you contend that God created all these things?"

"Officer," I said, "planting vegetables and creating vegetables or plant life are two entirely different things. The Bible says, 'In the beginning God created the heavens and the earth.' Before there were any material things in existence, and before there was man, God said, 'Let there be light, water, land,' and they were created. And he said, 'Let the earth bring forth grass, the herb that yields seed, and the fruit tree that yields fruit according to its kind' (Genesis 1:11). And thus were all things created and God saw that it was good. Now man produces everything that he needs by using the vegetation that God created. These men are planting, not creating."

"But," he said, "if man does not create plants how would they have seeds to plant? If man does not create and God does, why do not plants grow naturally for man's use without much labor?"

"When God created man he said to him, 'Of every tree of the garden you may freely eat; but of the tree of the knowledge of good and evil you shall not eat, for in the day that you eat of it you shall surely die' (Genesis 2:16). But man did not believe God's word; he ate of the fruit, and by disobedience became the enemy of God. As part of his punishment the earth was cursed, so that man must labor and suffer and till the ground in order to live and eat, even to this day.

"Do you not see that the wilderness has vegetation growing naturally that has not been planted, nor watered, nor cultivated by man? It is even more beautiful and useful than what man plants. Man must still, according to his God-given duty, plant and cultivate, but the life and blessing still come from God.

"Then there is the question of life. If God did not give life to the seeds of vegetation there would be no growth. Take this pencil, a thing without life; plant it by man's labor expecting a plant to grow from it. You would wait a year, two years, a lifetime, forever, and it would still be simply a pencil. Moreover, it would rot and never become a living plant. From the beginning of the world to the end of time, no man is able to produce life. How could he possibly create life? Therefore, when man plants he depends on God to make it grow and produce fruit."

The officer became impatient with my speech and said, "Now look at all the beautiful and useful things on the earth. Are they not the result of man's labor and industry and invention?"

"True," I said. "They do have important connections with man and his labor. Scientists study and teach such things. They 'bore holes with bowed heads' trying to understand things. We cannot say that man's labor is in vain; man has invented and manufactured many things, but even so he did not create them. He merely makes use of the things that God has created and by the knowledge God gives man he invents all these things. In the same way man's labor produces many things, but it is the living God who created all things."

Just then Liu Wen Xiao came and led me back to the cell. On May 30, 1953, I was given my freedom. The manager of the prison commanded me to go to the

Yamen to receive the personal things the government had confiscated when they took charge of the orphanage.

Among these things was a copy of the Bible. When the man saw it he asked, "What book is that?"

"This is the Holy Bible," I said. "It is the Word of God given to mankind. We who are Christians live according to the teachings of this book."

"Will you read and explain some of it for me?"

"If I do," I said, "then you might say that I am opposed to the government and am breaking the law."

"When I command you to read, then read," he said.

So I opened the Bible and read Genesis 1:1, "In the beginning God created the heavens and the earth." Then I stopped.

"Why don't you read?" he asked.

So I began again and read the whole chapter, then stopped. He took the book, looked at it, and gave it back to me.

"Why do you not see the importance of the book?" I asked. "If I were to lose this book along with everything else, the first thing I would buy would be a Bible. If I did not have this book I should be like a person alone and adrift in heavy seas with wild wind and waves, with no 'pointing-south needle.' I would not know where I was or where I was going and would have no power to move. This book is the compass for my life; it is a compass for every man's life. It tells us the way of life through Jesus the Son of God. It tells us of the love of God for us, and makes us willing to love our fellow men. So I cannot be without it."

"You are still obstinate and will not acknowledge your wrongdoings. All right. I'll let you keep it, and may you cherish it and carry it with you into your coffin."

"That satisfies my mind and heart, and I hope to carry it even to my coffin."

A person who was standing nearby said, "One who has had seventeen months of teaching and brainwashing and still resists, we certainly do not want."

The officer said, "It is her natural disposition to be hard-necked. We should get rid of her [by killing her]."

When I was told that I was to be freed from prison, I asked why I was being set free. When imprisoned I was accused of three misdemeanors or sins: being "a running dog" for Americans; stealing rice, clothing, and other things from the orphanage; and killing eighteen babies.

I had admitted working for and with Americans. Officers had investigated the thefts and found that not I, but the Communist workers they had put in charge, were guilty. As for killing babies, my record showed that only two children had died while I was in charge. After their many months of investigations, the witness of my neighbors and friends, and their own testimony that I had never told them a lie, they declared me *wu xu* (without sin) and set me free.

I refused to leave until they complied with my demand for an official statement in writing that I was freed as an innocent citizen and not as a pardoned criminal.[20]

I then went to the Li ancestral home, which was my legal and rightful home.

62

Life in Canton

When I was freed from prison, my address was 12 Gui Bei Street, Deqing, House of Li. I experienced many difficulties. After the Communist takeover in Guangdong Province they had compiled a complete and very strict census of the population and made special regulations to control all foodstuffs. In 1953 they made special laws for rationing rice and vegetables, so that if a person were not registered in a family, he or she could not buy food and was regarded by Communists as an alien without legal rights as a citizen. They also made it difficult for village people to come to the city. They had to show their census record and their former occupation, with a recommendation from their former employer, in order to have the rights of citizens.

Since I had no proper census record in Deqing, and no resident's transfer certificate for moving elsewhere, I could expect to be regarded as an undesirable and illegal resident and left to starve. I hoped, however, to be permitted to change my citizenship to Canton where Pei Deng, my daughter-in-law, was resident, and the Lord enabled me to do this. But the shadow of my imprisonment followed me through police records. The police notified a certain "Head of Ten Families" in Canton in which group I was living, and they continually spied on me. It was exactly a month and ten days after I got my freedom that I moved to Canton.

Christian friends in Canton were greatly concerned about me after my prison experiences. Mrs. Ao said to Pei Deng, "Though it is hot summer weather your mother is still wearing padded winter garments. She is not in good health and must see a doctor."

Pei Deng had already urged me to do so but I said it was not necessary. So I told them of my illness with dysentery and my promise to the Lord that, if he would heal me and free me so that the Communists could not gloat over my death, I would gladly give up my life at any time.

"While I was in prison," I said, "they made me carry water and do other hard labor, but now that I have become so weak it seems that the Lord may purpose to end my life here soon. I have nothing but a worn-out old body. My son is in America. Mrs. Ao, please help my daughter-in-law in all that concerns my funeral and burial."

Pei Deng tried to silence me by saying, "Who ever heard of a person welcoming death? People may say I was an undutiful daughter, causing you to wish to die!"

Mr. Zhang Min Fu said, "That is true; people would wonder about this. When you came from jail you were sick. This is Satan trying to terrify you, hoping to prevent you from doing God's work again. Will you allow him an easy victory? God has much work for you to do. You must see a doctor."

Next morning, Pei Deng said to me, "Mother, after breakfast I shall go with you to the doctor."

"Good," I said. "For your sake I will go. If I am not healed, I shall know I have not long to live, and you need not fear that people will blame you." My granddaughter, just five years old, was so glad that she ran to tell Mrs. Ao.

When the doctor saw how weak and emaciated I was he said, "Why have you waited until you are in this state? I am really worried about inserting a hypodermic needle, you are so very thin."

"No need to fear," I said. "Remember the proverb, 'A live tiger dares to fight a dead one.' I am as good as dead. If I become well and strong again, God is giving me life."

He then very slowly and carefully inserted the needle, watching closely lest I faint. Later I went back to show him that the swellings on neck and chest had disappeared, to his great surprise. When I went to a hospital for a thorough examination they found that a spot on my lung had healed, my heart was enlarged and weakened, my kidneys were affected, I had hookworms and other parasites in my intestines, my blood was impoverished and pressure was low. I obeyed the doctor's instructions and my health improved.

Truly, God wished me to live for him, and I have lived thirteen years since then in his love and grace. In all I have suffered, I am "more than a conqueror through him who loved me."

During the early days of my residence in Canton I was in touch with a number of other Christians who, like myself, were without "credentials." In order to earn our living we decided to join together to form a company for making soap.

We established this company after much prayer, for there were many details that required police permission. I was employed as cook for the company, hoping thus to avoid the special attention of spies appointed by the police. I spoke directly to the Lord and said, "Lord, it is not that I love the soap-making business, or that I love money; it is simply that I must make a living. If thou art not pleased for me to do this kind of work instead of church work, I trust thee to make a way out for me, even if we must go bankrupt."

Our three-point agreement was:

1) To observe the Sabbath as a day of rest.
2) To give a tithe of our earnings to the Lord's work.
3) Not to charge exorbitant prices, nor to make prices too low to enable us to meet expenses.

During the first four or five months we did passably well, and again I said, "Lord, if it is not thy will for us to continue this business, just allow us to suffer loss."

Some who heard my prayer said, "What merchant ever prayed to fail in business? Truly you are a strange person."

About the seventh or eighth month our soap was not selling well. In the next two months, we four in the company had made barely enough to feed ourselves, so we closed our business and sold all our stock with our equipment. Then we learned that the soap expert we had hired was dishonest and had substituted inferior oil for the good oil we had paid for, and our soap did not sell well because of its poor quality.

But thanks and praise be to God, my son in the United States was from this time onwards able to send money to me for my living, so henceforward I determined to give my whole time and energy to helping Miss Song in her work among our church people.

During the period when I helped Miss Song, who was allowed only the small attic room in the three-story church building, my special work was with children. The numbers grew from twenty or thirty to over 200, and I had to divide them into several groups because of the lack of seating space.

Of course the day came when the police were so worried that they came to investigate and to learn the source of my power over children.

"How much do you pay them for coming?" they asked.

"Not a brass penny," I said.

"Surely you give them picture cards or candy to attract so many?"

"Where would I get money to buy such things for so many?"

"Then how do you get them to come to your meetings? We have meetings for children and command them to come, but they will not come. You certainly have some mysterious power over them. What do you teach them?"

"I teach them the gospel of Jesus Christ and about how God loves them and how their conduct must always be good. That is all I have to give them."

"Well, we don't understand it. But we have to admit that nowadays the police are having much less trouble with the children than formerly."

Nevertheless the day soon came when the meetings were forbidden.

I met with other experiences also. May 1, 1954, was a festival celebrating International Labor Day. It fell on the Lord's Day.

At that time I was working in Western Canton. A young woman came and asked for me and said, "Today is Labor Day, and all engaged in Christian work are required to go about the city and visit in homes proclaiming the greatness and blessings of the People's Communist Government, so Miss Song wishes you to lead the meeting at the church. Your speech must be based on 'Labor.'" She gave me a pamphlet containing materials for the speech and slogans to use.

As I went to the church, I prayed for God's leading and help in the service.

My audience was greatly alarmed when I read Genesis 1:1-2 as the basis for my talk: "In the beginning God created the heavens and the earth." How dare I speak of God creating all things when the Communist teaching is that labor created all things? But I followed the Spirit's leading and God's Word on this most important subject.

"Today is May the first," I began, "a day regarded as very important by the government. So I invite you, brothers and sisters, to study with me the words of the Communists that 'Labor created the world.' Formerly I opposed this statement. I debated and argued with others, even until faces were red and ears tingling. But I did not fully understand these words, nor have I thoroughly studied the Bible on this subject until recently. Then I learned much about the manner in which the world was created, about the laborer who created it, his wisdom, power and authority, and about the beauty and mysteries of the creation. Therefore I speak to you today, May the first, about the fact that the world was created by labor.

"Who was the very first laborer? 'In the beginning God created the heaven and the earth.' The first two chapters of the Bible tell us how this was done. Thousands of years later a man named John, inspired by God, testified in these words: 'In the beginning was the Word, and the Word was with God, and the Word was God. He was in the beginning with God. All things were made through him, and without him nothing was made that was made' (John 1:1-3).

"With marvelous wisdom and order God made light, air, sun, moon, stars, water, and earth during four days. Then in his wonderful plan, he made all kinds of living things, vegetation with its life as a preparation for living birds, fish, and animals. All this was to provide for the life of God's greatest and most wonderful creation, man—man with an eternal soul and a mind to think—man in God's own likeness in knowledge, righteousness and holiness, with dominion over all other creatures.

"However, these first human beings were tempted by Satan, and they disobeyed God. Their natures became evil, bringing sin, sorrow, suffering, and death into the world. The earth also brought forth harmful things, and instead of being a pleasant thing, labor became drudgery and man had to live by 'the sweat of his brow.'

"In creating the world, God was the first laborer. And after his six days of labor, he rested. He put the first man and woman in a garden with instructions to labor there in caring for it. It was God's good will and plan that man should labor, and also to have a weekly day of rest from labor. Even though men labor, using all their energies of body and mind, they are not creating, but simply using the material things and powers that God gave them at creation. In Isaiah 42:5 and 8 we read: 'Thus says God the Lord, who created the heavens and stretched them out, who spread forth the earth and that which comes from it, who gives breath to the people on it, and spirit to those who walk on it…"I am the Lord, that is my name; and my glory I will not give to another."' Therefore the labor of God cannot be credited to man."

After this meeting some said, "Why were you so rash as to speak in the way you did on this important day? That stranger sitting near the door is officially sent to spy upon and report the behavior of the one who speaks."

"Thank you for your concern for me," I replied. "Have no fear. God will take the responsibility."

Afterwards, pastors who had already entered the Three-Self Church Organization and were on the board of managers, came to me in much confusion to criticize and judge me for what I had done. Some said, "She must go and be taught" (be brainwashed). Others said, "She is not a preacher; why do they want her to speak in the church?" Some wished to expel me from church work and sent a letter to church authorities saying I must be sent to the school at the YWCA for instruction by the proper authorities.

At that time I was a volunteer, unpaid worker in the Reformed Presbyterian Church in Canton, so rather than have the church troubled, I was willing to be taught at the Communist school. As I sat there in the school, I realized that everything I saw and all I heard had been instigated by the power and authority of the devil. All was lies, false doctrines, rumors, and gossip that they used as testimony. I hated them bitterly for this, and because of my discouragement and physical weakness I suffered greatly. I could not endure their vehement opposition and rage against the truth. On the advice of a doctor, I asked the church to release me from this work in order to avoid wearing this invisible *cangue* (a heavy wooden collar used in China for punishment, pronounced "kang").

63

Forever Free

I have mentioned earlier that when I moved from Deqing to Canton I went to live with Pei Deng, my daughter-in-law, who was then in that city. Soon, however, she was able to leave Canton with her two children and to go to Hong Kong. Naturally, I would like to have gone there too, but because I had been accused of being a spy for America, and of having connections with the rebels of Taiwan (Formosa), I was not granted the full freedom I needed for travel to Hong Kong. I decided therefore to remain in Canton until the Lord opened the way for me to leave.

One day while I was at my morning watch, a verse from God's Word came definitely to me: "Go to the other side."

At once I said, "Lord, art thou calling me to go to the other side? Where is the other side? If it is Hong Kong, then this must be the exact logical time for me to register for an exit permit. I pray thee to give me clear guidance. Without thee, it certainly will be in vain."

When I had finished my prayer and was reading my Bible, my eyes lit on exactly those words: "Go to the other side."

I was afraid and said, "Lord, give me peace. If thy time has come, calm my heart to see thy wonderful works. If it is from the evil one, help me to be victorious over him and not think of this again."

As soon as I finished praying, I got up and began to prepare my morning meal. Just as I entered the kitchen I saw Zhang Bao Wei carrying a letter in both hands and smiling happily as she said, "Yun Xian Shang, you have a letter."

"Why did the postman come so early today?" I asked.

"Probably the letter came yesterday when Mrs. Hou was not at home, so this morning she opened the mailbox and told me to bring this letter to you."

I opened the letter at once and saw that it was from my niece in Hong Kong. In it she said that my son was greatly worried about how I was able to live, so he had sent a large sum of money for me, but I must go to Hong Kong to receive it. It was to be deposited in the Bank of China in Hong Kong, and afterwards they would send it to me as I drew upon the account.

When I finished reading the letter, I half believed it and half doubted it, so I knelt and prayed again: "Lord, if this is from thee, calm my heart and show me the way I should go, and make my way prosperous as I attend to this."

When Mrs. Mei called to see me, I asked her to pray with me that I might be helped as I went to apply for a permit. She asked why I wanted to go to Hong Kong, so I showed her the letter.

She said, "If you really wish to go, come tomorrow." So she took the letter and showed it to the permit officer, and asked them to return it to me. The next day I received a blank form of application.

This form, I soon discovered, contained the instruction: write a history of the past twenty years of your life.

As soon as I saw this, I knew this one requirement would cause trouble. Actually, my life had been open and aboveboard; I was innocent of any crime. But the Communists had accused me of being a spy and a revolutionary, and I had been imprisoned. Should I write that part of my history? Even if I were to omit that part, the Communists certainly would have the record. If I wrote it they would refuse a permit. If I omitted it they would investigate and would doubt my integrity, and who could know the final result? In either case I would be in trouble.

So I went to see Mrs. Hou, who was ears and eyes for the Reds over Ten Families. She also saw the difficulties involved and hesitated to give an opinion. Thanks to my wonder-working Lord and Shepherd, he opened a way, a good way, for me. Mr. Liang, the officer who granted permits and passports, came to see Mrs. Hou and very naturally she said, "Mr. Liang, Wen Wei Zhen wishes to go to Hong Kong to receive some money that has been sent to her from abroad. She has filled out the application form in which she must write the history of the past twenty years of her life. To write this may make it very difficult for her to get a travel permit; not to write of her imprisonment would also cause trouble. So we ask you to decide whether or not she should write it."

"Write it," he said, and went away.

So I went home and was writing it when Mr. Liang came back to Mrs. Hou and said in a low voice, "Tell Wen Wei Zhen not to write it."

Mrs. Hou came quickly to me and whispered, "Mr. Liang told me to tell you not to write that."

I stood up, held Mrs. Hou's hand and said, "Jehovah be praised. He has led me on a right path."

"Why are you so very excited?" Mrs. Hou asked.

"You have helped me so much, and I am so thankful, though I troubled you so much."

After she left me I sang from my heart Psalm 23: "The Lord is my Shepherd. He leads me in the paths of righteousness for his name's sake."

I completed the application at once and took it to the office. For a week I had no news. Then one day I met Mr. Liang, but before I could open my mouth to ask about the permit he said, "You need not ask about a permit; if you keep asking, it certainly will not be granted."

Several days passed, then he came to see his friend Miss Mei.

She said, "Wen Wei Zhen…" He cut off her question and said, "Are you asking for her? Even if you ask, it won't be given. No matter who asks, I shall not give her a permit."

"I do not wish to interfere with your authority," said Miss Mei, "but that woman is all alone in the city. She has heart disease, high blood pressure. We live in the same house, and if she becomes ill it will be my responsibility and a great trouble. She is always sick, and sometimes at midnight or the third watch we have to take her to a doctor. I think it would be good to send her away so her own people could care for her."

"After this," said Mr. Liang, "will you please not bother me with other people's affairs?"

Again, several days later Mr. Liang came to see Mrs. Hou officially. Mrs. Hou was sympathetic toward me, and she and her neighbor had secretly agreed to talk to Mr. Liang about me. So when he came Mrs. Hou said, "Mr. Liang Tong Ji, why do you not allow Wen Wei Zhen to leave the city? She is very weak and often sick, and as I am head of Ten Families I have a great responsibility, and I often have to take her to see a doctor. The next time she is sick I shall call you to come and care for her."

Her neighbor Mrs. Liu now spoke up and said, "Speaking of that kind of person, just treat her like garbage and throw her out; why keep her here to clutter up the place and be in our way?"

"What Mrs. Liu says is right," agreed Mrs. Hou. "Every month we have to give her twenty *catty* of rice. Let her go, and we can take her ration of rice and vegetables and give them to some worthy person. Isn't that a good idea?"

Mr. Liang said not one word.

Three weeks after I had applied for a travel permit to leave Canton, Mrs. Hou came in after a visit to the police permit office and said, "The head man at the permit office told me to tell you to go to the office and change your residence certificate for a travel permit."

I was so happy that I laughed aloud and began to sing Psalm 103 and asked Mrs. Hou to join me in thanking God. I at once took my residence certificate and asked her to pray for me as I went to the office, because I truly feared what might take place there.

When Mr. Liang saw me, he led me to a room at the rear of the main office. How fearful I was at first! In my heart I fervently prayed, until I entered that place and saw trees and flowers, a stone table and benches. It was cool, clean, and beautiful; it seemed like a good place. Mr. Liang introduced me to a Mr. Hou who was sitting there, then he went away.

This Mr. Hou was the peace officer, and a Mr. Te Mao-he had the responsibility for brainwashing. He proceeded to ask me about my birth, my life and work, and my connection with society in general. He inquired particularly about my feelings—how I now regarded the accusations made against me, my imprisonment, and my present circumstances. He asked whether I harbored feelings of hatred and ill-will against the Communists for these things?

These and many other questions were those of extreme brainwashing tactics in order to judge if my mind was entirely clean and clear, and to see if I now regarded these things as even more cruel and unjust than when they happened.

When I answered him it was as if I took out my very heart and displayed my gall (the seat of courage) for his scrutiny. I felt I was walking on dangerously thin ice. My heart was very fearful lest I speak indiscreetly. If I did not answer wisely, it meant not only no exit permit, but also the possibility of going back to prison.

Mr. Hou reproved me for sending my son to America instead of to Russia to study.

I replied, "At that time I did not know that Russia was a land of great educators with the highest educational facilities."

He said I should urge my son to return to his native land and help his own people.

I replied, "Mr. Hou, it is not that I do not wish to help my own people; my son's original intention was to return to China. A medical college in North China had promised him a position as teacher and physician. All arrangements had been completed, and he expected to return to that work in 1952. But when he learned that his mother had been accused and cast into prison, he thought of all the work she had done for the church people through many years, and how she had worked in cooperation with American missionaries, and that for these things she had been accused, arrested, and cast into prison. He said, 'If I return to China after studying in America the Communists will certainly kill me.'

"If I were now to urge him to return," I went on, "would it not be like giving an innocent lamb into the mouth of a lion? How could I do such an unreasonable thing to my own life and to my son's life as well? For this reason," I said, "I cannot urge my son to return."

Mr. Hou said, "Write a letter to him and tell him that, though you had been put in prison, yet you did not suffer any great harm, and that you are now living in peace. Tell him to come back and visit you. If you will write this letter I shall send it for you. You need not spend money even for stamps."

I said, "I truly believe that no matter what good words I write, he will not believe them. What he may have learned of my experiences has become a power that rules in his heart. It is impossible for him to change. However, if I were allowed to go out to Hong Kong, he would know that in Communist China people are really given liberty, and it might counteract his ideas and doubts of communism.

"If I were to tell him the things I saw in communism that were good and profitable, he might believe it was true, because his mother has never deceived him in any way. I might then be able to say his country needed him. Whether or not he would return, I dare not promise. But if I wrote and told him of my imprisonment, it would grieve him and break his heart, and not only he but many others would be fearful. As the proverb says, 'When a snake sees the grass moving, it flees.' For us to be imprisoned is not to the advantage of the Communist Party, nor does it testify to the law of liberty, so the government would suffer from the bad impression on others."

"Now," he said, "I shall give you a permit to leave, and I shall expect you to make known and propagate the good things in communism so that it will become popular in Hong Kong. When police or others ask your opinion about the conditions in China you must tell only the good side. Do not hide the good. As you now see the admirable things about the government, always speak of that. Will you now please talk to me as you would to people in Hong Kong?"

"As for the government," I said, "I have had no experience in political affairs. All I know has been gained as an onlooker. I cannot explain what has never entered my mind. I can speak only of one or two things I have seen and heard. For one thing, I can speak of economics; the government has controlled the fluctuation of money, the prices of gold and silver, and the value of things is more settled.

"Another thing is the matter of education; you have made it mandatory that all should learn to read, and you have opened many schools to make this possible; you have swept away illiteracy. You have also improved conditions for sanitation and introduced better sewage disposal; you have trapped sparrows and other destructive birds; you have caught and destroyed rats, flies, mosquitoes, and other harmful insects, and thus prevented the spread of disease.

"A fourth thing is improvement in communications; you have built canals for travel; everyone has opportunity to learn the laws by which they are to live. Fifth: new factories and industries have provided work for every laborer, so that all have food. You generate electricity by the use of water. And sixth: you keep peace in the land by having police to protect every place and prevent theft and other crimes, so that people may live in safety.

"For these reasons one does not wish to leave the country. However, because of the money sent me by my son to support me, I must go to Hong Kong to arrange this satisfactorily."

As we talked together, time sped by like a black horse galloping, until three hours had passed. Mrs. Mei was worried and feared the police had put me in prison again. Mrs. Hou then sent her to the police office to inquire about me, and just as she left the house I returned.

I was granted a permit to leave Canton and China, so I arranged for my room and belongings which I had to leave. I also wrote to ask my niece to meet me when I arrived in Hong Kong. This took about five days. Comrade Liang came to my room and asked why I had not gone to Hong Kong; I understood his reason for inquiring.

Next morning at dawn I went to the boat-landing and waited. Before boarding the ship at nine o'clock I was examined. In my baggage I had my Bible, which I always kept with me. A person beside me urged me to throw it into the river lest it cause trouble and delay.

I said, "If the Lord allows me to go, the Bible will cause no difficulty or trouble. If he doesn't want me to go, throwing it into the river will make no difference."

When the inspector saw my Bible it raised many questions in his mind. In surprise he said, "Are you really a Christian?"

"Yes, I am a Christian," I said.

"How long have you been a believer in Jesus?" he asked.

"From my childhood I have believed in him," I replied.

"But so many people have changed their religion; they have abandoned their faith in Jesus. Why do you insist on being a Christian?"

"I cannot, as many have done, reject the grace of God to me. I cannot refuse his love to me which is like the love of father and mother. It is my duty to love him. Because the Lord Jesus loved me and gave his own life for me, I cannot but love him and also tell others about God's love for them. Therefore Christians are to spread the gospel and give it to others."

He said no more but put my Bible back in my baggage and closed the bag for me, then waved his hand in farewell as I went aboard the ship. He did not even examine the rest of my baggage. So I went in peace to Macao and thence to Hong Kong, where my niece Qian Chen awaited me.

This account of my travels covers about two months. When my travel permit expired, I returned it to the office that had issued it. This was to say that I was thus entirely and forever out from their jurisdiction and free from their oppression.

Epilogue

Let me add another chapter to the unfinished story of Jeanette Li's life. Mrs. Li had "preached to them the kingdom of God and taught them about the Lord Jesus Christ with boldness and quite openly" through her two years in Canton. Then she obtained her freedom in Hong Kong. Even there Communists were "planted" near her for some time, but she was not troubled.

Living at first in one room, sharing a kitchen with two other families, surrounded by hundreds of other refugees from Red China, she soon proved to be the confidant, the counselor, and the helper of scores of distressed sufferers.

When the Hong Kong government built "refugee estates," by special permission, Mrs. Li was assigned a 9 foot by 9 foot room on a seventh floor, with the luxury of living alone instead of with three others, because she wished to do social service, teach Bible classes, and serve the needy.

Her room was next to the laundry room used by all the twenty or more families on the seventh floor. It was also nearest the open public toilet which, by regulation, was flushed three or four times a day. Groups of children had only the narrow catwalk for games and noisy parades. Her room was often a gathering place for them, while their mothers did their laundry.

Women and children deserted by their Communist husbands and fathers came to her for counsel and comfort. Children whose parents had been cruelly murdered by the Reds, young men with no jobs, and others in distress, came to her, and she found jobs for them if only at breaking rock for the construction of the airstrip. One young man she started in a "little business," selling toothbrushes and pencils. He worked himself up and before long opened a factory for the making of children's clothing.

Mrs. Li substituted for a missionary who had a broken leg, until she injured her already weak heart by climbing the steps to the seventh floor every day for months, and then she was forced to retire from that service.

Churches needed workers, and she taught Bible classes and led meetings for women and children. She was friend and adviser to young men who today are pastors in Hong Kong or America, and at least one is in Indonesia.

She applied for a permit to enter the United States where her son and his family were living. Her visa was delayed year after year because of the small annual quota allowed to immigrants and because thousands were registered ahead of her.

At last, after an American missionary friend had come to her aid by wearying the officers in the consulate by her continuous requests (like the importunate widow with the judge in the Bible), Mrs. Li, on January 4, 1962, was able to enter the United States as a dependent of her son in New York City.

In America she was soon at work for the Lord. Her thrilling talks stirred and uplifted Christians and rebuked their indifference.

The young Chinese pastor with whom she worked in Los Angeles speaks of the footprints she left: of hardships she endured; of fervent sacrifice she made; of her contentment in all conditions; of her concern for others; of her joyful and untiring service. She constantly visited families of the Chinese in greater Los Angeles and was a blessing and an inspiration to the whole Chinese community.

A fitting close to the story of the life of Mrs. Jeanette Li is the tribute from her pastor, the Rev. Bruce C. Stewart, and his congregation:

> It has been a wonderful experience for the Los Angeles congregation to have Mrs. Jeanette Li in our midst during the last five years. Her radiant Christian faith and life has been a blessing to all of us.
>
> Mrs. Li was faithful in her attendance in the house of God. It was thrilling to hear her pouring out her heart in prayer in Chinese at our weekly prayer-meetings. Even though we could not understand her words, there was no mistaking her relationship with Christ. We remember also with joy the first time she read a Bible verse in English at the prayer meeting, and how determinedly she continued to improve her reading and speaking of English.
>
> Mrs. Li was always willing to speak to individuals or groups about her love for Christ. Her vivacity and expressiveness delighted the children and young people as well as adults even though she spoke through an interpreter.

We will ever remember the twinkle in her eye, her little chuckle, her wonderful Chinese cooking, her beautiful flower beds, her skill in games, her concern for the Christians still in China, and her testimony of God's grace in her life. Truly, she is one of the mighty host of women of whom the psalmist tells us "who make the tidings known."

After helping to translate the life of Rev. Wang Ming Dao into English, she wrote this autobiography in Chinese and it has been published in Taiwan. Her earthly life ended just when we had almost finished the translation into English.

—Rose A. Huston
1971

Life of Miss Rose A. Huston

Rose A. Huston, the translator of *Jeanette Li*, was an accomplished Christian woman in her own right. She was born in 1884, the ninth child in an Iowa farming family of fourteen children. After graduation from Amity College in Iowa and a few years' teaching experience, she sailed for China arriving at Deqing at the age of twenty-six to become the principal of the girls' school where Jeanette Li was a young convert. This was the just beginning, as these two strong Christian women would cross paths many times during their long productive lives.

Miss Huston's decision to go to China demonstrated great courage as three Reformed Presbyterian missionaries and one missionary child had already died in the unfriendly tropical climate and unsanitary conditions. The sacrifice of these precious lives had awakened the sympathies of the church and the largest party of new missionaries sent by any church to one field came to Deqing. Miss Huston was a student at the time of the tragic deaths and too young to go with them, but she dedicated her life to mission work and sailed for China in 1910 following the completion of her education. She would become fluent in Cantonese and serve in several capacities until forced by war in China to return to the United States in 1923.

While in the United States, Miss Huston earned a degree in nursing from Chautauqua School of Nursing, which she believed would be helpful in future missionary endeavors. Unable to return to China due to the still unsettled conditions, she served in the Reformed Presbyterian missions in Latakia, Syria, for two years and Nicosia, Cyprus, for one year, teaching English subjects and Bible.

Sometime around 1931 conditions in China improved, and she was asked to join a new Reformed Presbyterian effort in Northern Manchuria, which meant learning a new language: Mandarin. Jeanette Li was asked to join this group, and they became co-laborers. After eleven years of work, the missionaries witnessed the Japanese invasion, which ended their ministry there. Miss Huston was briefly incarcerated by the Japanese before being repatriated, arriving in New York in 1942 on the *Gripsholm*.

While World War II prevented her work in China, Miss Huston taught school in the rural mission school operated by the RP Home Mission Board in Kentucky. Following the war, Miss Huston returned with other missionaries to South China where they opened an orphanage in Deqing and engaged in relief work after the Japanese were driven out. Here again she labored with Jeanette Li, but their time together was brief as the Communists were taking over the government of China. In a matter of years, mission work became impossible and dangerous. All Reformed Presbyterian missionaries retired or were reassigned to Japan where a new work was started. Miss Huston was one of those who went to Japan. There she taught Bible classes and helped produce the first Japanese psalter.

Miss Huston retired from her Japan ministry in 1960 and at the age of seventy-six spent two years in Hong Kong with Jeanette Li doing evangelistic work among the refugees from the communist mainland. Although living conditions were primitive and unsanitary, Miss Huston refused to leave until she was successful in helping Mrs. Li obtain a visa for the United States where she could join her son in Los Angeles. From 1962 until Mrs. Li's death in 1968, the two women collaborated on the translation of the autobiography of the Rev. Wang Ming Dao and Mrs. Li's own biography.

No one was better suited to help Jeanette Li than Rose Huston. She had known her since her childhood and was fluent in both Cantonese and Mandarin, both necessary for undertaking this biography. Miss Huston's missionary service had required her to learn a new language every twenty years—Cantonese at the age of twenty-six, Mandarin at forty-six and Japanese at sixty-six. This accomplishment, along with her many other achievements, were recognized by Geneva College when they awarded her an honorary Doctor of Humane Letters.

Rose A. Huston was a remarkable Christian woman whose life deserves a book of its own. The ship's captain on her first voyage to China told her she was too beautiful to be a missionary and proposed marriage. She had a winning personality and a sense of humor. Even at age ninety, when asked if she were married, she answered, "Not yet." As a single woman without children of her own, she reached out to every child who came in contact with her and became known in mission circles and around the church as "Aunt Rose." She loved nothing more than to sit with a small child and tell them of her childhood on the farm and adventures over the sea—bandits, soldiers, highwaymen and travels on the Trans-Siberian Railway. She had an endless supply of stories.

Miss Huston spent her final years in the Reformed Presbyterian Home in Pittsburgh, Pa. She had hoped to use this time to get her own story down on paper, but her eyesight failed before that could be accomplished. She had faithfully written confidential letters to her family that she hoped would provide material for a final work, but a relative cleaning out the family home after her mother's death threw out all the letters. This is a great loss to the story of RP missions because she served in every RP mission of her period, both home and foreign, and had keen insight into people and wise opinions that would be worth our knowing.

Sometime before her death on April 27, 1978, Miss Huston accepted Dr. Li's offer of a cemetery plot beside his mother. Jeanette Li and Rose Huston lie side by side in Forest Lawn Cemetery (Hollywood Hills, Calif.) awaiting the resurrection.

—Faith M. Martin
Grandniece of Rose Huston
November 2014

A Brief History of China during the Twentieth Century

At the time of Mrs. Li's birth (1899), China was ruled from Beijing by the Manchu Dynasty, which had come to power in 1644. During the 19th century, it was in decline. It met with defeat as the European powers, Great Britain in particular, endeavored to force their way into China for reasons of trade. In the Opium War of 1839–42, Great Britain obtained trade concessions and compelled China to cede Hong Kong. In a second war, 1856–60, in which France joined with Great Britain, further concessions were made to the Western powers. Russia, too, became eager to benefit from China's weakness. In various treaties, China not only granted trade and diplomatic concessions, but recognized the right of Christian missionaries to propagate their faith, and the right of the Chinese to become Christians.

In the late 1890s came the Boxer rising against all "foreign devils," which led to the massacre of thousands of native Christians and many hundred foreign missionaries. As the foreign legations in Beijing were also besieged, the Great Powers intervened and made further inroads on China's sovereignty.

Japan, too, had designs on China. She had made war on her in 1894 and this had caused the Chinese to look to Russia for protection, especially on their northern frontiers. But the protecting power desired gain also and in 1900 she took military possession of Manchuria.

Since the 1860s, Japan had been copying the West and with astonishing speed had transformed herself into an industrial military state. The signing of a Treaty of Alliance between Great Britain and Japan in 1902 undoubtedly encouraged Japan to go to war with Russia in 1904. Russia was bitterly humiliated.

China was amazed and alarmed at Japan's success. A strong Nationalist

Movement began, led by Sun Yat-sen, with the ultimate aims of modernizing China's inefficient government and resisting aggression by all outside powers. In the outcome the Manchu Dynasty fell. It was replaced in February 1912 by a republic. The Nationalist Party now took the name of the Guomindang.

Intense internal conflicts quickly developed. Political and military groups struggled for the mastery during the next twelve years. In the world outside China World War I took place. The Russian czars were replaced by a Communist government under Lenin. While the Western powers were busy in Europe, Japan tried to get control of Manchuria. The Far Eastern situation was indeed chaotic.

About 1920, Sun Yat-sen was offered the friendship of the Russian Communists, but he was wary of accepting the doctrines of communism. He strengthened the Guomindang and seemed to be on the point of restoring good order in the land when his death occurred in 1925. Internal struggles continued.

In 1931 there was an ominous development. The Japanese overran Manchuria which they renamed Manchukuo. At its head they put Puyi, the last Manchu emperor of China. He was a mere puppet in their hands. Japan was rebuked by the League of Nations, the body formed at the close of World War I, of which both China and herself were members, but she defied world opinion and refused to back down. Indeed she extended her claims, destroyed China's air force and armies, and drove the Chinese government from Nanjing to take refuge in Chongqing in mid-China.

In 1939, World War II broke out. Japan was still bent on aggression. The collapse of France before German arms in 1940 was followed by a Japanese occupation of Indochina (Vietnam), hitherto largely under French influence. Made bold by success after success, Japan next launched a sudden attack on the United States naval base at Pearl Harbor in Hawaii on December 7, 1941, without a prior declaration of war. Hong Kong and Singapore were taken from Great Britain. China itself was easy prey. Against the common foe, Britain and the United States now negotiated agreements with the Chongqing government. The United States organized its immense resources. China received aid. After the collapse of Germany in Europe and the use of the atomic bomb, Japan capitulated in a hurry and withdrew its forces from China. The date was August 1945.

China's Nationalist Government, still dominated by the Guomindang, now moved back to Nanjing. At its head was Chiang Kai-shek who, with his wife, professed the Christian faith. Unhappily, communism had made rapid progress throughout the land by this time. Russia was not directly involved, though pledged to spread communism to all lands, but the presence of her victorious armies close to China's northern frontiers encouraged Chinese Communists to oppose the Nationalist Government. In 1949 Chiang Kai-shek and his government were driven out of China's mainland. They took refuge in the large island of Taiwan (Formosa), separated from the mainland by a strait 100 miles wide, and there they remained as Nationalist China.

On October 1, 1949, the "People's Republic of China" was proclaimed in Beijing. The Communist government set about the entire remodeling of Chinese society and institutions according to the doctrines of the Communist Party. All religion, including the Christian faith, was to be destroyed. The Christian church was to be denounced as a mere adjunct of imperialism and "annihilated." Church property was to be taken over by the state and turned to secular use. Atheism was to be relentlessly taught in all the schools of the land.

Remarkably, despite their declared hatred for imperialism, the Communist government of China has not attempted to remove the British from Hong Kong. The island itself has an area of 32 square miles. The strait that separates it from the mainland is but half a mile wide. The British "colony" also includes 3¼ square miles of the mainland peninsula of Jiulong, and certain other island territories amounting in all to between 300 and 400 square miles. Hong Kong soon became the overcrowded refuge of those Chinese who, for a variety of reasons, wished to escape from Communist China.

Outline of Jeanette Li's Life

1899	Born at Deqing, South China
1904	Begins her education
1906	Death of her father
	Enters hospital and, shortly, the Mission School of the Reformed Presbyterian Mission
1908	Her mother baptized in the Reformed Presbyterian Church
1909	Baptized in the Reformed Presbyterian Church
	Marriage arranged by her mother
1912	*The Manchu Dynasty overthrown and replaced by the Nationalist Government*
1915	Marriage
1918	Becomes teacher in the Qi Li Girls' School
1919	Birth of her son, Timothy, at the Mission Hospital
1920	Husband leaves for Canton (they rarely meet thereafter)
1921	Takes charge of a Girls' School
1922	A daughter (Man Shi) born but dies after eighteen days
	Becomes estranged from her husband
1923	Enters Normal School (for teacher training) at Canton
	At a gospel meeting promises to engage in missionary work
1926	Obtains diploma of the Normal School
	Takes teaching post near Canton
1928	Teaching post in Government School
	Takes short course in physical education at Canton
	Obtains post in school at Shuolong, but soon resigns

1929	Becomes principal of Mission School for Boys at Deqing
1932	Resigns principalship and enters Jinling Bible College, Nanjing
1934	Obtains diploma of Bible College, Nanjing
	Leaves Nanjing for Qiqihar, Manchuria
	Works for a time at Mingshui with Reformed Presbyterian Church
1936	Joined at Qiqihar by Timothy
1937	Working for the church at Yi An
1940	Working for the church at Daigang
1941	*Japanese attack Pearl Harbor in December*
	American missionaries in Manchuria become enemy aliens and are put under house arrest and later evacuated
1942-46	Carrying on the work of the mission in Manchuria
1946	*Japan's defeat in war, and surrender to America*
	Escape to Shenyang
1947	Begins work for the Lord in Changchun Hospital (capital of Manchukuo)
1948	[May] Flight to Shenyang from Communists
	Takes boat to Shanghai
1948	[Sept.] Returns to Deqing in South China
1949	*Communists obtain control in Deqing*
	American missionaries leave for Hong Kong
1949	Takes charge of the Mission Orphanage, Deqing
1949-51	Pays several visits to Hong Kong
1950-51	*Communists begin attempts to "annihilate" Christian Church*
1952	[Jan.] Imprisoned by Communists and brainwashed
1953	[May 30] Released from prison by Communists
1953	[July 1] Moves to Canton
	After two or three years is allowed to enter Hong Kong
1958-62	Engaged in Christian work in Hong Kong
1962	[Jan. 4] Enters United States
	Resides in Los Angeles
1968	Writes autobiography
	Death

Endnotes

1. Later the teacher of Classics in our school decided that *Dao Xing*, though a good name, was not suitable for one of her disposition and character, so he said, "I shall 'put on you' a suitable name: *Wei* (heroic) and *Jie* (extraordinary, admirable, powerful). In Mandarin it was *Wei He*. Her unusually strong character was impressive even in early school days. —R. A. H.

2. It may be of interest to know that, when baptized, a Chinese elder gave her, according to custom, a holy-name or sacred-name. It meant "grace-cheery." She disliked this name because it was so commonly used by new Christians, so she never used it; this proved a difficulty to us in finding the date of her baptism as no one knew it was her holy-name. —R. A. H.

3. In 1952 the Chinese Communists put a criminal accusation on my head, "International Spy," and put me in prison. One day, early in the morning when I was taken outside for some reason, I saw another woman at the building where they kept those in solitary confinement, but we showed no signs of recognition. Afterwards I talked with my fellow prisoners in the same room with me and learned that she was Wan Sao, the accountant I had known, who had been my mother's ideal for me to imitate. Because she had been a land owner, she had suffered extreme persecution. She was now like a very old person, "with fowl-like skin and crane-like hair." She had lost all her former spirit and energy because she had been reduced from riches to deepest poverty and shame, when cast into prison.

I sighed in sympathy for her and wished to share her unhappiness. Therefore, taking great risks, I broke the rules by writing a few characters on a scrap of paper and asking the water carrier to take it to her. She sent a reply to me on a small slip of paper, recalling the day we had talked together more than forty years earlier.

—J. L.

4. Actually I did agree with *Dao Xing* (Jeanette Li) but I consulted the senior missionary and was advised that it was best for her to submit to Chinese customs as long as no sin was involved. —R. A. H.

5. An expressive Chinese term for an oppressed or downtrodden person.

6. The founder of the Nationalist movement and first president of the Chinese Republic, 1912.

7. Afterward, Sing Kwok Ching and his mother studied chemistry and nursing under Dr. Edna Wallace in the Mission Hospital, and later he opened a chemist-shop. In 1950 he came to Deqing on business and called at the orphanage to visit me. He mentioned the voice I had heard in the night twenty years earlier. He still believed that it was God calling me. —J. L.

8. "Ya" is a prefix used with personal names, or one character of a name.

9. *Kao* (tall); *liang* (grain). Sorghum. Much like sugarcane, the stalk is used as fodder for animals and the grain, though coarse, for food. It provides a substitute for rice, which does not grow in the far North.

10. Mr. Vos was the minister in the first group from our church to go to Manchuria. He returned home after the Japanese closed the Bible school at Yingkou where he was principal. He then served as head of the Bible Department in Geneva College in Beaver Falls, Pennsylvania. —R. A. H.

11. The work in Taikang was not allowed to continue very long so she had returned to Qiqihar. —R. A. H.

12. The Rev. Philip W. Martin came to Manchuria in 1937 and his wife

(then Miss Peoples) in 1938. Because of ill health and the political situation they returned home in 1940. —R. A. H.

13. They did suggest that we sell off such articles as we did not need, which we did, largely things that the Martins had stored with us. I wove squares and made bags for sale, and also did sewing for the Chinese. —R. A. H.

14. The dropping of atomic bombs on Hiroshima and Nagasaki in Japan occurred on August 6 and 9. On August 14 came the cessation of hostilities. The actual surrender of Japan was signed on September 2.

15. Jiulong is the mainland peninsula separated from the island of Hong Kong by a narrow strait. Its southern tip is British territory, administered by the Hong Kong government. Canton lies about 80 miles upriver from Hong Kong.

16. I have never received them. I learned later that the Communists had opened my mail and confiscated them. —J. L.

17. In 1960, when I was in Hong Kong, a letter from Deqing told me that they were still worshiping under the tree on the grass. —J. L.

18. Since I have not asked permission to use the names of the other three, I am using fictitious names. —J. L.

19. Chiang Kai-shek had fled to Taiwan (Formosa), the large island off the mainland of China.

20. The judge said, as he set her free, "Don't go from this place with your head hanging like a criminal, but go unashamed with your head held high."
—R. A. H., from notes in 1958 diary.

Missions with a Reformed Perspective

Reformed Presbyterian Missions is a short-term missions organization that provides Christians with the opportunity to serve Christ's Church throughout the world.

- **RP Missions seeks to approach missions** from a biblical and historic Reformed perspective.
- **Short-term teams work alongside established churches** and missions to ensure that follow-up and discipleship continue after the team leaves, and to encourage local congregations.
- **RP Missions's goal is to aid and implement the programs of the host congregations,** instead of taking our own agendas or programs to mission sites.

RP Missions provides mission opportunities for individuals, small groups, and congregations to serve God together and become better acquainted with His global Church. To find out how to become involved, please visit **www.RPMissions.org**.

Serve. Proclaim. Disciple.
www.RPMissions.org

RP Missions

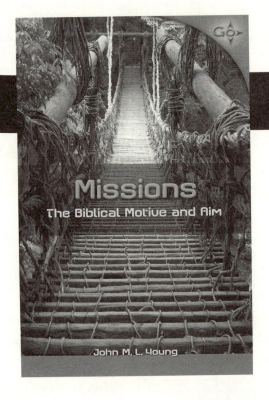

Whether you are trying to understand your calling to missions work, wanting your congregation to support missionaries more effectively, or are going on a short-term trip, this book is for you.

John M. L. Young's own mission work informed and nurtured his passion for missions, and he published his theology of missions in a ~ries of ten pamphlets in 1964. For the first time, these studies are ˙˙ᵈ in one volume.

Missions: The Biblical Motive and Aim
Paperback, 176 pages, Code: DS390, $10

412.241.0436